INVESTING THE ASEAN WAY

In recent decades, Southeast Asia has become one of the world's most popular destinations for foreign investment. The member states of the Association of Southeast Asian Nations (ASEAN) have employed varying modalities to pursue first security and then economic cooperation. This book explores regional law and governance in ASEAN through the lens of its regulation of foreign investment. It adopts a new framework to identify the unique ontological autonomy of the ASEAN Investment Regime beyond a simple aggregation of its individual member states. It deploys a sociology-led approach (especially constructivism) and emphasizes ideational factors (such as culture and norms) that guide state actions from within. The book explores the manner in which ASEAN's history and culture have fundamentally shaped its foreign investment policies, leading to outcomes that often depart fundamentally from the external structure and script of Global Investment Law.

SUNGJOON CHO is a Professor of Law at Chicago-Kent College of Law, Illinois Tech. He is a member of the arbitration panel roster under Chapter 14 (Dispute Settlement) of the Korea–European Union Free Trade Agreement. He is the author of *The Social Foundations of World Trade: Norms, Community, and Constitution* (Cambridge, 2015; paperback in 2017).

JÜRGEN KURTZ is a Professor of International Economic Law at the European University Institute. Jürgen is the author of *The WTO and International Investment Law: Converging Systems* (Cambridge, 2016) and co-editor of *International Trade, Investment and the Sustainable Development Goals* (Cambridge, 2020).

INTEGRATION THROUGH LAW
The Role of Law and the Rule of Law in ASEAN Integration

General Editors
J. H. H. Weiler, European University Institute
Tan Hsien-Li, National University of Singapore

The Association of Southeast Asian Nations (ASEAN), comprising the ten member states of Brunei Darussalam, Cambodia, Indonesia, Lao PDR, Malaysia, Myanmar, the Philippines, Singapore, Thailand and Vietnam, has undertaken intensified integration into the ASEAN Community through the Rule of Law and Institutions in its 2007 Charter. This innovative book series evaluates the community-building processes of ASEAN to date and offers a conceptual and policy toolkit for broader Asian thinking and planning of different legal and institutional models of economic and political regional integration in the region. Participating scholars have been divided up into six separate thematic strands. The books combine a mix of Asian and Western scholars.

Centre for International Law, National University of Singapore (CIL-NUS)
The Centre for International Law (CIL) was established in 2009 at the National University of Singapore's Bukit Timah Campus in response to the growing need for international law expertise and capacity building in the Asia-Pacific region. CIL is a university-wide research centre that focuses on multidisciplinary research and works with other NUS or external centres of research and academic excellence. In particular, CIL collaborates very closely with the NUS Faculty of Law.

INVESTING THE ASEAN WAY

Theories and Practices of Economic Integration in Southeast Asia

SUNGJOON CHO
Chicago-Kent College of Law

JÜRGEN KURTZ
European University Institute, Florence

CAMBRIDGE
UNIVERSITY PRESS

CAMBRIDGE
UNIVERSITY PRESS

Shaftesbury Road, Cambridge CB2 8EA, United Kingdom

One Liberty Plaza, 20th Floor, New York, NY 10006, USA

477 Williamstown Road, Port Melbourne, VIC 3207, Australia

314–321, 3rd Floor, Plot 3, Splendor Forum, Jasola District Centre, New Delhi – 110025, India

103 Penang Road, #05–06/07, Visioncrest Commercial, Singapore 238467

Cambridge University Press is part of Cambridge University Press & Assessment, a department of the University of Cambridge.

We share the University's mission to contribute to society through the pursuit of education, learning and research at the highest international levels of excellence.

www.cambridge.org
Information on this title: www.cambridge.org/9781009223362

DOI: 10.1017/9781009223331

First published 2023

A catalogue record for this publication is available from the British Library.

ISBN 978-1-009-22336-2 Paperback

CONTENTS

FIGURES

TABLES

PREFACE

This book aims to capture the complex history and culture of the Association of Southeast Asian Nations (ASEAN) as a way of understanding and evaluating the creation and utility of external and internal investment norms. ASEAN is our dominant analytical focus in this book as, we argue, its precepts have fundamentally configured the norms of international investment within the broader universe of bilateral investment treaties (BITs) and investment chapters under free trade agreements (FTAs) concluded by ASEAN member states. In doing so, this book critiques the clichéd assumption that thick (Western) legalization settings are the correct normative baseline for the ASEAN economic integration agenda.

In our view, this flaw is attributable to the unwillingness of the conventional scholarship on international investment law to interrogate the central assumptions underpinning the norms constructed around the protection of foreign investment, particularly as to their utility in a regional integration scheme.[1] The end result is a restatement of analytical positions and normative claims with a heavy focus on the benefits of third-party adjudication which seem especially poorly suited to

[1] For a rare and insightful analysis on how regional initiatives are fundamentally reshaping international regimes on trade and investment, see Damian Chalmers & Julia Slupska, *The Regional Remaking of Trade and Investment Law*, 30 (1) Eur. J. Int'l L. 169–7 (2019).

the ASEAN context. In this regard, this book intends to "shift the needle" in scholarly and policy discourse.

Our goal, however, is not to *only* focus on the development of treaty rules within ASEAN on foreign investment. Within the existing literature, there is already thoughtful and insightful engagement with the specific norms on foreign investment under the ASEAN treaties.[2] In fact, there are a number of existing books that already offer this type of dominant focus on investment law. We seek instead to investigate those norms against theories of economic integration in order to generate robust assessment as to strengths and weaknesses of the ASEAN investment project (which are combined in Chapters 5 and 6, the Conclusion).

It would be remiss of this book not to address the recent turbulence in international economic relations and their inevitable impacts on ASEAN economic integration. To be sure, a double tribulation of the United States–China trade war and the outbreak of the COVID-19 pandemic has dealt a blow to the ASEAN economy. Yet, it has also demonstrated remarkable levels of resiliency. While Asia's trade volume had contracted by 10 percent on a year-on-year basis by May 2020, "high frequency indicators" such as global

[2] For two recent examples, see Sufian Jusoh, *Investment Liberalization in ASEAN: Moving from Myths to Reality*, and Julien Chaisse, *The ACIA: Much More than a BIT of Protection for Foreign Investors*, in ASEAN Law in the New Regional Economic Order: Global Trends and Shifting Paradigms 209–51 (Pasha Hsieh & Bryan Mercurio eds., 2019).

shipping, packaging indexes and port calls, herald Asia's faster-than-expected economic rebound.[3]

In fact, Southeast Asia remains the most integrated area in Asia (driven by trade and investment) as measured by the Asia-Pacific Regional Cooperation and Integration Index (ARCII).[4] The pandemic has accelerated recent regionalization trends in ASEAN,[5] which have pushed *intra*-ASEAN trade fourfold from 2010 to 2017.[6] The United States–China trade war as well as the increasing labor cost in China have forced foreign investors to source their manufacturing to ASEAN members. In fact, Google and LG have already shifted their smartphone assembly operations to Vietnam. Malaysia has become the third-largest solar-cell-module maker outside of China, as it has launched manufacturing capacity of 4.3 gigawatts. Thailand has recently announced an ambitious plan of becoming an "electric vehicle hub" in next five years by popularizing electric buses and taxis for government and public transportation uses.[7]

This auspicious background lends credence to the main thesis of this book that timely economic integration within ASEAN, both deep and broad, is necessary to boost

[3] Asian Development Bank, *The ASEAN Economic Integration Report 2021: Making Digital Platform Work for Asia and the Pacific*, at xvii, 13 (Feb. 2021).

[4] *Id.* at xx.

[5] See Pasha L. Hsieh, New Asian Regionalism in International Economic Law (2021).

[6] Eoin Daly et al., *Reimagining Emerging ASEAN in the Wake of COVID-19*, McKinsey & Co. (Aug. 2020).

[7] *Id.*

the post-pandemic recovery.[8] Here, the ASEAN characteristics are uniquely situated to incentivize foreign investment into the region. In comparison to its equivalents in Europe or North America, the ASEAN Investment Regime (AIR) is distinct in the sense that it has evolved against the background of *open* regionalism as well as a robust working relationship between the government and the business sector.[9] Thus, any future legal and institutional upgrading of the AIR must be able to harness these rich traditions to contribute effectively to the common prosperity of the region. In particular, the clichéd Western style of formal legalism must be rethought and reinvented in a way which complements, rather than supplants, the deep-rooted cultural fore-structures within the region.

[8] See Juita Mohamad, *ASEAN Waits for RCEP Ratification – and Post-Pandemic Integration*, Hinrich Foundation (Sept. 7, 2021) www.hinrichfoundation.com/research/article/ftas/asean-waits-for-rcep-ratification-and-post-pandemic-integration/.

[9] Masahiro Kawai & Ganeshan Wignaraja, *Conclusion*, in Asia's Free Trade Agreements: How Is Business Responding? 261 (Masahiro Kawai & Ganeshan Wignaraja eds., 2011).

GENERAL EDITORS' PREFACE

This monograph is published within the context of a wide-ranging research project entitled, "Integration through Law: The Role of Law and the Rule of Law in ASEAN Integration" (ITL), undertaken by the Centre for International Law at the National University of Singapore and directed by J. H. H. Weiler and Tan Hsien-Li.

The Preamble to the ASEAN Charter concludes with a single decision: "We, the Peoples of the Member States of the Association of Southeast Asian Nations ... [h]ereby decide to establish, through this Charter, the legal and institutional framework for ASEAN." For the first time in its history of over four decades, the Legal and the Institutional were brought to the forefront of ASEAN discourse.

The gravitas of the medium, a Charter: the substantive ambition of its content, the creation of three interlocking Communities, and the turn to law and institutions as instruments for realization provide ample justification for this wide-ranging project, to which this monograph is one contribution, examining ASEAN in a comparative context.

That same substantive and, indeed, political ambition means that any single study, illuminating as it may be, will cover but a fraction of the phenomena. Our modus operandi in this project was to create teams of researchers from Asia and elsewhere who would contribute individual monographs within an overall framework which we had designed. The project framework, involving several thematic clusters within each monograph, is thus determined by the framework and the place of each monograph within it.

As regards the specific content, however, the authors were free, indeed encouraged, to define their own understanding of the problem and their own methodology and reach their own conclusions. The thematic structure of the entire project may be found at the end of this Preface.

The project as a whole, and each monograph within it, display several methodological sensibilities.

First, law, in our view, can only be understood and evaluated when situated in its political and economic context. Thus, the first studies in the overall project design are intended to provide the political, economic, cultural and historical context against which one must understand ASEAN and are written by specialists in these respective disciplines. This context, to a greater or lesser degree, also informs the sensibility of each monograph. There are no "black letter law" studies to be found in this project and, indeed, even in the most technical of areas we encouraged our authors to make their writing accessible to readers of diverse disciplines.

Comparative experience suggests that the success of achieving some of the more ambitious objectives outlined in Article 1 of the Charter will depend in no small measure on the effectiveness of legal principles, legal rules and legal institutions. This is particularly true as regards the success of establishing "an ASEAN Community comprising the ASEAN Security Community, the ASEAN Economic Community and the ASEAN Socio-Cultural Community as provided for in the Bali Declaration of ASEAN Concord II."

Article 2(2)(n) stipulates the commitment of ASEAN member states to act in accordance with the principle of "adherence to multilateral trade rules and ASEAN's rules-based regimes for effective implementation of economic commitments and progressive reduction towards elimination of all barriers to regional economic integration." The ASEAN member states therefore envisage that rules of law and the Rule of Law will become a major feature in the future of ASEAN.

Although, as seen, the Charter understands itself as providing an institutional and legal framework for ASEAN, the question of the "role of law and the rule of law" is not advocacy but a genuine enquiry in the various substantive areas of the project as to:

- the substantive legal principles and substantive rules of the various ASEAN communities;
- the procedural legal principles and rules governing institutional structures and decision-making processes;
- implementation, enforcement and dispute settlement.

One should not expect a mechanical application of this scheme in each study; rather, a sensibility that refuses to content itself with legal enactments as such and looks to a "living" notion of law and institutions is ubiquitous in all the studies. Likewise, the project is sensitive to "non Law." It variously attempts to locate the appropriate province of the law in this experience. That is, not only the role of law, but also the areas that are and should remain outside the reach of legal institutionalization with due sensitivity to ASEAN and Asian particularism and political and cultural identities.

The project, and the monographs of which it is made, are not normatively thick. They do not advocate. They are designed, for the most part, to offer reflection, discuss the pros and cons, and in this way enrich public awareness, deepen understanding of different options and in that respect contribute indirectly to policymaking.

This decisive development of ASEAN has been accompanied by a growing Asian interest in various legal and institutional forms of transnational economic and political cooperation, notably the various voices discussing and showing an interest in an East Asia Integration project. The number of Free Trade Agreements (FTAs) and Regional Trade Agreements (RTAs) has increased from six in 1991 to 166 in 2013, with an additional 62 in various stages of negotiations.

Methodologically, the project and many of the monographs are comparative in their orientation. Comparative law is one of the few real-life laboratories that we have in which to assess and understand the operation of different legal and institutional models designed to tackle similar objectives and problems. One should not need to put one's own hand in the fire to learn that it scorches. With that in mind, a couple of monographs offer both conceptual reflection and pragmatic "tool boxing" on some of the key elements featuring in all regional integration systems.

Comparative law is in part about divergence: it is a potent tool and means to understand one's own uniqueness. One understands better the uniqueness of apples by comparing them to oranges. You understand better the specialness of a Toyota by comparing it to a Ford.

Comparative law is also about convergence: it is a potent tool and means to understand how seemingly different phenomena are part of a broader trend, an insight which may enhance both self-understanding and policy potentialities.

Although many studies in the project could have almost immediate policy implications, as would the project as a whole, this is not its only or even principal purpose. There is a rich theory of federalism which covers many countries around the world. There is an equally rich theory of European integration, which has been associated with the advent Union. There is also considerable learning on Free Trade Areas and the like.

To date, the study of the legal aspects of ASEAN specifically, and other forms of Asian legal integration, has been derivative of, and dependent on, theoretical and conceptual insights which were developed in different contexts.

One principal objective of ITL and these monographs will be to put in place the building blocks for an authentic body of ASEAN and Asian integration theory developed in, and with sensitivity to, the particularities and peculiarities of the region and continent. A theory and conceptual framework of Asian legal integration will signal the coming of age of research and in the region itself.

Although the monographs form part of an overarching project, we asked our authors to write each as a "standalone" – not assuming that their readers would have consulted any of the other titles. Indeed, the project is rich and few will read all of the monographs. We encourage readers to pick and choose from the various monographs and design their own menu. There is, on occasion, some overlap in providing, for example, background information on ASEAN in different studies. That is not only inevitable but desirable in a project of this amplitude.

The world is increasingly witnessing a phenomenon of interlocking regional organization, where the experience of one feeds on others. In some way, the intellectual, disciplinary and comparative sensibility of this project is a microcosm of the world it describes.

The range of topics covered in this series comprises:
The General Architecture and Aspirations of ASEAN
The Governance and Management of ASEAN: Instruments, Institutions, Monitoring, Compliance and Dispute Resolution
Legal Regimes in ASEAN
The ASEAN Economic Community ASEAN and the World
The Substantive Law of ASEAN

ACKNOWLEDGMENTS

This book is part of the "ASEAN Integration Through Law" project at the Centre for International Law at the National University of Singapore. We are immensely grateful to Michael Ewing-Chow, Hsien-Li Tan and Joseph Weiler for their invitation to participate in this rewarding initiative. We have benefited enormously from their reflections and probing questions over the years. A special word of thanks also to the many participants at the ASEAN Law Academy, where we have jointly taught a course on investment regulation in the ASEAN Economic Community since 2018. Those private practitioners, government officials and scholars from the different member states of ASEAN have been a perfect laboratory to test the ideas presented in this book. Some of our earlier research has been published in different law review articles which we have used as a foundation in this book. Those articles are: "The Limits of Isomorphism: Global Investment Law and the ASEAN Investment Regime" (2016) 17 *Chicago Journal of International Law* 341; "International Cooperation and Organizational Identities: The Evolution of the ASEAN Investment Regime" (2017) 37 *North Western Journal of International Law and Business* 173; "Legalizing the ASEAN Way: Adapting and Reimaging the ASEAN Investment Regime" (2018) 66 *American Journal of*

Comparative Law 233. Lastly, we wish to express particular thanks to Ahhyun Ryu (PhD researcher at the European University Institute) and Rachel Gray (Editor-in-Chief at *Chicago-Kent Law Review*) for their superb research and formatting assistance.

GATT/WTO Reports

Canada – FIRA

GATT Panel Report, *Canada – Administration of the Foreign Investment Review Act*, BISD 30S/140 (adopted Feb. 17, 1984).

Argentina – Textiles

Appellate Body Report, *Argentina – Measures Affecting Imports of Footwear, Textiles, Apparel and Other Items*, WTO Doc. WT/DS56/AB/R (adopted Mar. 27, 1998).

Indonesia – Automobile

Panel Report, *Indonesia – Certain Measures Affecting the Automobile Industry*, WTO Doc. WT/DS54/R (adopted July 2, 1998).

Indonesia – Iron or Steel

Panel Report, *Indonesia – Safeguard on Certain Iron or Steel Products*, WTO Doc. WT/DS496/R (adopted Aug. 18, 2007).

Thailand – Cigarettes

Panel Report, *Thailand – Customs and Fiscal Measures on Cigarettes from the Philippines*, WTO Doc. WT/DS371/R (adopted Nov. 15, 2010).

WTO Requests for Consultations

Malaysia – Polyethylene

Request for Consultations Under Article XXIII.1 of the GATT 1994, *Malaysia – Prohibition of Imports of Polyethylene and Polypropylene*, WTO Doc. WT/DS1/R (adopted Jan. 13, 1995).

Investor-State Dispute Settlement

Maffezini v. *Spain*

Emilio Agustín Maffezini v. *The Kingdom of Spain*, ICSID Case No. ARB/97/7, Decision of the Tribunal on Objections to Jurisdiction (Jan. 25, 2000).

SD Myers v. *Canada*

SD Myers v. *The Government of Canada*, UNCITRAL Partial Award (Nov. 13, 2000).

Philippe Gruslin v. *Malaysia*

Philippe Gruslin v. *Malaysia*, ICSID No. ARB/99/3, Award (Nov. 27, 2000).

Pope & Talbot v. *Canada*

Pope & Talbot v. *The Government of Canada*, UNCITRAL Award on the Merits of Phase 2 (Apr. 10, 2001).

Mexico v. *Metalclad*

The United Mexican States v. *Metalclad Corporation*, Supreme Court of British Columbia, Judgment of the Honourable Mr. Justice Tysoe, 2001 BCSC 664 (May 2, 2001).

Yaung Chi Oo v. *Myanmar*

Yaung Chi Oo Trading Pte Ltd. v. *Gov't of the Union of Myanmar*, ASEAN I.D. Case No. ARB 01/1 (Mar. 31, 2003), 42 ILM 540 (2003).

SGS v. *Philippines*

SGS Société Générale de Surveillance S.A. v. *Republic of the Phil.*, ICSID Case No. ARB/02/6, Decision of the Tribunal on Objections to Jurisdiction (Jan. 29, 2004).

Malaysian Historical Salvors Award on Jurisdiction

Malaysian Historical Salvors, SDN, BHD v. *Malaysia*, ICSID Case No. ARB/05/10, Award on Jurisdiction (May 17, 2007).

Desert Line Projects v. *Yemen*

Desert Line Projects LLC v. *The Republic of Yemen*, ICSID Case No. ARB/05/17, Award (Feb. 6, 2008).

Malaysian Historical Salvors Annulment Decision

Malaysian Historical Salvors SDN BHD v. *The Government of Malaysia*, ICSID Case No. ARB/05/10, Decision on the Application for Annulment (Apr. 16, 2009).

Churchill Mining v. *Indonesia*

Churchill Mining PLC & Planet Mining Pty Ltd v. *Republic of Indonesia*, ICSID Case No. ARB/12/14 & 12/40, Award (Dec. 6, 2016).

Lao Holdings v. *Laos*

Lao Holdings N.V. v. *The Lao People's Democratic Republic*, ICSID Case No. ARB (AF)/12/6, Award (Aug. 6, 2019).

Sanum Investments v. *Laos*
Sanum Investments Ltd v. *The Government of the Lao People's Democratic Republic*, UNCITRAL, PCA Case No. 2013-13, Award (Aug. 6, 2019).

International Court of Justice

Nuclear Weapons case
Legality of the Threat or Use of Nuclear Weapons, Advisory Opinion, 1996 I.C.J. 226 (July 8).

Reparation case
Reparation for Injuries Suffered in the Service of the United Nations, Advisory Opinion, 1949 I.C.J. 174 (Apr. 11).

Domestic Court Decisions

Penn Central Transportation Co. v. *New York City*
Penn Central Transportation Co. v. *New York City*, 438 U.S. 104 (1978).

ICM Agriculture v. *Commonwealth*
ICM Agric. Pty, Ltd. v. *Commonwealth*, [2009] HCA 51, 81–86 (French, C.J., Gummow, & Crennan, JJ.); *id.* at 142–54 (Hayne, Kiefel, & Bell, JJ.).

ABBREVIATIONS

ACIA	ASEAN Comprehensive Investment Agreement
ADB	Asian Development Bank
AEC	ASEAN Economic Community
AFTA	ASEAN Free Trade Area
AHKFTA	ASEAN–Hong Kong Free Trade Agreement
AIA	ASEAN Investment Area
AIR	ASEAN Investment Regime
APEC	Asia-Pacific Economic Cooperation
ARCII	Asia-Pacific Regional Cooperation and Integration Index
ASA	Association of Southeast Asia
ASEAN	Association of Southeast Asian Nations
ASEAN Charter	Charter of the Association of Southeast Asian Nations
BIT	Bilateral Investment Treaty
CAI	EU–China Comprehensive Agreement on Investment
CCI	Coordinating Committee on Investment
CEP	Comprehensive Economic Partnership
CIM	Contract Intensive Money
COVID-19	Coronavirus Disease 2019
CPTPP	Comprehensive and Progressive Agreement for Trans-Pacific Partnership

DNA	Deoxyribonucleic Acid
DSB	Dispute Settlement Body
EEC	European Economic Community
EFTA	European Free Trade Association
EU	European Union
EVSL	Early Voluntary Sectoral Liberalization
FAO	Food and Agricultural Organization
FDI	Foreign Direct Investment
FTA	Free Trade Agreement
GATS	General Agreement on Trade in Services
GATT	General Agreement on Tariffs and Trade
GDP	Gross Domestic Product
GIL	Global Investment Law
GVC	Global Value Chain
HIV/AIDS	Human Immunodeficiency Virus/ Immunodeficiency Syndrome
ICJ	International Court of Justice
ICR	Interstate Cooperative Regime
ICSID	International Centre for Settlement of Investment Disputes
ICSID Convention	Convention on the Settlement of Investment Disputes between States and Nationals of Other States
IMF	International Monetary Fund
IO	International Organization
IR	International Relations
ISDS	Investor-State Dispute Settlement
MFN	Most-Favored-Nation
MNE	Multinational Enterprise
MRA	Mutual Recognition Arrangement

NAFTA	North American Free Trade Area
OECD	Organisation for Economic Co-operation and Development
PECC	Pacific Economic Cooperation Council
RCEP	Regional Comprehensive Economic Partnership
ROO	Rules of Origin
SME	Small or Medium-sized Enterprise
SOM	Senior Officials Meeting
TRIMs	Trade-Related Investment Measures
TRN	Trans-governmental Regulatory Network
UN	United Nations
UNCITRAL	United Nations Commission on International Trade Law
UNCTAD	United Nations Conference on Trade and Development
USTR	United States Trade Representative
VAP	Vientiane Action Programme
VCLT	Vienna Convention on the Law of Treaties
WHO	World Health Organization
WTO	World Trade Organization
WTO Agreement	Agreement Marrakesh Agreement Establishing the World Trade Organization

Chapter 1

Introduction

1.1 Background and Context

Southeast Asia is characterized by remarkable diversity, dynamism and, at times, tragedy. The current ten members of the Association of Southeast Asia Nations (ASEAN) span a political spectrum that extends from thin and thick models of democracy, to authoritarian regimes (whether under military or monarchical rule) to states with one-party, communist systems. Culturally, this extraordinary region encompasses a rich set of linguistic traditions, diverse customs and religious beliefs encompassing Islam, Buddhism, Hinduism and Christianity. Its modern history too is a study in turbulence. Other than Thailand, all of the member states of ASEAN were colonized by Western (mainly European) states. The post–Second World War project of acquiring independence and self-determination has deeply shaped the political and economic contours of the region.

Indeed, some of the independence movements and post-colonial states in Southeast Asia began to experiment with political (and economic) models influenced by Marxist principles through the 1950s and 1960s. Tragically, that would in turn trigger (overt or covert) hostile interference by Western states (particularly the United States). Post-colonial turbulence though is not only a story of disastrous Western interventions in this region. Internal conflicts too are an essential background script. Perhaps most significantly of all, there was the violent episode of *Konfrontasi* that stemmed from Indonesia's opposition to the amalgamation of the Federation of Malaya, Singapore and the crown colony/British protectorates of North Borneo and Sarawak.[1] Spanning 1963 to 1966, *Konfrontasi* was triggered by Indonesia's increasingly aggressive post-colonial foreign policy in the period, leading to overt and covert military operations in the region with hundreds of casualties.[2]

Shortly after the end of *Konfrontasi*, the Bangkok Declaration[3] established ASEAN in 1967 to prevent destructive behavior by embedding security cooperation among the five founding members (Indonesia, Malaysia, the Philippines, Thailand, and Singapore). The timing here is significant and telling. While ASEAN sought to develop regional *security* cooperation, its economic mandate was almost non-existent in this early period. In fact, when dealing with economic matters, the 1967 ASEAN Declaration focuses only on trade in goods and even then, on a sub-set of agricultural trade. This omission is by no means accidental. It reflects, at first instance, existing colonial-era patterns at that time of agricultural specialization among individual ASEAN members, largely in commodity trade.[4]

Of course, a number of ASEAN states were implementing (non-liberal) strategies throughout the 1950s–1970s

[1] *See generally* J.A.C. Mackie, Konfrontasi: The Indonesia – Malaysia Dispute 1963–6 (1974).

[2] *Id.*

[3] The ASEAN Declaration (Bangkok Declaration), Aug. 8, 1967, 6 I.L.M. 1233 (1967).

[4] Rodolfo C. Severino, Southeast Asia in Search of an ASEAN Community: Insights from the Former ASEAN Secretary-General 213 (2006).

(usually of import substitution) that were designed to move their economies toward rapid industrialization. A curious collective instrument supplemented these strategies that sharply elucidates the limits of economic cooperation between the ASEAN members in this period. By the mid-1970s, the idea had begun to form that ASEAN should be employed as a system of *managed* industrialization through the centralized allocation of different industrial sectors and projects among the member states. At the first ASEAN Summit in 1976, the member states called for the establishment of large-scale industrial projects in ASEAN countries that would use available materials, increase food production, augment or save foreign exchange and create jobs.[5] At a later meeting of economic ministers, a decision was made to allocate different industrial projects among the grouping – a urea fertilizer plant each for Indonesia and Malaysia, superphosphates for the Philippines, diesel engines for Singapore and soda ash for Thailand.[6] The goal of state-managed industrialization reaches its early and short apotheosis in this period with ministers even agreeing to consult with one another on plans to establish other industries with a view to "avoiding unnecessary duplication and competition."[7]

Needless to say then, the origin of ASEAN as a "security community" is fundamentally different to other regional settings such as the European Union (EU).[8] Famously, the EU's evolution follows something of a reverse sequence, with

[5] *Id.* at 214. [6] *Id.* [7] *Id.*

[8] Amitav Acharya, Constructing a Security Community in South East Asia: ASEAN and the Problem of Regional Order, at chp. 7 (3rd ed. 2014).

a choice to begin with, facially at least, economic integration. The variances between these two regional schemes transcend start-points. The story of integration in the European Union is, to a very large degree, one of law and legal actors.[9] The intergovernmental structure of ASEAN, by contrast, is characterized by more fluid arrangements, with stronger reliance on informality and consensus coupled with domestic implementing measures. There is a danger then of making false comparisons here. Researchers and policymakers must be mindful of the diversity of geneses, traditions and political economies of different regional organizations, which is itself a fundamental premise of this book.

On the economic front, ASEAN members would only shift their dominant paradigm from a closed to open strategy in the 1980s.[10] By that time, of course, inward-orientated models (such as import substitution) had proved disappointing in their ability to deliver sustainable levels of economic growth and development outcomes.[11] Some ASEAN states even signed their first bilateral investment treaties (BITs) from the late 1980s onwards, such as Brunei (with Germany

[9] On the role of judicialized dispute settlement in driving integration in the European setting, *see* Miguel Maduro, We the Court: The European Court of Justice and the European Economic Constitution (1998).

[10] *See generally* The Politics and Economics of Integration in Asia and the Pacific (Shiro Armstrong ed., 2011).

[11] For exploration of the theory, adoption, and subsequent limits of import substitution as a development strategy, *see* Michael J. Trebilcock & Robert Howse, The Regulation of International Trade 486, 486–88 (3rd ed. 2005).

in 1998), Cambodia (with Malaysia in 1994), Laos (with France in 1989), Myanmar (with the Philippines in 1998) and Vietnam (with Italy in 1990). For the other ASEAN members, while there was sporadic use of BITs during the 1960s–1980s, there were exponential growth and clustering of BIT activity throughout the 1990s.[12] More significantly, the late 1980s witnessed the first attempt by the ASEAN states to develop a dedicated ASEAN treaty on foreign investment in the form of the 1987 ASEAN Agreement on the Promotion and Protection of Investment. Strikingly, the ASEAN members would refine legal tools and develop deeper normative commitments in two further iterations culminating in the 2009 ASEAN Comprehensive Agreement on Investment.

In comparison to significant liberal and protective grants to foreign investment, the ASEAN states moved relatively cautiously on the trade front. It was only by the 1990s that the ASEAN members had established the ASEAN Free Trade Area (AFTA).[13] At inception, the AFTA was a cautious free trade area. Originally, the members committed to only reduce tariffs on intra-ASEAN trade to 0–5 per cent on non-sensitive goods over a 15-year period.[14] Moreover, the AFTA's complicated administrative procedures required to meet rules

[12] Zachary Elkins, Andrew Guzman & Beth Simmons, *Competing for Capital: The Diffusion of Bilateral Investment Treaties, 1960–2000*, 60 International Organization 811, 821 (2006) (outlining the clustering of BIT signings by developing states through the late 1980s and 1990s).

[13] Agreement on the Common Effective Preferential Tariff Scheme for the ASEAN Free Trade Area, Jan. 28, 1992, 31 I.L.M. 513 (1992).

[14] *Id.* art. 4.

of origin led to low levels of utilization by businesses.[15] Yet political commitment to economic integration would advance throughout the 1990s with governmental change in key ASEAN member states.[16] By 2003, in the Bali Concord, the ASEAN members had committed to establishing a single market and production base by 2020,[17] with a later detailed plan targeting trade liberalization in 11 sectors.[18] With the adoption of the ASEAN Charter in 2008, the members articulated their vision of an Economic Community which would comprise:

> [A] single market and production base which is stable, prosperous, highly competitive and economically integrated with effective facilitation for trade and investment in which there is free flow of goods, services and investment: facilitated movement of business persons, professionals, talents and labour; and freer flow of capital.[19]

[15] Bryan Mercurio, *Trade Liberalization in Asia: Why Intra-Asian Free Agreements Are Not Utlilised by the Business Community*, 6 (1) ASIAN J. WTO & INT'L. HEALTH L. & POL. 109, 110–36 (2011).

[16] Richard Stubbs, *Signing on to Liberalization: AFTA and the Politics of Regional Economic Cooperation*, 13 PACIFIC REV. 297 (2000).

[17] Declaration of ASEAN Concord II (Bali Concord II), Oct. 7, 2003, 43 I.L.M. 18 (2004).

[18] Vientiane Action Programme (VAP) 2004–2010, Nov. 29, 2004, https://asean.org/wp-content/uploads/images/archive/VAP-10th%20ASEAN%20Summit.pdf.

[19] Charter of the Association of Southeast Asian Nations art. 1(5), Nov. 20, 2007, 2624 U.N.T.S. 223 (hereinafter ASEAN Charter).

Indeed, across this time frame, trade and investment flows have been nothing short of spectacular. Between 1990 and 2014, the investment inflow to, and outflow from, this region has increased approximately 10 times and 34 times, respectively.[20] By 2014, foreign direct investment (FDI) flows to ASEAN exceeded inflows to China, making it the largest recipient of FDI in the developing world.[21] More recently, ASEAN has been a center of gravity in global economic developments. The disastrous trade war between the United States and China, as well as the subsequent outbreak of the COVID-19 pandemic, have pushed multinational enterprises (MNEs) to diversify their supply chains – especially from China – to some ASEAN nations, such as Vietnam. The United States–China trade war has even pushed Chinese investors to move labor-intensive manufacturing facilities from China to ASEAN nations.[22] Strikingly, in the middle of the pandemic, FDI flows to Vietnam have remained relatively robust.[23]

[20] UNCTAD, *FDI Statistics Division on Investment and Enterprise* (April 2, 2016) http://unctad.org/en/Pages/DIAE/FDI%20Statistics/FDI-Statistics.aspx.

[21] ASEAN Secretariat & UNCTAD, *ASEAN Investment Report 2015*, at xv (Nov. 2015), https://perma.cc/W7YR-KJTB.

[22] Alistair Gray, *US Retailers Accelerate Shift away from Chinese Suppliers*, FIN. TIMES (Sept. 10, 2019); Steve Johnson, *Trump's Trade War: Which of China's Neighbours Are Set to Profit?*, FIN. TIMES (Dec. 3, 2018).

[23] *See* John Reed, *Vietnam Prepares for Supply Chain Shift from China*, FIN. TIMES (Dec. 28, 2020).

Moreover, the newly-minted Regional Comprehensive Economic Partnership (RCEP)[24] is hailed as a golden opportunity for ASEAN members to deepen trade and investment liberalization among themselves to maximize the RCEP's true potential being the synthesis of *extra*-ASEAN and *intra*-ASEAN economic flows. Indeed, RCEP can be said to be a brainchild of the "ASEAN Centrality"[25] or the "Global ASEAN" under the AEC Blueprint 2025.[26] The potential benefits

[24] ASEAN, *Joint Leaders' Statement on the Negotiations for the Regional Comprehensive Economic Partnership (RCEP)* ¶ 5, Nov. 14, 2018, https://asean.org/asean2020/wp-content/uploads/2021/02/18.-RCEP-Summit-2_Joint-Leaders-Statement_FINAL2.pdf.

[25] Peter A. Petri & Michael Plummer, *RCEP: A New Trade Agreement That Will Shape Global Economics and Politics*, Brookings (Nov. 16, 2020) (attributing the launch of RCEP to the notion of "ASEAN Centrality").

[26] "Create a deeply integrated and highly cohesive ASEAN economy"; "to increase ASEAN's competitive edge in moving the region up the global value chains (GVCs) into higher technology and knowledge-intensive manufacturing and services industries." ASEAN, *ASEAN Economic Community Blueprint 2025*, ¶ 6 (Nov. 2015) www.asean.org/wp-content/uploads/2012/05/8.-March-2016-ASCC-Blueprint-2025.pdf; "ASEAN is continuing to make steady progress towards integrating the region into the global economy through FTAs and comprehensive economic partnership agreements (CEPs) with China, Japan, Republic of Korea, India, Australia and New Zealand. Negotiations to conclude the Regional Comprehensive Economic Partnership (RCEP) and the ASEAN-Hong Kong FTA (AHKFTA) are also ongoing. These FTAs/CEPs have been strengthening ASEAN's position as an open and inclusive economic region, and lay the foundation for ASEAN to retain its centrality in global and regional engagements, where possible. ASEAN Member States are also engaged in FTAs and CEPs with their strategic trade partners to complement the regional FTAs/CEPs." ASEAN, *ASEAN Economic Community Blueprint 2025*, ¶ 79 (Nov. 2015).

of using foreign investment to position ASEAN as an integrated production base are extraordinary, including the possibility of higher employment, wages and overall development throughout the region. As about a quarter of total FDI flows into the ASEAN region originate from non-ASEAN RCEP member countries, ASEAN economies are expected to benefit greatly from the RCEP connectivity through a deep nexus between trade and investment.[27] Consider the telling point that the top 100 multinational enterprises (MNEs) from non-ASEAN RCEP member countries retain commercial presence in the ASEAN region, holding an enormous investment potency of $13.6 trillion in assets and $1.1 trillion in cash as of 2019.[28] As ASEAN economies have committed to unprecedented improvements in infrastructure (such as power, telecommunication and transportation) since the COVID-19 pandemic, foreign investors from RCEP states are critically positioned in infrastructure development, where the investment need is estimated to be between $110 billion and $184 billion annually from 2015 to 2030.[29]

1.2 The COVID-19 Pandemic and ASEAN Investment

The ASEAN region has recently been one of the most popular FDI destinations across the globe. In 2019, ASEAN was the

www.asean.org/wp-content/uploads/2012/05/8.-March-2016-ASCC-Blueprint-2025.pdf.

[27] ASEAN Secretariat & UNCTAD, *ASEAN Investment Report 2020–2021: Investing in Industry 4.0*, at 32–4 (Sept. 2021), https://asean.org/wp-content/uploads/2021/09/AIR-2020-2021.pdf.

[28] *Id.* at 35.

[29] *Id.* at 43.

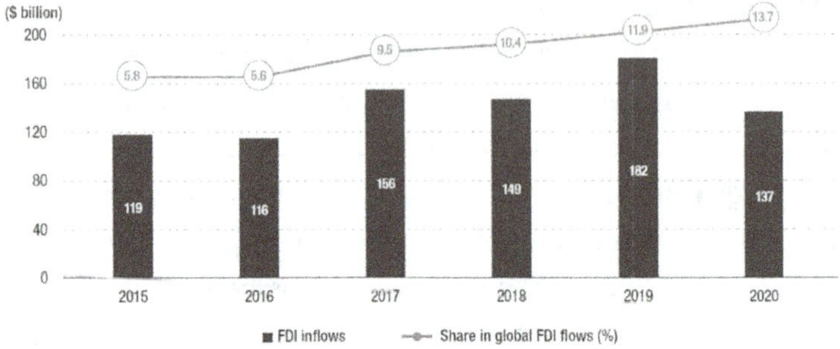

Figure 1.1 FDI flows in ASEAN and share in the world (%)[30]

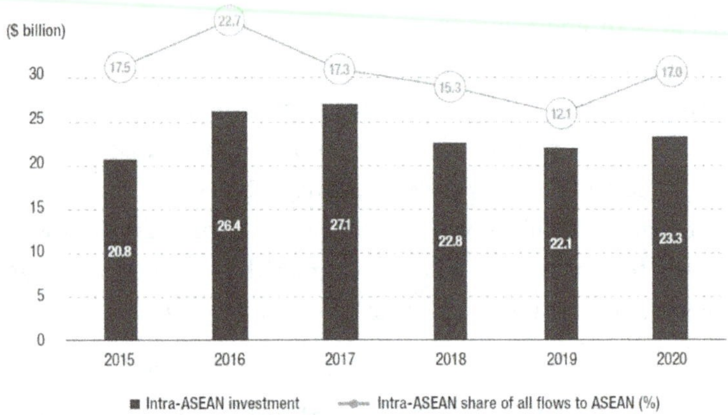

Figure 1.2 Intra-ASEAN FDI flows and shares (%)[31]

largest recipient of FDI among developing economies, as the region witnessed the highest-ever FDI inflows in history ($182 billion). Despite a temporary decline due to the COVID-19 pandemic in 2020, the region's share of global FDI actually rose from 11.9 percent to 13.7 percent that year. (Figure 1.1) At the same time, *intra*-ASEAN investment flows have also

30 *Id.* at 3–4. 31 *Id.* at 24–5.

demonstrated a steady growing trend. The pandemic pushed the *intra*-ASEAN share of FDI in the region from 12 percent in 2019 to 17 percent in 2020 (Figure 1.2).

ASEAN members have continued to adopt and implement economic recovery packages, especially under the auspices of the "2020 ASEAN Comprehensive Recovery Framework," which coordinates ASEAN economies' post-pandemic recovery as well as FDI strategies.[32] In the same vein, they have also upgraded the ASEAN Comprehensive Investment Agreement and the ASEAN Trade in Services Agreement.[33] In June 2020, ASEAN members launched the Fourth Protocol to amend the ASEAN Comprehensive Investment Agreement. The Fourth Protocol augments investor protection by incorporating the prohibition of "performance requirements" and further promotes investment liberalization by converting preexisting reservations on restricted investment areas and non-conforming measures into two annexes in accordance with a "negative-list" approach. In October 2020, ASEAN members replaced the ASEAN Framework Agreement on Services with the ASEAN Trade in Services Agreement, which provides an enhanced level of investor protection and investment liberalization in the services sector. Individual ASEAN members have also persisted in incentivizing FDI as a post-pandemic recovery strategy. The ratio of domestic measures between protection/liberalization and restriction/regulation has shifted from 27:2 in 2019 to 51:0 in 2020.[34]

Ironically, the pandemic has highlighted the vitality of the ASEAN region as a new FDI hot spot. In

[32] *Id.* at 55–6. [33] *Id.* at 61. [34] *Id.* at 64.

particular, the dramatic increase of online activities during government-mandated lockdowns has attracted FDI in the area of "digital infrastructure," such as data centers and 5G networks across the ASEAN region.[35] In fact, the region is expected to rise as a prominent global data center within next five years, surpassing the rest of the world, including North America.[36] In this regard, the Asian Development Bank (ADB) aptly observes that:

> The ongoing pandemic also highlights the benefits of rapid technological progress, digitalization, and increasing services trade in connecting the global economy even closer and providing new forms of global linkages.[37]

Tellingly, a number of MNEs handling data centers and cloud services have already increased their investments in the region, which eloquently demonstrates their optimism toward the region's transformation into "Industry 4.0."[38] Against this background, the challenge for ASEAN members is to collectively harness the new pandemic-driven FDI environment in the region. ASEAN members need to recalibrate the micro-operation of their characteristic "ASEAN Way" in a manner that refrains from parochialism and instead channels synergistic cooperation, with or without preexisting treaty mandates.

[35] *Id.* at 12. [36] *Id.* at 52.

[37] Asian Development Bank, *The ASEAN Economic Integration Report 2021: Making Digital Platform Work for Asia and the Pacific*, at xvii (Feb. 2021).

[38] ASEAN Secretariat & UNCTAD, *ASEAN Investment Report 2020–2021*, *supra* note 27, at 51–2.

1.3 Our Thesis in Summary

Against this exhilarating background of the vitality of Southeast Asia as a site of economic growth and innovation, this book explores regional economic law and governance in ASEAN through a lens of its regulation of foreign investment. ASEAN economic law and governance features a complex yet distinct set of traits, which can be epitomized as a dynamic legal interaction of *centripetal* force (represented by global economic norms) and its *centrifugal* counterpart (defined by ASEAN's unique historical and cultural traits). Rather than defending a narrowly articulated thesis, our goal in this book is threefold in a broad sense.

First, we aim to interpret legal and institutional fore-structures of the ASEAN Investment Regime (AIR) through the lens of the ASEAN Way. The political, diplomatic and cultural traits that comprise the ASEAN Way have been constructed from the region's unique historical legacies, including colonialization, external interventions during the Cold War and the *Konfrontasi.* The ASEAN Way can be symbolized by its emphasis on the principle of non-interference and consensus decision-making engineered by informal working-level deliberations prior to high-level summitries.[39] Under the ASEAN Way, legalization may be "neither inevitable nor desirable."[40]

[39] *See* Peter Boyce, *The Machinery of Southeast Asian Regional Diplomacy,* in New Directions in the International Relations of Southeast Asia: Global Powers and Southeast Asia 175 (1973).

[40] Miles Kahler, *Conclusion: The Causes and Consequences of Legalization,* in Legalization and World Politics 299 (Judith L. Goldstein et al. eds., 2001).

The creation of "Senior Officials Meetings" (SOM) in various sectors, such as economics, the environment and science, as well as national secretariats in the foreign ministry of each member, has prioritized trans-governmental cooperation in the ASEAN over more legalistic/judicial strategies (that are so prominent in other regional settings such as the EU).[41] Thus, the ASEAN Way provides an "institutional point of reference" against which the opportunity costs of undermining sovereignty can be measured.[42]

Second, we seek to identify apposite theoretical paradigms that capture the unique realities of the AIR. While recent controversies in international economic law are mostly directed at Western phenomena, such as those related to Brexit and the new trade politics of the United States, the legal academy has been slow to recognize the richness and distinctiveness inherent in the legal facets of ASEAN. To be sure, there are a number of valuable explorations of the ASEAN investment system from a doctrinal perspective.[43] In this book however, we focus on the many non-legal forms of cooperation and characteristic flexibilities in ASEAN's economic regulation which we argue provide both scholars and policymakers with new insights on the conceptualization of law and legalization in global economic governance.

[41] *Id.*

[42] Michael Leifer, ASEAN and the Security of South-East Asia 151 (1989).

[43] *See especially* Julien Chaisse & Sufian Jusoh, The ASEAN Comprehensive Investment Agreement: The Regionalization of Laws and Policy on Foreign Investment (2016).

Third, informed by these rich theoretical frameworks, this book seeks to chart not only the past and present, but the future of the AIR. It elucidates the historical evolution of AIR as it explores the incorporation of external norms (Global Investment Law) and the adaptation of those norms in light of the specific needs and deliberative modalities of the ASEAN states. AIR subscribes, superficially at least, to the Western legalization paradigm in the form of Global Investment Law, which might be a (regrettable) tendency as a (soft or hard) benchmark. Yet, ASEAN states have transcended this external start-point to endogenously (and strategically) position ASEAN as an integrated production base. Properly implemented, this normative goal promises much. For the many developing countries within the ASEAN grouping, the unbundling of production facilities embedded in global value chains (GVC) can be a significant opportunity. Participation in a GVC holds out enormous promise of development spillovers at a lower entry cost than past strategies, particularly those focused on jurisdictionally bounded industrialization.[44] That said, there is cause for caution in some of the puzzling implementation modalities employed within AIR, not least the relative absence of liberalization of services in ASEAN together with "reverse open regionalism" and its attendant disadvantages.

[44] Richard Baldwin, The Great Convergence: Information Technology and the New Globalization, at chp. 9 (2016).

1.4 Theoretical Paradigms

As flagged above, to properly understand the foundation and evolution of the AIR, we need first to identify an appropriate theoretical framework.

Conventional international relations theories[45] mostly adopt a micro framework. Agency-oriented theories, such as neorealism, rational choice theory and neoliberal institutionalism, employ methodological individualism that is largely state oriented. Neorealists tend to dismiss international legal regimes like the AIR, trivializing its constitutive infrastructure.[46] To them, any interstate cooperation is tantamount to a mere "epiphenomenon of underlying power" or a "coincidence of state interests or coercion by powerful states."[47] On the other hand, rational choice theory views any institution as a program that *ex ante* maps out actors' rational strategies.[48] In this regard, AIR could be seen as a welfare-maximizing contract in which states' interests and preferences determine

[45] Regarding various strands of IR theories, *see generally* Sungjoon Cho, The Social Foundations of World Trade: Norms, Community and Constitution (2014).

[46] *See* Richard H. Steinberg & Jonathan M. Zasloff, *Power and International Law*, 100 Am. J. Int'l L. 64, 73–76 (2006); *see also* Kenneth N. Waltz, Theory of International Politics 105 (1979); Stephen D. Krasner, *Structural Causes and Regime Consequences: Regimes as Intervening Variables*, in International Regimes 1 (Stephen D. Krasner ed., 1983); Jack L. Goldsmith & Eric A. Posner, The Limits of International Law 36–7, 118, 225 (2005).

[47] Steinberg & Zasloff, *supra* note 46, at 74–5.

[48] *See* Kenneth A. Shepsle, *Rational Choice Institutionalism, in* Oxford Handbook of Political Institutions (R.A.W. Rhodes, Sarah A. Binder & Bert A. Rockman eds., 2008).

various institutional choices.[49] Cooperation here is a result of a complicated calculation of various utilities (such as positive reputation and reciprocal cooperation by others) and disutilities (such as negative reputation and penalties).[50] Neoliberal institutionalism shares a set of premises with neorealism and rational choice theory. As with neorealists, neoliberal institutionalists' main analytical focus is individual actors (states).[51] Meanwhile, similar to rational choice theorists, neoliberal institutionalists argue that individual actors (states) basically pursue competing interests, subject to various (material and non-material) constraints.[52] Based on an integrated view of a domestic and international sphere,[53] neoliberal institutionalists' main concern is how to coordinate diverging domestic preferences with a minimum cost.[54]

These conventional international relations (IR) theories are collectively coined "rationalism," in that they presuppose isotropic, rational actors (states) whose actions are

[49] *See generally* Sungjoon Cho, *Beyond Rationality: A Sociological Construction of the World Trade Organization*, 52 VA. J. INT'L L. 321 (2012).

[50] *See id.* at 36–40, 45, 47–8.

[51] *See* Claire R. Kelly, *The Value Vacuum: Self-Enforcing Regimes and the Dilution of the Normative Feedback Loop*, 22 MICH. J. INT'L L. 673, 681–3 (2001).

[52] *See* Andrew Moravcsik, *Taking Preferences Seriously: A Liberal Theory of International Politics*, 51 INT'L ORG. 513, 516 (1997).

[53] Anne-Marie Slaughter, *A Liberal Theory of International Law*, 94 AM. SOC'Y INT'L L. PROC. 240, 241 (2000).

[54] Robert O. Keohane, AFTER HEGEMONY: COOPERATION AND DISCORD IN THE WORLD POLITICAL ECONOMY (1984) (viewing that international institutions facilitate decentralized cooperation among state actors).

guided by a common thesis of substantive rationality represented by efficiency, power and interest.[55] While these conventional IR theories offer useful heuristics in understanding the *origin* of AIR, they cannot fully capture the complex "changes" that AIR makes over time. One of the structural qualities of the AIR is its evolution over time across multiple iterations (1987, 1998 and 2009). Yet the paradigms provided by conventional IR theories are necessarily functional and therefore inherently static. Their characteristic methodological individualism adopts states (agency) as a primary analytical unit.[56] Under this view, AIR is merely an instrument that serves various utilitarian functions that rational states would desire, such as providing information, reducing uncertainties and monitoring cheating.[57] Functionalism cannot bestow ontological autonomy[58] onto AIR that enables us to observe its post-creation evolution process in which AIR adapts

[55] Robert O. Keohane, *International Institutions: Two Approaches*, 32 Int'l Stud. Q. 379, 386–7 (1988).

[56] Alexander Wendt, *The State as Person in International Theory*, 30 Rev. Int'l Stud. 289, 299 (2004) ("We-intentions are *nothing but* interlocking I-intentions toward a group.").

[57] *See* Michael N. Barnett & Martha Finnemore, *The Politics, Power, and Pathologies of International Organizations*, 53 Int'l Org. 699, 702 (1999); *see also* The New Institutionalism in Organizational Analysis 3–4 (Walter W. Powell & Paul J. DiMaggio eds., 1991); Anna Grandori, *Notes on the Use of Power and Efficiency Constructs in the Economics and Sociology of Organizations*, in Interdisciplinary Perspectives on Organization Studies 61 (Siegwart M. Lindenberg & Hein Schreuder eds., 1993).

[58] Barnett & Finnemore, *supra* note 57, at 704.

itself, on its own terms, to environmental challenges.[59] In sum, conventional IR theories may offer various functional snapshots of AIR, but not its panoramic identity *qua* organization.

Therefore, we need a new theoretical framework through which we can conceptually embrace the ontological autonomy of AIR so as to investigate its dynamic institutional development. AIR's institutional decision, or collective consciousness, cannot be the result of an aggregation of the interests of its individual member states. Although its member states are building blocks of AIR, AIR "emerges" on its own, rather than being simply created by those states.[60] Our preferred theoretical underpinning of AIR's organizational autonomy is one of constructivism. A sociology-led approach, especially constructivism, distinguishes itself from conventional IR theories as it highlights a social *structure*, rather than agency, that constructs the culture and identities of those actors.[61] Constructivists emphasize ideational factors, such as culture and norms, that guide state actions from within.[62] States build a collective identity as they share common goals and norms. Such a collective identity often bonds those participating states, *with or without material incentives*, and enables cooperation among them. While constructivism provides our theoretical underpinning of AIR's

[59] Laurence R. Helfer, *Understanding Change in International Organizations: Globalization and Innovation in the ILO*, 59 VAND. L. REV. 662 (2006).

[60] Wendt, *supra* note 56, at 301, 304.

[61] Martha Finnemore, *Norms, Culture, and World Politics: Insights from Sociology's Institutionalism*, 50 INT'L ORG. 325, 333 (1996).

[62] *See generally*, Wendt, *supra* note 56.

organizational autonomy, we also seek to explain: first, when and how certain institutional changes transpire, and, second, what kinds of changes take place in the process of AIR's institutional development. Here, one critical aspect of AIR's institutional development is that as an autonomous organization, AIR incessantly interacts with its surrounding environment for its growth and survival. That external environment is both a resource and a threat to an organic entity like AIR. Harnessing and adapting to its environment is essential to AIR's survival.[63]

Our critique of the Western orthodoxy on economic governance could be seen, on first view, as aligned with the field of post-colonial legal criticism. These scholars tend to characterize "Global Investment Law" (GIL) and its characteristic pro-investor bias as exploitive and thus detrimental to host (developing) countries. For example, Ntina Tzouvala argues that GIL has "consistently subjected nature to the imperatives of capital" and has forced host states to be "the primary bearers of the bulk of the (not-legally binding) responsibilities," while responsibilities of land-grabbing foreign investors (transnational corporations) remain vague.[64] Likewise, B.S. Chimni accuses the "transnational capitalist class" of having "used its economic clout and ideological primacy to shape the foreign *economic* policy

[63] *See* Richard W. Scott, Organizations: Rational, Natural, and Open Systems 57 (3rd ed. 1991); Alvin W. Gouldner, *Organizational Analysis*, *in* Sociology Today 404–5 (Robert K. Merton et al. eds., 1959).

[64] Ntina Tzouvala, *A False Promise?: Regulating Land-Grabbing and the Post-Colonial State*, 32 Leiden J. Int'l L. 235, 239 (2019).

of emerging powers" in the area of foreign investment.[65] Muthucumaraswamy Sornarajah makes a critical observation that the repeated appointment of pro-investor panelists of investor-state arbitration tribunals tends to entrench the neoliberal agenda in GIL.[66] James Gathii also concludes that various regional trade and investment agreements, through liberalization, deregulation and privatization, aim to "fortify the neoliberal agenda of the Washington Consensus."[67]

Relatedly, ASEAN's selective adaption of GIL may be perceived as ASEAN governments' collective struggle in maintaining the continuing relevancy of the ASEAN "developmental state" engineered by "elite technocracies" amid the increasingly salient trend of the reinvention of the neoliberal economic order.[68] According to Toby Carroll and Darryl Jarvis, the Asian developmental state has encountered the phenomenon of "heterodoxy" when its originally interventionist policy orientation was subsequently transmuted into an evolving neoliberal position that brought the market

[65] B.S. Chimni, *Capitalism, Imperialism, and International Law in the Twenty-First Century*, 14 Or. Rev. Int'l L. 17, 34 (2012) (emphasis original).

[66] Muthucumaraswamy Sornarajah, *Mutations of Neo-Liberalism in International Investment Law*, 3 Trade L. & Dev. 203, 224 (2011).

[67] James Thuro Gathii, *The Neoliberal Turn in Regional Trade Agreements*, 86 Wash. L. Rev. 421, 460–71 (2011).

[68] Toby Carroll & Darryl S. L. Jarvis, *Disembedding Autonomy: Asia after the Developmental State*, in Asia after Developmental State: Disembedding Autonomy 7 (Toby Caroll & Darryl S. L. Jarvis eds., 2017).

back in.[69] Ironically, however, China's enduring adherence to state capitalism or "capitalism with Chinese characteristics" might rekindle the case for the ASEAN developmental state "in ways that are at odds with the conventional and increasingly discredited Western wisdom."[70]

Our critique of the Western orthodoxy of market normalcy remains however a "comparativist" enterprise, distinct from these structure-laden approaches. The main goal of this book is to explore the manner in which ASEAN's history and culture has fundamentally shaped its foreign investment policies, leading to outcomes that often depart from the external structure and script of GIL. Human agency and complex private–public partnerships are core components of this distinctive approach to economic integration. Indeed, the very notion of "ASEAN Centrality" – so critical to the launch and conclusion of RCEP – is based on the progressive, active and constructive participation of individual ASEAN member states.

1.5 Overview

The regulation of foreign investment in the ASEAN legal order is facially characterized by thick complexity. As a start-point, Chapter 2 begins the inquiry into the collective ASEAN rules on investment by assessing the bilateral

[69] For example, the World Bank has continued to advance the "Good Governance" agenda. *Id.* at 20.

[70] Mark Beeson, *What Does China's Rise Mean for the Developmental State Paradigm*, in ASIA AFTER DEVELOPMENTAL STATE: DISEMBEDDING AUTONOMY 192 (Toby Caroll & Darryl S. L. Jarvis eds., 2017).

investment treaties (BITs) entered into by individual member states within ASEAN. Much of that dense BIT network temporally predates the construction of the ASEAN investment treaties, and thus operates as the legal and conceptual scaffolding for the construction of those dedicated collective rules. Yet the collective rules themselves are characterized by multiple iterations (1987, 1998 and 2009), with distinct heterogeneities in normative orientation and doctrinal choices that depart from the individual BIT commitments of the ASEAN member states.

As flagged earlier, to accurately understand the organizational development of AIR, we need a targeted conceptual or theoretical framework. In Chapter 2, we critique the various state-orientated theories – such as neorealism or neoliberal institutionalism – entrenched in the rationalist tradition. Our guiding premise in this book is to construct ASEAN's identity *qua* organization using different insights from constructivism to probe ASEAN's institutional evolution for the past several decades. Although ASEAN encompasses multiple economic and political dimensions, Chapter 2 focuses on the initial formation of ASEAN's identity – in the 1987 ASEAN Agreement on the Promotion and Protection of Foreign Investment – as it concerns the *intra*-regional investment regime. To the extent that this investment regime is an important factor driving economic integration among the ASEAN states, scrutinizing ASEAN's identity formation in that particular area offers a unique way of understanding ASEAN's institutional development.

In the next stage of the evolution of the AIR, the ASEAN member states shift dramatically from the start-point of 1987 ASEAN Investment Agreement. Chapter 2 shows that this start-point was marked by a remarkable degree of conservativism, with the member states unwilling to extend fundamental liberal and protective guarantees typically found in their BITs with third countries among themselves. By contrast, Chapter 3 traces a fundamental shift by the late 1990s, where a series of internal and external events would push those members to dramatically reshape their approach to investment rules. The combination of the disastrous effects of the 1997–1998 Asian financial crisis and the rise of China as a serious economic competitor would force those states to begin to develop a deeper level of integration. That identity crisis fundamentally shapes both the normative orientation and legal norms within the 1998 ASEAN Framework Agreement. Though limited when measured against conventional legalization indicators, any such critique ignores the vitality and creativity of the key choices made in this time of crisis. In fact, we find a remarkable pattern of treaty innovation in certain areas, especially financial sector flexibilities.

Chapter 4 builds upon the legalization assessment by focusing on the latest (and current) iteration of the AIR: the 2009 ASEAN Comprehensive Investment Agreement (ACIA). What is distinct about the ASEAN investment project – and potentially transformative – is the evolution in objectives surrounding the role of treaty disciplines. By the time of the ACIA, those treaty constraints would no longer be used as part of a simple BIT-style project of delivering investment protection with the hope that this would somehow translate into greater flows of foreign investment. Instead, the ASEAN members now sought to strategically position their region as an integrated production base for foreign investment, thereby leveraging one of the fastest and most dynamic aspects of the global economy. There is also a good degree of innovation at play in the expressed desire of the ASEAN members to construct an investment treaty representing global best practice. Yet clearly, the AIR continues broadly to exhibit a low degree of legalization measured against conventional benchmark indicators. Chapter 4 seeks to contextualize and explain this low degree of legalization through both the ASEAN Way and negative social learning. The adaptation and reimagination embedded into the AIR calls into question universalist assumptions underpinning the concept of legalization and highlights the idiographic nature of legalization from a comparative law perspective. We argue instead that delegalization can be an independent and entirely legitimate mode of legalization.

In Chapter 5, we synthesise our analysis and identify targeted normative reforms. To our mind, ASEAN leaders need a new cost–benefit analysis on political economy as their broader domestic constituencies, such as consumers, have recently demonstrated robust support for free trade.[71] ASEAN leaders will eventually need to defy political demands for protectionism to establish a stable foundation for economic growth as they harness the development potential within the ASEAN region. Here, the post-pandemic trend of "regionalization" of supply chains, which is to establish multiple regional sourcing hubs close to consumer markets, has

[71] Andi Haswidi, *ASEAN Governments Out of Step on Free Trade*, Fin. Times (Feb. 12, 2019).

emerged.[72] An empirical study has shown that positive welfare effects from the creation of the RCEP could help repair economic damage to ASEAN economies inflicted by the United States–China trade war.[73] Considering that these trends are likely to continue, the inauguration of the RCEP provides a golden opportunity for ASEAN members to deepen trade and investment liberalization among themselves to maximize the RCEP's true potential – the synthesis of *extra*-ASEAN and *intra*-ASEAN economic flows.

While the ASEAN Way has been criticized, rightly or wrongly, as a hindrance to ASEAN investment, we suggest that the Western style of legalization is not the right answer. Promoting *intra*-ASEAN investment flows should be pursued *alongside*, not against, the ASEAN Way. What seems essential in soliciting cooperation from ASEAN members is to gradually expand shared grounds and consolidate the ASEAN identity pronounced in the ASEAN Charter. By embracing a constructivist logic, ASEAN members need a new paradigm of integration based on trust and confidence in their common market project. Here, an earlier success of the APEC regime offers an illustrative case in point.[74] Considering the critical space occupied by the ASEAN within the Asia Pacific Economic

[72] *See* Mike Cherney, *Firms Want to Adjust Supply Chains Post-Pandemic, but Changes Take Time*, Wall St. J. (Dec. 27, 2020).

[73] *See* Peter A. Petri & Michael G. Plummer, *Trade War, RECP and CPTPP: Will East Asia Decouple from the United States?* (Nov. 28, 2020), https://papers.ssrn.com/sol3/papers.cfm?abstract_id=3630294.

[74] *See generally* Sungjoon Cho, *Rethinking APEC: A New Experiment for a Post-Modern Institutional Arrangement*, *in* WTO and East Asia: New Perspectives 381 (Mitsuo Matsushita & Dukgeun Ahn eds., 2004).

Cooperation (APEC) regime, it is no coincidence that the latter's strengths, such as effective human agency (trans-governmental bureaucrats) and soft law instruments, correspond with the ASEAN Way. Indeed, the recent successful delivery of RCEP has also been attributed to a similar low-profile yet practical *modus operandi*, which may be labeled "quiet diplomacy."[75] Touting human agency and soft law, ASEAN leaders may rebalance domestic political economy and collective economic interests, thereby synthesizing global and regional (ASEAN) value chains and linking a single ASEAN market to the global market. ASEAN leaders should promote and upgrade ASEAN investment in the same manner.

The final concluding chapter provides a summary and recount of the main observations and arguments in previous chapters from the standpoint of regionalist dynamics in ASEAN investment regulation. It also offers several policy proposals to harness the potential of the ASEAN Investment Regime (AIR) and achieve the mega-goal of "ASEAN Centrality."

[75] *See* Khairy Tourk, *Asia-Pacific Pact Is a Triumph for the Region's 'Quiet Diplomacy'*, FIN. TIMES (Nov. 19, 2020).

Chapter 2

The Foundation of the ASEAN Investment Regime

2.1 Introduction

The regulation of foreign investment in the ASEAN legal order is facially characterized by thick complexity. As a start-point, any inquiry into the collective ASEAN rules necessarily requires assessment of the bilateral investment treaties (BITs) entered into by individual member states within ASEAN. Much of that dense BIT network temporally predates the construction of the ASEAN investment treaties, and thus operates as the legal and conceptual scaffolding for the construction of those dedicated collective rules. Yet the collective rules themselves are characterized by multiple iterations (1987, 1998 and 2009), with distinct heterogeneities in normative orientation and doctrinal choices that depart from the individual BIT commitments of the ASEAN member states.

To fully understand the organizational development of the ASEAN Investment Regime (AIR), we must first choose a conceptual or theoretical framework. One set of possibilities are the various state-orientated theories – such as neorealism or neoliberal institutionalism – entrenched in the rationalist tradition. Yet these state-oriented theories often give remarkably short shrift to the ontology of international organizations as independent entities, rather than as instruments of those states who founded them.[1] Our guiding premise in this book is to construct ASEAN's identity *qua* organization as it probes ASEAN's institutional evolution for the past several decades. Although ASEAN encompasses multiple economic and political dimensions, this chapter focuses on the initial formation of ASEAN's identity as it concerns the *intra*-regional investment regime. To the extent that the investment regime is an important factor driving economic integration among the ASEAN states, scrutinizing the ASEAN's identity formation in that particular area offers a unique way of understanding ASEAN's institutional development.

This chapter proceeds in the following sequence. Section 2.2 conceptualizes an interstate cooperative regime based on our preferred conceptual approach of constructivism. It defines an Interstate Cooperative Regime (ICR) as a stable interstate cooperative nexus or relationship on a particular regulative subject, such as the treatment of investment within the AIR. Section 2.3 demonstrates why rationalism cannot fully capture an organizational structure of an ICR due mainly to its methodological individualism. Constructivism, on other hand, enables a structural and holistic investigation of the AIR and therefore offers an especially useful analytical tool to map an ICR's evolution. It then introduces Erik Erikson's identity-formation theory to undertake a dynamic investigation of the evolution of AIR. Section 2.3 then begins to apply constructivism and identify-formation theory to the AIR and explains its organizational development process. Charting a chronology, we begin

[1] *See* Sungjoon Cho, *An International Organization's Identity Crisis*, 34 Nw. J. Int'l L. & Bus. 359 (2014).

with the general account of the formation of BITs in the 1960s and 1970s, set against a backdrop of post-colonial political and legal contestation. Our focus then turns to the distinct conservatism that characterizes the specific BITs entered into by many (though not all) ASEAN member states. The chapter concludes with the first set of collective ASEAN investment rules (in 1987) which, remarkably, offer even fewer liberal and protective guarantees than what ASEAN members would extend to third-party states (in their BITs). Put starkly, the AIR's foundational position was a loose interstate arrangement with limited levels of cooperation. Importantly, however, the past is not destiny. As we will see in later chapters, the AIR would eventually develop a collective (integrationist) identity as an investment community, though the process is by no means linear and one can detect sovereigntist regressionism in certain areas.[2]

2.2 Conceptualizing an Interstate Cooperative Regime

To truly understand both the foundation and later evolution of the ASEAN investment regime, we must first choose a

[2] A word of caution is in order. This chapter does not address the ASEAN as a whole, but only its investment regime (AIR). AIR is entitled as a subject of serious investigation as a separate system – both functionally and culturally – distinct from the ASEAN in its entirety. Likewise, there could be other operational areas of ASEAN, such as security, that might or might not warrant the same approach as the one this chapter adopts. Therefore, the ASEAN's identity in terms of security may exhibit different properties from the one discussed here, although the two identities could be interrelated.

conceptual or theoretical framework. Such a framework may represent a micro foundation focusing on individual members and their interactions or a macro foundation concerning a systematic, organizational structure. Conventional IR theories[3] mostly adopt the micro framework. Agency-oriented theories, such as neorealism, rational choice theory and neoliberal institutionalism, adopt methodological individualism (state-oriented). Based on a Hobbesian view of international anarchy, neorealists adopt something of a dismissive view of an ICR, in particular trivializing its constitutive infrastructure, such as international law and institutions.[4] To them, any interstate cooperation is tantamount to a mere "epiphenomenon of underlying power" or a "coincidence of state interests or coercion by powerful states."[5]

Informed by an economic methodology, rational choice theory views any institution as a program or script that *ex ante* maps out actors' rational strategies as well as their

[3] Regarding various strands of IR theories, *see generally* Sungjoon Cho, The Social Foundations of World Trade: Norms, Community and Constitution (2014).

[4] *See* Richard H. Steinberg & Jonathan M. Zasloff, *Power and International Law*, 100 Am. J. Int'l L. 64, 73–6 (2006). *See also* Kenneth N. Waltz, Theory of International Politics 105 (1979); Stephen D. Krasner, *Structural Causes and Regime Consequences: Regimes as Intervening Variables*, in International Regimes 1 (Stephen D. Krasner ed., 1983); Jack L. Goldsmith & Eric A. Posner, The Limits of International Law 36–7, 118, 225 (2005).

[5] Steinberg & Zasloff, *supra* note 4, at 74–5.

results.[6] These institutions bind and shape actors' behaviors only because choices over them can be measured and predicted through a rational (cost–benefit) analysis.[7] In this regard, an ICR may be seen as a welfare-maximizing contract in which states' interests and preferences determine various institutional choices.[8] The theoretical assumption behind rational choice theory leads naturally to a proposition that a state will respect an ICR *if and only if*, its payoff from compliance (cooperation) is greater than the cost incurred through such compliance.[9] In other words, cooperation is a result of a complicated calculation on various utilities (such as positive reputation and reciprocal cooperation by others) and disutilities (such as negative reputation and penalties).[10]

Neoliberal institutionalism shares a set of premises with neorealism and rational choice theory. As neorealists do, neoliberal institutionalists' main analytical focus is individual

6 *See* Kenneth A. Shepsle, *Rational Choice Institutionalism*, in OXFORD HANDBOOK OF POLITICAL INSTITUTIONS (R.A.W. Rhodes, Sarah A. Binder & Bert A. Rockman eds., 2008).

7 *See* Oliver E. Williamson, THE ECONOMIC INSTITUTIONS OF CAPITALISM (1985) (using the "transaction cost" approach in analyzing institutions); Douglas C. North, INSTITUTIONS, INSTITUTIONAL CHANGE AND ECONOMIC PERFORMANCE 3 (1990).

8 *See generally* Sungjoon Cho, *Beyond Rationality: A Sociological Construction of the World Trade Organization*, 52 VA. J. INT'L L. 321 (2012).

9 *See* Andrew T. Guzman, HOW INTERNATIONAL LAW WORKS: A RATIONAL CHOICE THEORY 55–60 (2008).

10 *See id.* at 36–40, 45, 47–48.

actors (states).[11] Meanwhile, similar to rational choice theorists, neoliberal institutionalists argue that individual actors (states) basically pursue competing interests, subject to various (material and non-material) constraints.[12] Based on an integrated view of a domestic and international sphere,[13] neoliberal institutionalists' main concern is how to coordinate diverging domestic preferences with a minimum cost. In this sense, an ICR can be an important avenue to facilitate such coordination by creating norms, supplying useful information and monitoring compliance.[14]

These conventional IR theories are collectively coined "rationalism" in that they presuppose isotropic, rational actors (states) whose actions are guided by a common thesis of substantive rationality represented by efficiency, power and interest.[15] While these conventional IR theories offer useful heuristics in understanding the *origin* of an ICR (explaining why states cooperate at first instance), they cannot fully capture the complex "changes" that an ICR makes over time. The paradigms provided by conventional IR theories are

[11] *See* Claire R. Kelly, *The Value Vacuum: Self-Enforcing Regimes and the Dilution of the Normative Feedback Loop*, 22 MICH. J. INT'L L. 673, 681–83 (2001).

[12] *See* Andrew Moravcsik, *Taking Preferences Seriously: A Liberal Theory of International Politics*, 51 INT'L ORG. 513, 516 (1997).

[13] Anne-Marie Slaughter, *A Liberal Theory of International Law*, 94 AM. SOC'Y INT'L L. 240, 241 (2000).

[14] Robert O. Keohane, AFTER HEGEMONY: COOPERATION AND DISCORD IN THE WORLD POLITICAL ECONOMY (1984) (viewing that international institutions facilitate decentralized cooperation among state actors).

[15] Robert O. Keohane, *International Institutions: Two Approaches*, 32 INT'L STUD. Q. 379, 386–87 (1988).

necessarily functional and therefore inherently static. Their characteristic methodological individualism adopts states (agency) as a primary analytical unit.[16] Under this view, an ICR is merely an instrument that serves various utilitarian functions that rational states would desire, such as providing information, reducing uncertainties and monitoring cheating.[17] Under functionalism, the only occasion in which states are compelled to retool their ICRs is when they face extreme external shocks, such as catastrophes.[18] By definition, functionalism cannot bestow ontological autonomy[19] onto an ICR that enables us to observe its post-creation evolution process in which an ICR adapts itself, on its own terms, to environmental challenges.[20] In sum, conventional IR theories may offer various functional snapshots of an ICR, but not its panoramic identity *qua* organization.

[16] Alexander Wendt, *The State as Person in International Theory*, 30 Rev. Int'l Stud. 289, 299 (2004) ("We-intentions are *nothing but* interlocking I-intentions toward a group.").

[17] *See* Michael N. Barnett & Martha Finnemore, *The Politics, Power, and Pathologies of International Organizations*, 53 Int'l Org. 699, 702 (1999); *see also* The New Institutionalism in Organizational Analysis 3–4 (1991) (Walter W. Powell & Paul J. DiMaggio eds., 1991); Anna Grandori, *Notes on the Use of Power and Efficiency Constructs in the Economics and Sociology of Organizations*, *in* Interdisciplinary Perspectives on Organization Studies 61 (Siegwart M. Lindenberg & Hein Schreuder eds., 1993).

[18] *See* Laurence R. Helfer, *Understanding Change in International Organizations: Globalization and Innovation in the ILO*, 59 Vand. L. Rev. 649, 662 (2006).

[19] Barnett & Finnemore, *supra* note 17, at 704.

[20] Helfer, *supra* note 18, at 662.

Moreover, as long as ICRs are viewed as tools, their unique institutional contexts tend to be underappreciated. As Gayl Ness and Steven Brechin aptly observe, "[ICRs] differ over time, or . . . they perform differently from one another, or . . . they achieve their ends with varying effectiveness or efficiency."[21] Thus, conventional IR theories cannot fully capture the various contexts of each ICR endemic to its unique subject matter, history and culture.

Therefore, we need a new theoretical framework through which we can conceptually embrace the ontological autonomy of an ICR so that we can investigate its dynamic institutional development. An ICR's institutional decision, or collective consciousness, cannot be the result of an aggregation of the interests of its individual member states. Although its member states are building blocks of an ICR, an ICR "emerges" on its own, rather than being simply created by those states.[22] In this regard, a sociology-led approach, especially constructivism, distinguishes itself from those conventional IR theories as it highlights a social *structure*, rather than agency, that constructs the culture and identities of those actors.[23] Constructivists emphasize ideational factors, such as culture and norms, that guide state actions from within.[24] States build a collective identity as they share common goals

[21] Gayl D. Ness & Steven R. Brechin, *Bridging the Gap: International Organizations as Organizations*, 42 INT'L ORG. 245, 247 (1988).

[22] Wendt, *supra* note 16, at 301, 304.

[23] Martha Finnemore, *Norms, Culture, and World Politics: Insights from Sociology's Institutionalism*, 50 INT'L ORG. 325, 333 (1996).

[24] *See generally*, Alexander Wendt, THE SOCIAL THEORY OF INTERNATIONAL POLITICS (1999).

and norms. Such a collective identity often bonds those participating states, with or without material incentives, and enables cooperation among them. In this regard, the International Court of Justice (ICJ) ruled that:

> The resolutely positivist . . . approach of international law . . . has been replaced by an objective conception of international law, a law more readily seeking to reflect a *collective juridical conscience* and respond to the social necessities of States organized as a community.[25]

This "collective juridical conscience" is a normative manifestation of social identity that cannot be reduced to a mere aggregation of individual, subjective intentionalities.[26] Once we conceptualize an ICR as an autonomous institution or structure that is ontologically independent from its creators (states), we can observe its development (evolution) in a dynamic fashion.

Here, a note of caution is in order. Although this collective bond generates an "ontological security"[27] among states and provides a source of cooperation within an ICR,

[25] Legality of the Threat or Use of Nuclear Weapons, Advisory Opinion, 1996 I.C.J. 226, 268, ¶ 13 (July 8) (Declaration of President Bedjaoui) (emphasis added).

[26] *See* Judith Goldstein & Robert O. Keohane, *Ideas and Foreign Policy: An Analytical Framework*, in IDEAS AND FOREIGN POLICY: BELIEFS, INSTITUTIONS, AND POLITICAL CHANGE 3 (Judith Goldstein & Robert O. Keohane eds., 1993) (observing that ideas, as well as material interests, shape behavior and noting the impact of beliefs shared by large numbers of people, such as world views).

[27] *See generally* Jennifer Mitzen, *Ontological Security in World Politics: State Identity and the Security Dilemma*, 12 EUR. J. INT'L REL. 341 (2006).

these intersubjective qualities of social interaction should not be equated with cooperation itself. As witnessed in the Cold War, social dynamics can be conflictual.[28] Neither should consequences of social interaction be necessarily celebratory: even slavery and Apartheid were once social norms.[29]

Markedly, the recent development of public international law has countenanced an ICR's ontological autonomy in the form of "legal personality." As a departure from its traditional obsession with state sovereignty, postwar international law is characterized by the prominence of a thick set of International Organizations (IOs). Although the legal status of an IO was deeply contentious in the prewar period,[30] a number of postwar IOs (such as the UN and the WTO) explicitly claimed their autonomous legal personalities separate from their member states.[31] Now, an IO (ICR) is a "subject of international law and capable of possessing international rights and duties."[32] Likewise, such legal personality is

[28] Alexander Wendt, *Collective Identity Formation and the International State*, 88 Am. Pol. Sci. Rev. 384, 386 (1994).

[29] Martha Finnemore, National Interests in International Society 128 (1996); Audie Klotz, Norms in International Relations: The Struggle against Apartheid 19–20 (1995).

[30] *See* Giuseppe Marchegiano, *The Juristic Character of the International Commission of Cape Spartel Lighthouse*, 25 Am. J. Int'l L. 339, 339 (1931).

[31] U.N. Charter art. 104; Marrakesh Agreement Establishing the World Trade Organization, Apr. 15, 1994, 1867 U.N.T.S. 154 [hereinafter WTO Agreement].

[32] Reparation for Injuries Suffered in the Service of the United Nations, Advisory Opinion, 1949 I.C.J. 174, 179 (Apr. 11); *see also* International Law Commission, *Responsibility of International Organizations*, http://legal.un.org/ilc/guide/9_11.shtml (last updated June 19, 2016);

deemed to be inextricably linked to a unique institutional specialty of each IO (ICR).[33] This specialty-laden legal personality promotes the "*mentalités collectives*" within an ICR by professionalizing its daily operation, relatively detached from direct interventions from the headquarters.[34] Juridical personhood tends to also bestow upon an IO (ICR) an institutional compass, in the form of object and purpose, by which it can maintain its permanency. In other words, an IO, and the ICR it espouses, can secure its survival through persistent normative engagement with, and even transformation of, its object and purpose. For example, an IO (ICR) brings meanings to its operation by interpreting various situations, such as disputes, based on the object and purpose.[35]

While constructivism provides a theoretical underpinning of an ICR's organizational autonomy, we need another theoretical framework in which we can explain: first, when and how certain institutional changes transpire, and second, what kinds of changes take place in the process of an ICR's institutional development. Here, one critical aspect of an ICR's institutional development is that as an autonomous organization, an ICR incessantly interacts with its surrounding environment for its growth and survival.

International Law Commission, *Draft Articles on the Responsibility of International Organizations* (2011), http://legal.un.org/ilc/texts/instruments/english/commentaries/9_11_2011.pdf.

[33] Legality of the Threat or Use of Nuclear Weapons, Advisory Opinion, 1996 I.C.J. 226 (July 8).

[34] John Gerard Ruggie, *Territoriality and Beyond: Problematizing Modernity in International Relations*, 47 INT'L ORG. 139, 157 (1993).

[35] *See* Cho, *supra* note 1, at 381, 390.

The environment is a source for both resources and a threat to an organic entity like an ICR. Harnessing and adapting to its environment is essential to an ICR's survival.[36]

Here, the identity formation theory in developmental psychology can be a plausible candidate in explaining an ICR's evolution as a dynamic process of its adaption to its environment. Admittedly, this particular interdisciplinary attempt – an IR theory (constructivism) borrowed from psychology – is not without controversies.[37] Put simply, an IO cocooning an ICR is not a complex human being. As Alexander Wendt observes, a corporate identity might not be of the same quality as that of a human being as a biological entity.[38] Nonetheless, this particular form of anthropomorphism is still conceivable in particular dimensions, especially considering the *open* operational structure shared by an IO and a human being: as an organic system, both an IO (juridical person) and a natural person must interact with their respective environments.[39] Maintaining a meaningful whole or integrity (that is, an identity) is a serious constitutive process both to an IO and an individual. Indeed, business administration scholars have already embraced this notion of corporate identity in illuminating the life cycle of a corporation.[40]

[36] *See* Richard W. Scott, ORGANIZATIONS: RATIONAL, NATURAL, AND OPEN SYSTEMS 57 (3rd ed. 1991); Alvin W. Gouldner, *Organizational Analysis*, in SOCIOLOGY TODAY 404–05 (Robert K. Merton et al. eds., 1959).

[37] *See* Cho, *supra* note 1, at 376–78. [38] Wendt, *supra* note 24, at 221.

[39] Walter Buckley, SOCIOLOGY AND MODERN SYSTEMS THEORY 50 (1967).

[40] *See* Dennis Bromley, *Relationships between Personal and Corporate Reputation*, 35 EUR. J. MARKETING 316, 318 (2001) (observing the tendency to "personify" an organization); Stuart Albert & David

Against this background, Erik Erikson's identity formation theory appears to offer a useful analogy for understanding an ICR. For Erikson, a human being's (subjective) identity is negotiated with that person's understanding of its (objective) social environment.[41] Erikson's identity formation model presupposes various stages that an individual developmentally experiences in his or her lifetime. Each stage is characterized by "its own set of circumstances of particular sensitivity, identity crisis, and potential."[42] Erikson observed that:

> Identity formation employs a process of simultaneous reflection and observation, a process taking place on all levels of mental functioning, by which the individual judges himself in the light of what he perceived to be the way in which others judge him in comparison to themselves and to a typology significant to them; while he judges their way of judging him in the light of how he

A. Whetten, *Organizational Identity, in* 7 RESEARCH IN ORGANIZATIONAL BEHAVIOR 265 (Larry L. Cummings & Barry M. Staw eds., 1985); Peter Gorb, *The Psychology of Corporate Identity*, 10 EUR. MGMT. J. 310, 312 (1992); Henry Mintzberg, *Power and Organizational Life Cycles*, 9 ACAD. MGMT. REV. 207, 210 (1984); Andrew D. Brown & Ken Starkey, *Organizational Identity and Learning: A Psychodynamic Perspective*, 25 ACAD. MGMT. REV. 102, 104 (2000); Dennis A. Gioia et al., *Organizational Identity, Image, and Adaptive Instability*, 25 ACAD. MGMT. REV. 63, 65 (2000).

[41] *See generally* Erik H. Erikson, IDENTITY, YOUTH AND CRISIS (1968). *See also* Willem L. Wardekker, *Identity, Plurality, and Education, in* PHILOSOPHY OF EDUCATION 1995 (Alven Neiman ed., 1995).

[42] Cho, *supra* note 1, at 374; ERIKSON, *supra* note 41, at 91–141 (describing the different stages of the human life cycle).

> perceived himself in comparison to them and to types that have become relevant to him.[43]

An adolescent defines his or her own existence as he or she transitions from childhood to adulthood.[44] At the end of adolescence, an individual person replaces his or her earlier identifications (with parents or other admirable adults) with a new identity resulting from socialization that reflects that person's own unique value system.[45] Yet, this identity formation process is not necessarily uneventful. Adolescents often experience "a war within themselves"[46] as they suffer from multiple identifications and the role confusion therefrom.[47] It is only after they survive this rite of passage that they finally discover their place in society.[48]

An ICR, just like an individual person, is given its original institutional DNA from its creators (states). An organizational history of an ICR starts with the founding member states. The initial goals those member states intended to achieve through that ICR leave a deep, if not indelible, path-dependency within the ICR. Particular texts or arrangements engraved in an initial form of ICR tend to determine or explain what may be permitted or prohibited in the ICR's institutional manifestations. For example, as stipulated in the Vienna Convention on the Law of Treaties (VCLT), "preparatory work of the treaty and the circumstances of its

[43] Erikson, *supra* note 41, at 22–3.

[44] Erik H. Erikson, Childhood and Society, 156–65 (1950).

[45] *Id.* at 155.

[46] Erikson, *supra* note 41, at 17.

[47] Erikson, *supra* note 44, at 163–4.

[48] *Id.* at 161.

conclusion" may guide that treaty regime (ICR)'s present or future activities.[49]

Yet, as the ICR responds to various challenges given by its environment, these institutional vestiges may lessen or even become obsolete. The ICR is often forced to "bring organizational structure, culture, and purpose in line with perceived environmental requirements."[50] Erikson's identity theory aptly captures this struggle with the environment and a subsequent adaption as an "identity crisis." An ICR can be said to form its unique identity as it assimilates complex information from its broader environment. Importantly, the legal personality of an IO enshrining an ICR tends to facilitate such adaptation process. Social interactions within an IO are mediated by discourse and communication among member states. As a juridical person, discourse and communication within an IO are based on normative goals and legal principles.[51] If an ICR is forced to modify its initial *raison d'etre* after an identity crisis, such modification will be accompanied invariably by some kind of legal change, such as amendment or teleological interpretation. The World Bank's

[49] Vienna Convention on the Law of Treaties art. 32, May 23, 1969, 1155 U.N.T.S. 331.

[50] Matthias Finger & Bérangère Ruchat, *The Transformation of International Public Organizations: The Case of UNCTAD* 3 (Institut de Hautes Etudes en Administration Publique, Working Paper No. 14/2000, 2000); Howard E. Aldrich, Organizations and Environments 252–5 (1979).

[51] *See generally* Alexander Wendt, *Anarchy Is What States Make of It: The Social Construction of Power Politics*, 46 Int'l Org. 391 (1992).

widely documented "mission creep" is a case in point.[52] The World Bank's original mission was a narrow goal of facilitating economic development as stipulated in Article I of its Charter (Articles of Agreement). Subsequently, however, social pressures from its various constituencies forced the World Bank to adopt an evolutionary interpretation of Article I that turned that narrow mission into a broad vision, requiring it to consider such diverse impacts as heath, education, the environment, and women's rights.[53]

2.3 Establishment of the ASEAN Investment Regime

These IR theories provide useful analytical lenses through which one can understand the commencement and later dynamic evolution of the ASEAN investment regime (AIR). Each theoretical framework, be it neorealism, neoliberal

[52] *See, for example*, Jessica Einhorn, *The World Bank's Mission Creep*, 80 Foreign Aff. 22 (2001) (arguing that member countries of the World Bank should control the currently unwieldy status of mission creep by devolving some of its derivative missions to other institutions and focus more on the original, basic mission of the Bank); Sarah Babb & Ariel Buira, *Mission Creep, Mission Push and Discretion in Sociological Perspective: The Case of IMF Conditionality* (Mar. 9, 2004), http://web.archive.org/web/20070719172319/http://www.g24.org/012gva04.pdf (discussing the IMF's expanded mandate over the years).

[53] *See* Ibrahim F.I. Shihata, *The Dynamic Evolution of International Organizations: The Case of the World Bank*, 2 J. His. Int'l L. 217, 249 (2000); Georg Ress, *The Interpretation of the Charter*, in The Charter of the United Nations – A Commentary 28 (Bruno Simma et al. eds., 1994) (discussing "evolutionary dynamic interpretation").

institutionalism, or constructivism, can shed its distinct light on the AIR and its practices. Yet, relying entirely on insights offered by a single theory risks generating only a static snapshot of the regime, neglecting its panoramic nature. In this regard, this chapter begins the process of matching theoretical insights against temporal contexts by choosing and employing a given theory (at particular points in time) that is best equipped to capture the corresponding identity and properties of the regime. In that way, we seek throughout the book to dynamically use identity formation theory to map and explain the sequential development of the regime.

In describing a macro structure (culture) in each stage of AIR's organizational development, we adopt metaphoric representations, such as Hobbesian, Lockean and Kantian, developed by Alexander Wendt.[54] This metaphor signifies a dominant role, such as adversary, competitor and fellow, that each developmental stage may assign in the Self–Others configuration. These are not necessarily empirical manifestations at each stage, but highly abstract ideal types of structural logic that hold unique explanatory power in social, rather than material, terms.[55] In general, these three cultures parallel neorealism (Hobbesian), neoliberal institutionalism (Lockean), and constructivism (Kantian), respectively. Although these three cultures tend to demonstrate a sequential development – from Hobbesian to Lockean to

[54] *See* Wendt, *supra* note 24, at 247.

[55] In this sense, the social approach this article takes is distinguishable from Kenneth Waltz's traditional realist (materialist) one that emphasizes distribution of power or capabilities. *See id.* at 249.

Kantian – a later stage may still retain certain theoretical properties from an earlier stage, depending on degrees of norm internalization.[56] For this particular section, our focus is on the AIR's earliest development stages, where we see strong embodiments of Hobbesian traits (such as mutual suspicion among the members of the AIR). This section will then trace moves to deeper levels of cooperation and the political, economic and social forces driving those changes. But even AIR's later stages in its organizational development (embodying strong components of Kantian culture) still hold neorealist traits, such as internal sovereignty (suspicion of Others or an inward-looking mentality).

2.3.1 1950s – 1970s: Sovereigntist Foundation and Early BITs

Turning then to ASEAN, any inquiry into the creation of the collective rules governing foreign investment obviously requires assessment of the bilateral investment treaties (BITs) entered into by individual member states within ASEAN. Much of that BIT network temporally predates the construction of the ASEAN investment treaties, and thus operates as the legal and conceptual scaffolding for the construction of those dedicated collective rules. The historiography of those BITs is marked by features common to the investment treaty universe, such as the original desire by capital-exporting states to use BITs to counter downward shifts in the protection of foreign property under customary

[56] *See id.* at 250.

international law.[57] But from the specific perspective of the Asian states (as capital-importing countries in this unsettled period), their general approach to foreign investors (and by extension, international investment law) was characterized by a deep-seated desire to acquire and defend state sovereignty.[58]

Likewise, the original intentions and disposition of the individual members of ASEAN heavily influenced ASEAN's early institutional format. The collective memory of colonialism and post-colonial political and economic chaos borne by ASEAN members imbued its members with an obsession with survival and worst-case scenarios. As long as each member views another member as a potential adversary, negative reciprocity tends to prevail and complicates cooperation. This adversarial dimension is aptly illustrated by the violent conflict of *Konfrontasi* that stemmed from Indonesia's opposition to the amalgamation of the Federation of Malaya, Singapore and the crown colony/British protectorates of North Borneo and Sarawak.[59] Spanning 1963 to 1966, *Konfrontasi* was triggered by Indonesia's increasingly aggressive post-colonial foreign policy in the period, leading to overt and covert military operations in the region, with hundreds of casualties.[60] In the economic sphere, too, we find similar

[57] Andrew Newcombe & Lluis Paradell, Law and Practice of Investment Treaties – Standards of Treatment 18–44 (2009).

[58] Simon Chesterman, *Asia's Ambivalence About International Law & Institutions: Past, Present and Futures*, 27 Eur. J. Int'l L. 945, 947–51 (2016).

[59] *See generally* J.A.C. Mackie, Konfrontasi: The Indonesia–Malaysia Dispute 1963–66 (1974).

[60] *Id.*

levels of suspicion (albeit directed largely outwards at former colonial powers) and attachment to sovereignty. Not surprisingly then, the early stages of investment rules only occasioned weak levels of cooperation among the ASEAN states.

In fact, the immediate decades following the Second World War were marked by a wave of forced takings of foreign assets throughout the developing world.[61] Expropriation was no longer an isolated and exceptional event; its frequent invocation reflected a fundamental realignment of inter-state interests. An array of peoples and groups demanded political independence from the strictures of colonial power relations including those within Asia. The demand for political independence was not surprisingly accompanied by a desire for economic sovereignty. Yet, the productive capacity of many of these states remained dependent on infrastructure and investment from former colonial powers. Foreign investment came in turn to be seen as a continuing proxy for colonialism, with expropriation being used as a visible mechanism to complete the decolonization process. Formal laws passed to effect nationalization were often explicitly targeted at enterprises of the former colonial power. Thus, the 1958 Indonesian nationalization law was directly solely at Dutch enterprises.[62] The political sensitivity of the priority accorded to national ownership of state assets often transcended the immediate

[61] Thomas L. Brewer & Stephen Young, The Multilateral Investment System and Multinational Enterprises 53 (1998).

[62] The Indonesian Act No. 86 of 1958 concerning "the nationalization of property of Dutch-owned enterprises within the territory of the Republic of Indonesia." Martin Domke, *Indonesian Nationalization Measures before Foreign Courts*, 54 Am. J. Int'l L. 305 (1960).

project of expelling nationals of the former colonial power. Wells and Ahmed capture this heightened sensitivity in their case analysis of Indonesia's much later nationalization (in the late 1970s) of a telecommunications satellite facility constructed by ITT. Writing of the political sensitivity of the pro-investor clauses in the initial infrastructure contract, the authors perceptively note:

> [O]ne may dismiss a critique of these non-economic issues as "emotional". But in the real world, these very issues can cause discontent and conflict, particularly in countries that believe they have been subject to long periods of colonial suppression and exploitation – a feeling that was alive in Indonesia at the time. Although it found little voice in the tightly controlled press, that feeling would erupt in riots targeting Japanese investments in 1974.[63]

The push to expropriate was further driven by the spread of alternative political models during this period. States that had adopted Marxist principles were hostile to *all* forms of private property, whether foreign or domestic. But even for other states, hostility to foreign investment is a natural consequence of strategies employed to achieve developmental outcomes. For instance, the tendency of most ASEAN states through the 1950s–1970s was to engage in import substitution as a means

[63] Louis T. Wells & Rafiq Ahmed, Making Foreign Investment Safe: Property Rights and National Sovereignty 38 (2007). On the parallel between colonialism and the modern phenomenon of "market-dominant minorities," *see* Amy Chua, World On Fire: How Exporting Free Market Democracy Breeds Ethnic Hatred and Global Instability 120–1 (2003).

of transitioning to a particular level of industrialization.[64] The import substitution model posited the development of indigenous industrial capacity as the primary mechanism for countries to achieve comparative advantage in manufactured trade.[65] Such an indigenous industry was to be nurtured through restrictions on competitive imports[66] but constraints on entry of foreign investors (who would also act as potential competitors to domestic industry) were a further necessary complement to this program.

The common outcome of these diverse tensions is a general opposition in developing states – albeit at different degrees – to the free entry and operation of foreign investment in this period. This generated significant political conflict between capital importing and exporting states on whether and how traditional customary international rules should apply to newer instances of forced taking of foreign

[64] For an overview of the influence of import substitution-based theory on development strategies throughout the 1950s and 1960s, *see* Michael Trebilcock & Robert Howse, The Regulation of International Trade (3rd ed. 2005), 486–8.

[65] For a historical overview of the origins and influence of the infant industry argument from Alexander Hamilton and Friedrich List to John Stuart Mill, *see* Douglas Irwin, Against the Tide: An Intellectual History of Free Trade 116–37 (1996).

[66] The dominance of this view of development is even reflected in post-war efforts to multilateralize trade liberalization. The GATT 1947 countenances the use of trade barriers to nurse the indigenous infant industry. *See* General Agreement on Tariffs and Trade art. XVIII (2), Oct. 30, 1947, 61 Stat. A-11, 55 U.N.T.S. 194.

property and particularly nationalization of industry.[67] Despite these significant advances in the multilateral sphere, these same states began to slowly enter into bilateral investment treaties (BITs) with capital exporting states to govern regulation of foreign investment. The first BIT was concluded between West Germany and Pakistan in 1959[68] and soon thereafter, other European nations followed suit by building their own BIT programs.[69] Yet, in comparison to the frenetic treaty making of later periods, BIT growth throughout the 1960s to 1970s proceeded at a "largely desultory pace."[70] There were only 72 BITs signed between 1959 and 1969, half of which were concluded by Germany.[71] The pace of negotiations accelerated slightly throughout the 1970s, with a further 166 BITs concluded by the end of 1979.[72]

The problem, then, in this early period is one of strident political and ideological conflict between developing

[67] *See, for example*, S.N. Guha Roy, *Is the Law of Responsibility of States for Injuries to Aliens a Part of Universal International Law?* 55 AM. J. INT'L L. 866–86 (1961); Chittharanjan Felix Amerasinghe, STATE RESPONSIBILITY FOR INJURIES TO ALIENS 128–9 (1967).

[68] UNCTAD, *Bilateral Investment Treaties* 1959–1999 57 (2000).

[69] Between 1960 and 1966, Belgium, Denmark, France, Italy, Luxembourg, the Netherlands, Norway, Sweden and Switzerland all concluded their first BITs. UNCTAD, *International Investment Law Rule-Making: Stocktaking, Challenges and The Way Forward*, 11, U.N. Doc. UNCTAD/ITE/IIT/2007/3 (2008).

[70] Kenneth J. Vandevelde, *The Political Economy of a Bilateral Investment Treaty*, 92 AM. J. INT'L. L. 621, 627 (1998).

[71] UNCTAD, *International Investment Law Rule-Making, supra* note 69, at 1–5.

[72] *Id.* at 13.

and developed states. With this in mind, BITs play an important role over and above the immediate functional goal (for host states) of attracting foreign capital. They also represent a mechanism by which treaty partners could anticipate and manage the deep schisms concerning political ideology and variances in economic models. Specifically, BITs have a function of depoliticizing and preventing escalation of interstate conflict by carving out a zone of protection for foreign economic actors.[73] Newly independent states (including in Asia) could use entry into BITs to signal that, regardless of the level of experimentation in development strategy, their overall political program was not driven by Marxism or its variants. In return, the major powers would refrain from various strategies of covert intervention and tolerate – at the margins – economic models that deviated from preferred liberal precepts. The zone of protection in the typical BIT model of this period assumes – not without cause – an embedded hostility to foreign investors in the domestic political and judicial processes of host states.

In sum, the unique collective historical consciousness that derived from the colonial past and internal struggle within some states (*Konfrontasi*) embedded a strong ideology of non-interference and self-determination among ASEAN members, which is often broadly defined as the

[73] For a similar account of the early BIT movement but one that focuses on "tribunalization" to manage interstate political and ideological conflict, *see* Ruti Teitel & Robert Howse, *Cross-Judging: Tribunalization in a Fragmented but Interconnected Global Order*, 41 N. Y. J. Int'l L. & Pol. 959 (2009).

"ASEAN Way."[74] This centrifugal political ideology would eventually compound the difficulties of seeking *intra*-ASEAN investment liberalization as each ASEAN member sought to retain firm control of investment flows in and out of its own territory. Protectionist policies (such as through import substitution) are a natural reflection of this general goal, as they deter foreign investment in areas where there is potential competition and conflict with domestic rivals.

2.3.2 1980s – 1990s: BIT Network Expansion

By the 1980s, a broad array of political and economic factors had begun to coalesce that forced and shaped change in the investment policy pursued by ASEAN members. First, expropriation declined sharply as now-independent states had largely completed the post-colonial project of acquiring control of natural resources and infrastructure.[75] Second, many of those states had begun to move away from political

[74] Regarding the history of the ASEAN Way, *see* Lee Jones, *ASEAN and the Norm of Non-Interference in Southeast Asia: A Quest for Social Order*, Nuffield College Politics Group Working Paper (Mar. 2009). *See also* Gillian Goh, *The "ASEAN" Way: Non-Intervention and ASEAN's Role in Conflict Management*, 3 Stan. J. East Asian Aff. 113 (2003) (shedding a positive light on the ASEAN Way); Vinod K. Aggarwal & Jonathan T. Chow, *The Perils of Consensus: How ASEAN's Meta-Regime Undermines Economic and Environmental Cooperation*, 17 Rev. Int'l Pol. Econ. 262 (2010) (shedding a negative light on the ASEAN Way).

[75] Michael S. Minor, *The Demise of Expropriation as an Instrument of LDC Policy 1980–1992*, 25 J. Int'l Bus. Stud. 177 (1994) (discussing the reduction of expropriations of foreign assets amongst developing countries).

and developmental models predicated on opposition to foreign and private capital. The continuing feasibility of the import substitution approach to economic development had always depended on its ability to generate successful and competitive industrial champions. Yet by the late 1980s, it became clear that this model was producing disappointing results for those countries (especially in Sub-Saharan Africa and Latin America) that had chosen this development path.[76] On the other hand, policies linked to export growth and market openness had led to demonstrable economic growth in the newly industrializing "tiger" states of East Asia.[77] Meanwhile, the collapse of the Soviet Union weakened the case for Marxism as a realistic alternative to economic and political liberalism. And finally, the sovereign debt crisis of the 1980s reduced developing state access to private bank loans. Unable to borrow to finance policies of economic development, developing states increasingly sought to attract foreign direct investment for their development needs.

The net effect of these trends was the emergence of, as Vandevelde aptly describes it, "a consensus in the developing world about the desirability of attracting foreign investment

[76] For an overview of the policy failures associated with import substitution, *see* Trebilcock & Howse, *supra* note 64, at 486–7.

[77] These countries though did not by any means simply adopt policies of unconstrained market liberalization. Some of them offered a range of targeted industrial policies including export incentives to specific firms. South Korea, for instance, prominently used a range of subsidies and incentives to encourage private investment in strategic industries. *See generally* Alice Amsden, Asia's Next Giant: South Korea and Later Industrialization (1989).

through free market policies."[78] This is illustrated first, and sharply, by the direction of changes in domestic laws. States took *unilateral* steps to liberalize domestic restrictions on the entry and operation of foreign investment throughout the 1990s. Between 1991 and 2006, out of 2533 national legal and regulatory changes relevant to foreign investment, 91 percent were in the direction of making the host country more favorable for FDI.[79] This trend encompassed widespread expansion in practices of positive discrimination as both developed and developing states offered locational incentives to attract foreign capital into their jurisdictions.[80] Even for those developing states that remained skeptical of the merits of the market model, the ideological structural adjustment policies imposed on them by the Bretton Woods institutions left many of them with little alternative but to liberalize their domestic economies.[81]

The constellation of these various factors drove explosive growth in investment treaty making throughout the 1990s. State parties had concluded a relatively modest

[78] Kenneth Vandevelde, *Sustainable Liberalism and the International Investment Regime*, 19 MICH. J. INT'L. L. 373, 390 (1998).

[79] Lisa Sachs & Karl Sauvant, *BITs, DTTs and FDI Flows: An Overview, in* THE EFFECT OF TREATIES ON FOREIGN DIRECT INVESTMENT: BILATERAL INVESTMENT TREATIES, DOUBLE TAXATION TREATIES AND INVESTMENT FLOWS xlix (Karl P. Sauvant & Lisa E. Sachs eds., 2009).

[80] *See generally* UNCTAD, *Incentives and Foreign Direct Investment*, U.N. Doc. UNCTAD/DTCI/28 (1996).

[81] Robert Gilpin, GLOBAL POLITICAL ECONOMY: UNDERSTANDING THE INTERNATIONAL ECONOMIC ORDER 313–7 (2001).

385 BITs in the 30 years from 1959 to 1989.[82] In comparison, 1857 BITs were concluded in the next 10 years.[83] With this dramatic expansion of the BIT network, José Alvarez has argued that "[t]he 1990s, not the 1980s and certainly not the 1970s, were the era when the modern investment regime was born."[84] Not surprisingly, then, we begin to see a range of individual ASEAN states also beginning to accelerate their entry into BITs during this period. Indeed, some ASEAN states sign their first BITs from the late 1980s onwards, such as Brunei (with Germany in 1998), Cambodia (with Malaysia in 1994), Laos (with France in 1989), Myanmar (with the Philippines in 1998) and Vietnam (with Italy in 1990). For the other ASEAN members, while there is sporadic use of BITs during the 1960s–1980s, there is exponential growth and clustering of BIT activity throughout the 1990s.[85] Generally speaking though, there is stability in the underlying form and structure of treaty making by individual ASEAN states as the basic features of the classic BIT model continue

[82] UNCTAD, *Bilateral Investment Treaties 1959-1999*, at 1, U.N. Doc. UNCTAD/ITE/IIA/2 (2000).

[83] *Id.*

[84] José Alvarez, *The Once and Future Foreign Investment Regime, in* Looking to the Future: Essays on International Law in Honor of W. Michael Reisman 15 (Mahnoush H. Arasanjani et al. eds., 2010).

[85] Beth Simmons, *East Asia, investment and International Law: Distinctive or Convergent?*, 13(3) Kor. J. Int'l. Stud. 461, 469–71 (2015) (outlining the "timing of Asia's [international investment agreements]"); Zachary Elkins, Andrew Guzman & Beth Simmons, *Competing for Capital: The Diffusion of Bilateral Investment Treaties, 1960–2000,* 60 Int. Org. 811, 821 (2006) (outlining the clustering of BIT signings by of Malaysia and Indonesia throughout the 1990s as well as by other developing states).

to be replicated in this fertile growth period. Put differently, the core DNA within BITs created by capital exporting states – national and most-favored-nation treatment, the amorphous guarantee of fair and equitable treatment, the obligation to compensate for direct and indirect expropriation and investor-state arbitration – appear with regularity throughout most of the BITs entered into by individual ASEAN members. Yet underlying this general degree of conformity is a highly distinct degree of conservatism within specific elements of Asian investment treaty practice.[86]

2.3.3 *Early Conservatism in ASEAN BIT Practice*

Most early BITs concluded by ASEAN member states fully preserve the right of the signatory host state to regulate the question of admission of foreign investment. The myriad of strong BIT protections thus only applies on a post-establishment basis, being after foreign investment has been admitted into the host state. At its most extreme, this structure entitles a state to exclude entire economic sectors from participation by foreign investors, which may well be necessary if those sectors are targeted as part of an infant industry strategy. Even if a state chooses to open a given economic sector to foreign competition, they are free to impose conditions upon the entry of a foreign investor. In this respect, most ASEAN BITs are conceptually different from a stronger liberalization

[86] Mohd Haflah Piei, *An East Asia FTA: A Malaysian Perspective*, in East Asian Regionalism: Feasibilities and Challenges 109 (Choong Yong Ahn, Richard E. Baldwin & Inkyo Cheong eds., 2005).

model that characterizes the investment treaty practice of a number of developed countries, especially the U.S. and Canada. Those states typically require combined national treatment and most-favoured-nation treatment at the pre-admission stage, thus severely restricting discretionary regulatory mechanisms that prohibit entry or offer it only on conditions that reduce the overall value of the investment to the investor.[87]

Relatedly, many early ASEAN BITs delineate the operation of substantive investment treaty protections (even on a post-admission basis) by reference to compliance by the foreign investor with some element of domestic law. At the outset, however, it is important to note that there is heterogeneity on this key point across the entire field of ASEAN investment treaty practice.[88] Thailand, for instance, tends to sit at the most conservative end of the spectrum, as evident in Article 3(1) of the 1978 Thailand – UK BIT which provides:

> The benefits of this Agreement shall apply only in cases where the investment of capital by the nationals and companies of one Contracting Party in the territory of the other Contracting Party *has been specifically approved in*

[87] On what the authors call a "full liberalization model," *see* Ignacio Gómez-Palacio & Peter Muchlinski, *Admission and Establishment*, in The Oxford Handbook of International Investment Law 243 (Peter Muchlinski, Federico Ortino & Christoph Schreuer eds., 2008).

[88] Dato Cecil Abraham, *State Approval in South East Asian Bilateral Investment Treaties*, in Investor-State Arbitration: Lessons for Asia 123 (Michael J. Moser ed., 2008).

> *writing by the competent authority of the latter Contracting Party.* (emphasis added)[89]

This formula requires a foreign investor to prove that they have met very specific and formalized preconditions to entry, not least approval in writing by the host state. Without clear proof of compliance with this one discrete element across a possible spectrum of entry conditions, foreign investment will not be protected by the BIT. An affirmative act of this sort is thus a necessary and sufficient condition of conferring treaty protection. This mechanism enables a state to calibrate its investment treaty exposure by reference to approval (which will often take the form of registration) of foreign investment under domestic law. Registration itself is often a technique used by states to supervise the grant of benefits to attract foreign investment in key economic sectors (including through investment incentives)[90] and to monitor specific conditions imposed on foreign investors to maximize the development benefits to the host state

[89] Agreement between the Government of the United Kingdom of Great Britain and Northern Ireland and the Government of the Kingdom of Thailand for the Promotion of the Investment of Capital and for the Protection of Investments art. 3(1), Nov. 28, 1978, 1172 U.N.T.S. 211. For a more recent example of this strategy in Thai BIT practice, *see* Treaty Between the Kingdom of Thailand and the Federal Republic of Germany concerning the Encouragement and Reciprocal Protection of Investments art. 2(2), June 24, 2002, 2286 U.N.T.S. 159.

[90] For explanation by Malaysia of its rationale in using this technique, *see* *Philippe Gruslin* v. *Malaysia*, ICSID No. ARB/99/3, Award, ¶ 17.1 (Nov. 27, 2000).

from foreign investment in those sectors (through employment of performance requirements such as local content conditions).[91]

This type of stringent precondition – requiring a discrete and affirmative act on the part of the host state to guarantee coverage of investment protection – is also a characteristic of Indonesian[92] and Malaysian[93] BIT practice. Yet

[91] For the use of local content conditions by Indonesia when regulating foreign investment in the automotive sector (which were ruled contrary to the WTO Agreement on Trade-Related Investment Measures), *see* Panel Report, *Indonesia – Certain Measures Affecting the Automobile Industry*, WTO Doc. WT/DS54/R (adopted July 2, 1998). *See also* GATT Panel Report, *Canada – Administration of the Foreign Investment Review Act*, BISD 30S/140 (adopted Feb. 17, 1984) (ruling that the Canadian practice of enforcing certain undertakings given by foreign investors in order to gain discrete regulatory approval to invest in Canada breached the obligation of national treatment in GATT Article III(4)).

[92] For example, Article 9 of the 1970 Belgium – Indonesia BIT provides:

"The protections afforded to investors by the provisions of the present Agreement shall apply: in the territory of the Republic of Indonesia only to investments *which have been approved by the Government of the Republic of Indonesia pursuant to stipulations contained in the Foreign Investment Law No. 1 of 1967 or other relevant laws and regulations of the Republic of Indonesia.*" (emphasis added). Agreement Between the Kingdom of Belgium and the Republic of Indonesia on the Encouragement and Reciprocal Protection of Investments art. 9, Jan. 15, 1970, 843 U.N.T.S. 19. For a more recent example of this strategy in Indonesian BIT practice, *see* Agreement Between the Government of Australia and the Government of the Republic of Indonesia concerning the Promotion and Protection of Investments art. III(1)(a), Nov. 17, 1992, 1993 Australian Treaty Series No. 19.

[93] For example, under 1981 Malaysia – United Kingdom BIT:

"The said term [investment] shall refer . . . in respects of investments in the territory of Malaysia, to all investments made in projects classified

this limitation strategy is by no means uniformly employed by all ASEAN member states in their BITs. The Philippines, for instance, has only reserved this possibility in its two oldest BITs, with the United Kingdom (1981)[94] and the Netherlands (1987).[95] More commonly, the Philippines has delineated the definition of "investment" as found in the 1997 Germany – Philippines BIT:

> The term "investment" shall mean any kind of asset *accepted in accordance with the respective laws and regulations of either Contracting State*, and more particularly though not exclusively:
>
> (a) movable and immovable property as well as other rights in rem, such as mortgages, liens, pledges, usufructs and similar rights;
> (b) shares of stocks and debentures of companies or interest in the property of such companies;

by the appropriate Ministry of Malaysia in accordance with its legislation and administrative practice as an "approved project." Agreement between the Government of the United Kingdom of Great Britain and Northern Ireland and the Government of Malaysia for the Promotion and Protection of Investments art. 1(b)(ii), May 21, 1981, 1579 U.N.T.S. 11.

94 Agreement Between the Government of the United Kingdom of Great Britain and Northern Ireland and the Republic of the Philippines for the Promotion and Protection of Investments art. II(1), Dec. 3, 1980, United Kingdom Treaty Series 007/1981: Cmnd 8148.

95 Agreement Between the Kingdom of the Netherlands and the Republic of the Philippines for the Promotion and Protection of Investments art. 2, Feb. 27, 1985, 1985 Tractatenblad (Neth.) No. 86.

> (c) claims to money utilized for the purpose of creating an economic value or to any performance having an economic value;
> (d) intellectual property rights, in particular copyrights, patents, utility-model patents, registered designs, trade-marks, trade-names, trade and business secrets; technical processes, know-how and good will;
> (e) business concessions conferred by law or under contract, including concessions to search for, extract or exploit natural resources;
>
> any alteration of the form in which assets are invested shall not affect their classification as an investment. (emphasis added)[96]

The Philippines here seems to adopt a slightly more liberal strategy to the extension of BIT coverage than some of the other ASEAN member states. There is no explicit requirement of discrete approval for a given foreign investor to gain the protection of the BIT. Instead, provided that a foreign investor had met all Philippines entry requirements at the time of their investment (even without specific registration), one might logically then suggest that the state has "accepted" that investment (for the purposes of Article 1(1)). Of course, this general legality condition can still be an important mechanism to vet problematic investments. In a series of BIT cases involving select ASEAN member states, investor-state arbitral tribunals have invoked the legality condition as a means of denying

[96] Agreement Between the Federal Republic of Germany and the Republic of the Philippines on the Promotion and Protection of Investments art. 1 (1), Apr. 18, 1997, 2108 U.N.T.S. 19.

admissibility (or otherwise constraining claims) where the underlying investment had been tainted by bribery and corruption, either on the part of an investor or a third party.[97]

These key differences in BIT coverage across ASEAN member states have two key fundamental impacts on the construction of investment treaty rules within ASEAN. First, the tension between restrictive and liberal preferences plays out later in sensitive scoping choices when constructing dedicated investment rules within the ASEAN group. And second, investment treaty adjudication under some of these treaties – especially the 1997 Germany – Philippines BIT – reveals a deep-seated failure among arbitral tribunals to recognize the heterogeneity among individual ASEAN states in their preferred approach to investment treaty exposure. This too would begin to shape the extent of both substantive and procedural protections for foreign investment in later dedicated ASEAN rules.

2.3.4 1987: First Dedicated ASEAN Investment Treaty – A Lockean Construct?

The inception of ASEAN is characterized by silence both on the role and treatment of foreign investment within the new regional grouping. When dealing with economic matters, the

[97] *See, for example, Churchill Mining PLC & Planet Mining Pty Ltd* v. *Republic of Indonesia*, ICSID Case No. ARB/12/14 & 12/40, Award (Dec. 6, 2016); *Lao Holdings N.V.* v. *The Lao People's Democratic Republic*, ICSID Case No. ARB (AF)/12/6, Award (Aug. 6, 2019); *Sanum Investments Ltd* v. *The Government of the Lao People's Democratic Republic*, UNCITRAL, PCA Case No. 2013-13, Award (Aug. 6, 2019).

1967 ASEAN Declaration focuses only on trade in goods and even then, on a sub-set of agricultural trade. This omission is by no means accidental. It reflects, at first instance, the strategic importance of agricultural specialization among individual ASEAN members – particularly in commodity trade.[98]

Of course, as touched upon earlier, a number of ASEAN states were implementing individual strategies throughout the 1950s to the 1970s (usually of import substitution) that were designed to facilitate rapid industrialization. A curious collective instrument supplemented these strategies. By the mid-1970s, the idea had begun to form that ASEAN should be employed as a system of managed industrialization through the centralized allocation of different industrial sectors and projects among the member states. At the first ASEAN Summit in 1976, the member states called for the establishment of large-scale industrial projects in ASEAN countries that would use available materials, increase food production, augment or save foreign exchange and create jobs.[99] At a later meeting of economic ministers, a decision was made to allocate different industrial projects among the grouping – a urea fertilizer plant each for Indonesia and Malaysia, superphosphates for the Philippines, diesel engines for Singapore and soda ash for Thailand.[100] The goal of state-managed industrialization reaches its early and short apotheosis in this period, with ministers even agreeing to consult

[98] Rodolfo C. Servino, Southeast Asia in Search of an ASEAN Community: Insights from the Former ASEAN Secretary-General 213 (2006).

[99] *Id.* at 214. [100] *Id.*

with one another on plans to establish other industries with a view to "avoiding unnecessary duplication and competition."[101]

Yet deep and enduring divisions between key members had begun to form behind the façade of collective cooperation. Among the approved ASEAN industrial projects, only the urea fertilizer plants in Indonesia were developed. Real or perceived self-interest soon began to trump common instrumental objectives. Put simply, no ASEAN state was willing to accept curbs on its freedom to establish industrial projects similar to those allocated to another ASEAN member.[102] More deeply, some states were opposed at the outset from the very philosophy underpinning collective industrialization with Singapore, for instance, antagonistic to a system that it regarded as profoundly anti-competitive.[103]

Yet, by the mid-1980s, the ASEAN states had themselves begun the process of constructing a dedicated ASEAN treaty on foreign investment. The negotiations toward the 1987 ASEAN Agreement for Promotion and Protection of Investments ("1987 ASEAN Agreement")[104] coincide with the fertile period of BIT-making by individual ASEAN member states. Unsurprisingly then, the *strategic* direction and tenor of those BITs have clearly influenced this early

[101] *Id.* [102] *Id.* at 217 [103] *Id.* at 218–19.

[104] Agreement among the Government of Brunei Darussalam, the Republic of Indonesia, Malaysia, the Republic of the Philippines, the Republic of Singapore and the Kingdom of Thailand for the Promotion and Protection of Investments, Dec. 15, 1987, https://asean.org/wp-content/uploads/2020/12/Agreement-for-the-ASEAN-Promotion-and-Protection-of-Investments-or-the-Investment-Guarantee-Agreement-ASEAN-IGA.pdf [hereinafter 1987 ASEAN Agreement].

iteration of the ASEAN investment project. Most visibly, there is a distinct shift from earlier (state-driven) assumptions that the ASEAN parties can or should control the factors leading to the establishment of industrial economic activity. It is certainly true that "acceleration of industrialization of the region" remains as a core objective in the 1987 ASEAN Agreement. But there is now explicit recognition that freer "flow of *private* investments" is the preferred mechanism to achieve that goal.[105]

This type of normative shift can be explained through Erikson's identity-formation theory, whereby an adolescent defines his or her own existence (identity) as he or she incessantly explores his or her right place in society.[106] The adolescent experiments with various roles and replaces earlier identifications with parents with a new identity as he or she socializes and competes with peers.[107] The AIR's embrace of neoliberal prescriptions in the 1980s–1990s can be understood as its members' socialization with peers (such as the Asian "tigers") as well as with global institutional partners (such as the IMF and the World Bank). The zeitgeist of the Washington Consensus pushed the AIR from old inward-looking development strategies to trying to find identification with the ideological preferences of the Bretton Woods institutions. The functional appeal of the AIR, such as investment liberalization of both *intra*- and *extra*-ASEAN regions, reflected a Lockean culture as its members demonstrated a limited trust among themselves based on self-

[105] *Id.* Preambular Recitals 2 and 3.
[106] Erikson, *supra* note 44, at 261–3.
[107] *Id.* at 155.

interest. Nonetheless, cooperation remained fragile, given stubborn vestiges of mercantilist competition.

Indeed there is a clear mismatch between this new normative direction (of facilitating greater flows of foreign investment within ASEAN) and the substantive content of the obligations within the 1987 ASEAN Agreement. This tension illustrates the limits of Lockean cooperation in given settings. On the scope of operation for instance, the definition of covered investment encompasses a wide variety of foreign capital extending beyond foreign direct investment (FDI) to less permanent sources including debt capital and portfolio investment.[108] The latter would become a focal point for dissatisfaction by key ASEAN members in the aftermath of the 1997–1998 Asian financial crisis, feeding eventually into key changes to the ASEAN investment treaty landscape. But even at this early stage, the new ASEAN investment treaty offered a far more restrictive standard of protection than most (although not all) BITs entered into by individual ASEAN members. In particular, there is a distinct ambivalence to the lauded goal of ensuring free operation of foreign capital within the ASEAN grouping. The substantive treaty obligations only apply if an ASEAN member has "specifically approved in writing" and "registered" an investment, upon which it can impose "such conditions as it deems fit for the purposes of this Agreement."[109] As we have seen, strict threshold conditions of this sort are certainly at play in the BIT practice of certain ASEAN members (including Indonesia and Thailand) but others (such as the Philippines) offer a far more liberal

[108] *Id.* art. I(3). [109] *Id.* art. II(1).

admission regime in their BITs.[110] The framers then have thus chosen to elevate into the collective sphere the most restrictive mechanism in operation across the entire suite of individual BITs entered into by ASEAN members.[111]

Strict threshold conditions of this sort theoretically offer ASEAN members an important flexibility to vet and control their exposure to investment disciplines. Yet, it may well be that the balance is tilted too far in favor of the host state vis-à-vis foreign investors. This precondition to legal coverage in the 1987 ASEAN Investment Agreement was examined in some detail in *Yaung Chi Oo Trading Pte Ltd* v. *Myanmar.* The Tribunal in that case declined jurisdiction precisely because the claimant was unable to prove that its existing investment (which had received earlier acceptance by Myanmar under domestic law) had been officially approved in writing at the time the 1987 ASEAN Agreement came into operation.[112] Yet Myanmar had not at that time implemented such a formal process of investment approval (for the specific

[110] On the differences in admissions clauses in BITs concluded by these various Southeast Asian countries, *see* Dato' Cecil Abraham, *State Approval in South East Asian Bilateral Investment Treaties*, 123. *See also* Ignacio Gómez-Palacio & Peter Muchlinski, *Admission and Establishment*, 227.

[111] Along these lines, when ruling on this part of the 1987 ASEAN Agreement, the *Yaung Chi Oo* v. *Myanmar* Tribunal expressly noted that "[t]he 1987 Agreement was thus subject to important limitations in terms of its coverage, as compared with other bilateral and multilateral investment protection treaties." *Yaung Chi Oo Trading Pte Ltd.* v. *Gov't of the Union of Myanmar*, ASEAN I.D. Case No. ARB 01/1, ¶ 23 (Mar. 31, 2003), 42 ILM 540 (2003).

[112] *Id.* at paras 60–2.

purposes of the 1987 ASEAN Agreement), making it simply impossible for the claimant to discharge this burden. Outside of the ASEAN context, certain arbitral tribunals have criticized the way in which formalized preconditions of this sort "advance no real interest of either signatory State" and "constitute an artificial trap depriving investors of the very protection the BIT was intended to provide."[113]

But even assuming this artificial and highly restrictive threshold condition is met, the remaining substantive provisions of the 1987 ASEAN instrument offer little promise of meaningful market access for flows of intra-ASEAN investment. Like most of the BITs entered into by the ASEAN members, those substantive obligations only apply on a post-admission basis. In other words, the sensitive determination of when and under what conditions foreign investment from one ASEAN member may enter the economy of another ASEAN member is purely a question for the latter to decide in exercise of full sovereignty. However, there is a fundamental and inexplicable omission in the 1987 ASEAN Agreement compared to that universe of BITs, even when the latter are also operating on a more conservative post-admission basis. There is no targeted obligation[114] on ASEAN members to extend national treatment to foreign investors and

[113] *Desert Line Projects LLC* v. *The Republic of Yemen*, ICSID Case No. ARB/05/17, Award, ¶ 106 (Feb. 6, 2008).

[114] To be sure, there is a provision constraining "unjustified or discriminatory measures" in Article IV(2) of the 1987 ASEAN Agreement. However, it is highly likely that this was not intended to operate as a guarantee of national treatment in the sense of requiring members to extend equal competitive opportunities to foreign investors

investments from another ASEAN state (which are typically present in almost all Asian BITs).[115]

The absence of national treatment (even on a post-admission basis) is deeply problematic from an economic perspective. Such an obligation ensures that an ASEAN member extends equal competitive opportunity to foreign investment established in accordance with domestic entry laws. Put differently, it precludes an ASEAN state from intervening in the domestic economy (whether through tax or regulation) in such a way as to intentionally advantage domestic actors to the detriment of competing foreign investors (from another ASEAN state). Without such a guarantee, the most efficient and innovative (foreign) producers could be precluded from serving customers in the host state's market where there is successful protectionist lobbying of regulators by a competing domestic industry. Consumers would suffer as a result when denied the benefits of lower prices, greater product variety and/or higher service quality where provided by foreign investors. National treatment thus has a critical role in establishing a fundamental liberal guarantee against protectionism, as evidenced in its common employment across the suite of BITs entered into by individual ASEAN

because the ASEAN members explicitly reserve the question of national treatment protection for future negotiation under Article IV(4).

115 Instead, the ASEAN members simply reserve the possibility for future bilateral or plurilateral commitments on national treatment to be struck under the framework of the 1987 ASEAN Agreement:

"Any two or more of the Contracting Parties may negotiate to accord national treatment within the framework of the Agreement."

1987 ASEAN Agreement, *supra* note 104, art. IV(4).

members. This omission in the 1987 ASEAN Agreement thus evidences a highly significant variance in strategic focus to those BITs. Liberalization of investment restrictions is simply not something that the ASEAN members as a collectivity were able or prepared to commit to in 1987. Their collective focus instead was simply, and only, one of investment protection. These elements are characteristic of a weak integrationist identity represented by the ASEAN investment regime in the 1980s–1990s. Put simply, at this stage, the ASEAN investment regime was barely a community.

On the other hand, the investment protection provisions of the 1987 ASEAN Agreement closely track and mirror the strong BITs characteristic of this period (and the preferences of the Bretton Woods institutions). Thus, there are the usual clauses obliging an ASEAN member to pay adequate compensation where engaging in (direct or indirect) expropriation of foreign investment.[116] Similarly, the 1987 ASEAN Investment Agreement obliges members to extend "fair and equitable treatment" whose content, in line with treaty practice in the 1980s, is left undefined and ambiguous.[117] The 1987 instrument also extends a strong treaty right for foreign investors to repatriate their capital and earnings, subject only to the national laws of the ASEAN state from which transfers were to be made.[118] This too is an area in which later parts of the ASEAN investment project would diverge significantly, especially as members digested the lessons and implications of the 1997–1998 Asian financial crisis.

[116] *Id.* art. VI. [117] *Id.* art. IV(2). [118] *Id.* art. VII.

The analysis so far has identified a set of stringent protective obligations imposed on ASEAN members. To put this slightly differently, the many constraints on state action directed at foreign investment are not balanced in any significant way by flexibilities that would permit state regulation in key areas of public interest. In this respect, the 1987 ASEAN Investment Agreement matches most of the investment law universe at play in the 1980s, which stands in contrast to the law of the WTO.[119] In the latter, there has always been a set of important exceptions for state regulation to pursue key public objectives that had been formalized at inception of the General Agreement on Tariffs and Trade (GATT) 1947. These mechanisms reflect a set of shared social purposes among the membership which, as John Ruggie has argued, has led to historical norm-governed change *within* the dictates of the system rather than an irretrievable decline in multilateralism (given the slow erosion of the U.S. as a dominant hegemon over time).[120]

Of course, the absence of exceptions is not the only significant departure from the WTO model in the 1987 ASEAN Investment Agreement. Dispute settlement in the WTO is reserved for states parties with, since the completion of the Uruguay Round in 1994, a complex set of

[119] Regarding a discussion on the GATT/WTO's legal and institutional arrangement for legitimate public objectives, *see* Sungjoon Cho, FREE MARKETS AND SOCIAL REGULATION: A REFORM AGENDA OF THE GLOBAL TRADING SYSTEM (2003).

[120] John Ruggie, *Embedded Liberalism and Postwar Economic Regimes*, *in* CONSTRUCTING THE WORLD POLITY: ESSAYS ON INTERNATIONAL INSTITUTIONALIZATION 82–3 (John Ruggie ed., 1998).

procedures formalized within the WTO Dispute Settlement Understanding. By contrast, there is no dedicated or specialized institution to monitor state compliance with the 1987 ASEAN Agreement. Perhaps reflecting ASEAN's then rudimentary nature as an interstate negotiating forum to advance economic cooperation (in line with a Lockean conception), state-to-state disputes concerning the interpretation or application of the 1987 instrument were to be "settled amicably between the parties" and, failing settlement, were simply to be "submitted to the ASEAN Economic Ministers."[121] Yet we are then faced with a fundamental disjuncture with the harder and formalized mechanisms to resolve disputes between foreign investors (as non-state actors) and member states under the 1987 ASEAN Agreement. Once again, the influence of the universe of BITs entered into by individual ASEAN members (and by extension, the Bretton Woods institutions) is apparent and explains this discrepancy. In line with standard BIT practice by the 1980s, the 1987 ASEAN Agreement extends standing to foreign investors (from an ASEAN state) who could bring a complaint against a signatory (ASEAN) member for breach of the treaty, which could be ultimately resolved by arbitration whose outcome would be "binding" as a matter of treaty obligation.[122] Although used relatively sparsely in the future, the few cases brought against individual ASEAN members (both under their BITs and the 1987 ASEAN Agreement)

[121] 1987 ASEAN Agreement, *supra* note 104, art. IX. [122] *Id.* art. X.

would eventually usher in treaty change based on the reasoning and outcome of those particular disputes. There seems then to be a selective learning effect from these BIT experiences. While the 1987 ASEAN Agreement adopted the investor-state investment arbitration mechanism, the Agreement was not as open as those individual BITs in key substantive areas of investor protection and investment liberalization, especially national treatment. This partly explains why there were so few disputes that arose under the early collective ASEAN rules. The general orientation of the regime closely mirrors the strongly pro-state decisions (especially on jurisdiction) made by certain arbitral tribunals.

In sum, during the 1980s–1990s the AIR grew out of the earlier Hobbesian mutual suspicion and embraced a neo liberalist identity as ASEAN's global partners disabused the ASEAN economies of an outmoded development model, such as import substitution. The 1987 ASEAN Agreement provided the AIR with an operable organizational avenue in expanding *intra*-ASEAN investment flows. Nonetheless, the AIR during this period betrayed the limits of Lockean cooperation. Indeed, an ethos of *intra*-ASEAN investment was preceded by zeal for deep *extra*-ASEAN investment evidenced by a dense web of BITs between individual members of ASEAN and other developed countries. Markedly, *extra*-ASEAN capital flow dwarfed *intra*-ASEAN flows during the BIT growth period of the mid- to late 1990s. This puzzling irony, which might be dubbed "reverse open regionalism," eloquently demonstrated the embedded rivalry among members of the AIR fueled by protectionist (mercantilist) competition (see Table 2.1).

Table 2.1 *ASEAN Net FDI on a Balance of Payments Basis 1995–1999 (Unit: U.S. Million)*[123]

Year	Intra-ASEAN FDI	Extra-ASEAN FDI	Total ASEAN FDI	Share of Intra-ASEAN FDI in Total ASEAN FDI (%)
1995	4,653.0	16,668.0	21,321.0	21.8
1996	2,777.7	23,238.4	26,061.0	10.7
1997	5,537.05	22,597.5	28,135.0	19.7
1998	2,019.8	17,575.2	19,595.0	10.3
1999	1,217.5	15,693.5	16,911.0	7.2

2.4 Conclusion

This chapter began by conceptualizing the ASEAN Investment Regime (AIR) as an Interstate Cooperative Regime (ICR), defined as a stable interstate cooperative nexus on a particular regulative subject, comprising the regulation of foreign investment in this particular case. It has sought to develop a framework that, deployed both here and in later chapters, would describe and explain the complex evolution of the AIR in terms of its identity formation. To that end, we have presented three ideal types of cultural logic (Hobbesian, Lockean and Kantian), largely overlapping with the three main IR theories of neorealism, neoliberal institutionalism and constructivism respectively. For the purposes of this chapter, AIR's start-point is modest as a model of integration. The member states barely transcended mutual Hobbesian

123 Mohd Haflah Piei, *An East Asia FTA: A Malaysian Perspective, in* East Asian Regionalism: Feasibilities and Challenges 109 (Choong Yong Ahn, Richard E. Baldwin & Inkyo Cheong eds., 2005).

suspicion to engage limited Lockean cooperation in the first (1987) iteration of the AIR.

Later chapters will chart the evolutionary pathway that transcends this modest beginning as the AIR transitioned toward a closer, regional investment community. Importantly, however, this sequential evolution is not always linear and non-retrogressive. Indeed, one can still detect Hobbesian relics, such as sovereignty-preserving protectionism, even in the latest and most advanced form of AIR. While this regressionism challenges any uncritical application of identity-formation theory to AIR, it also eloquently demonstrates that an ICR is indeed a complex social organization whose institutional evolution may not be isomorphic. To that extent, "path-dependency," such as the "ASEAN Way," remains as a critical factor in mapping and understanding the nuances of AIR's evolution.

Chapter 3

Tracing Influences on the ASEAN Investment Regime

3.1 Introduction

In the previous chapter, we have seen that those states interlinked around the Association of Southeast Asian Nations (ASEAN) shifted their economic paradigm from a closed to open economy in the 1980s.[1] Ever since, trade and investment flows in and out of this area have been nothing short of spectacular. Between 1990 and 2014, the investment inflow to, and outflow from, this region has increased approximately 10 and 34 times, respectively.[2] By 2014, foreign direct investment (FDI) flows to ASEAN exceeded inflows to China, making it the largest recipient of FDI in the developing world.[3] Notably, this paradigm shift from a closed to an open economy through liberalization of trade and investment restrictions by ASEAN countries has been powered by a thick set of global norms. A variety of treaties provided ASEAN nations with modern regulatory platforms necessary to integrate their

[1] *See also generally* The Politics and Economics of Integration in Asia and the Pacific (Shiro Armstrong ed., 2011).

[2] UNCTAD, *FDI Statistics Division on Investment and Enterprise* (Apr. 2 2016), http://unctad.org/en/Pages/DIAE/FDI%20Statistics/FDI-Statistics.aspx.

[3] ASEAN Secretariat & UNCTAD, *ASEAN Investment Report 2015*, at xv (Nov. 2015), https://perma.cc/W7YR-KJTB.

economies into the global market. At the same time, as the ASEAN nations were becoming more involved in the global market, policymakers and private practitioners from developed countries, as well as international organizations – such as the International Monetary Fund (IMF) and the World Bank – offered their technical assistance to the ASEAN nations in adopting neoliberal reform in the areas of trade and investment liberalization.[4] Naturally, ASEAN nations relied heavily on general legal principles and templates, such as model bilateral investment treaties (BITs) originally created by developed states and then dispersed mimetically.

Nonetheless, isomorphism of this benchmarking type (mimetic isomorphism)[5] does not necessarily mean identical treaty products ("equifinality").[6] As we have already seen, despite general convergence into global patterns in the basic legal structure and tenets, both the individual ASEAN BITs (signed between ASEAN nations and non-ASEAN nations) and the collective ASEAN investment regime (AIR) (addressing intra-ASEAN investment flows) feature unique departures from the global investment model. There is a temptation to dismiss these departures as mere outliers. This chapter,

[4] On the imposition of structural adjustment conditions in the lending policies of international financial institutions such as the International Monetary Fund, *see* Michael Trebilcock & Robert Howse, The Regulation of International Trade (3rd ed. 2005), 486–91.

[5] *See generally* Paul J. DiMaggio & Walter W. Powell, *The Iron Cage Revisited: Institutional Isomorphism and Collective Rationality in Organizational Fields*, 48 Am. Soc. Rev. 147 (1983).

[6] Martha Finnemore, National Interests in International Society 138–9 (Peter J. Katzenstein ed. 1996).

however, continues to take those heterogeneities seriously and explores a structural explanation. Here our focus is on the next iteration of the AIR – the 1998 Framework Agreement on the ASEAN Investment Area – whose negotiation was characterized by an identity crisis which forced the ASEAN members toward a deeper level of integration and community-building.

In addition, this chapter also begins the process of the exploring the legalization characteristics of the AIR. Measured against orthodox and external benchmarks, ASEAN's investment regime is relatively limited. In this chapter, however, we begin to build the argument that while ASEAN members have subscribed to global norms in their own collective rules, they have done so in an intentionally selective manner shaped fundamentally by key contextual dynamics. These encompass a complex combination of ASEAN members' unique deliberation modality (the "ASEAN Way") informed by their shared historical experience coupled with negative social learning. Using those insights over the course of the next chapters, we argue that it is both possible and desirable to understand the ASEAN approach as an independent and legitimate form of legalization, rather than as a failed or flawed model.

This chapter is structured as follows. Section 3.2 establishes the conventional orthodoxy of legalization according to the indicators developed by Kenneth Abbott, Robert Keohane, Andrew Moravcsik, Anne-Marie Slaughter and Duncan Snidal.[7] Although formulated for descriptive purposes, these

[7] Kenneth W. Abbott, Robert O. Keohane, Andrew Moravcsik, Anne-Marie Slaughter & Duncan Snidal, *The Concept of Legalization*, *in* Legalization and World Politics 17 (Judith L. Goldstein et al. eds., 2001).

indicators nonetheless connote, albeit implicitly, certain normative assumptions in their design. Components of "obligation," "precision" and "delegation," especially when coupled with proffered examples, tend to signify that a higher degree of legalization is necessarily *better* than a lower degree of legalization. However, by expanding and deepening the notion of legalization, we will argue (both in this chapter and the next) that the AIR's deliberate departure from Global Investment Law (GIL), which we define as "delegalization," is indeed a *different*, but not necessarily worse, form of legalization. Section 3.3 then turns to the identity crisis that reshapes the evolution of the AIR, comprising the devastating 1997–1998 Asian financial crisis and the rise of China as a serious economic threat. It was only after the AIR experienced these diverse crises that it firmly constituted its collective, integrationist identity as an investment community, rather than as a loose arrangement among individual members. Section 3.4 then uses both sets of insights in measuring both formation of an ASEAN community identity and idiographic nature of legalization in the 1998 Framework Agreement on the ASEAN Investment Area.

3.2 The Orthodoxy of Legalization as a Rationalist Benchmark

In a broad sense, legalization is a conscious employment of norms, both soft and hard, in an institutionalized setting. Both international legal scholars and political scientists, of a rationalist bent, in the study of international relations (IR) widely embrace the thesis of legalization in explaining and understanding various aspects and properties of international law and international politics.[8] While this concept remains contested, a paradigmatic working definition can be found in a collaborative work commissioned by a group of pre-eminent international law/international relations scholars, Kenneth Abbott, Robert Keohane, Andrew Moravcsik, Anne-Marie Slaughter and Duncan Snidal.[9] Their definition of legalization focuses on textual and institutional factors in a given international setting. Such definition is a formalistic, ex ante concept, rather than one informed by practical (empirical), ex post characteristics.[10] The three main properties that Abbott and colleagues elected in delineating legalization are "obligation," "precision" and "delegation."

First, obligation refers to a legal rule's *binding* commitment. Indicators of obligation range from unconditional commitments, such as UN General Assembly declarations that invoke *jus cogens*, to overt negation of a binding effect, such as treaty reservations.[11] Importantly, the concept of obligation not only exhibits substantive norms but also implicates derivative procedures and particular forms of discourse.[12] For example,

[8] *See, for example*, Beth A. Simmons & Richard H. Steinberg, International Law and International Relations (2007); Christian Brütsch & Dirk Lehmkuhl, Law and Legalization in Transnational Relations (2007); American Society of Comparative Law (ASIL), Legalization of International Relations/Internationalization of International Law, Proceedings of the 96th Annual Meeting (2002).

[9] Abbott et al., *supra* note 7.

[10] *Id.* at 18 ("Note that we have defined legalization in terms of key characteristics of rules and procedures, not in terms of effects.").

[11] *Id.* at 26. [12] *Id.* at 24–8.

failing to comply with a binding obligation entails certain legal consequences, such as "state responsibility" under public international law. Granted, determining eventual violation is a complicated issue, subject to a plethora of precluding circumstances (or exceptions) ranging from a doctrine of *rebus sic standibus* to self-defense.[13] Also, remedial issues, such as cessation, restitution, compensation and satisfaction (apology), derive from binding obligation.

Second, precision engages the level of textual ambiguity (or determinacy) that shapes subsequent interpretation in practice.[14] Indicators of precision spread from determinate rules that are self-evident and therefore leave little room for interpretation to self-judging provisions subject to autonomous (sovereign) interpretation.[15] Legal scholars from various theoretical positions impute to precision certain properties or virtues of law, such as rationality (James Morrow), compliance pull (Thomas Frank) and predictability (Lon Fuller).[16] As to the degree of precision (or imprecision) of legal provisions, an oft-invoked dichotomy of "rules" and "standards" may be relevant to international law, despite its domestic law origin.[17] Under the *thick* institutional context that features a rich set of both administrative (secretarial) and judicial apparatus, as seen in the European Union, there is a textual division of labor between rules and standards (such as EU Regulations and Directives, respectively). Nonetheless, most international organizations display *thin* institutional contexts that lack equivalence to this

[13] *Id.* at 25. [14] *Id.* at 28–31. [15] *Id.* at 30–1. [16] *Id.* at 29.
[17] *Id.* at 29–30.

apparatus and leave issues of implementation and interpretation in the hands of contracting parties themselves.

Third, delegation denotes the extent to which states authorize third-party institutions, such as courts, arbitration panels and administrative organs, to interpret legal rules, resolve disputes and oversee treaty implementation.[18] Indicators of delegation vary from non-delegation (pure diplomacy) to binding arbitration (arbitral panel) to full adjudication (international court).[19] The most representative form of delegation in most international organizations is through third-party dispute settlement. For example, the European Union (EU) has highly advanced international courts, such as the Court of Justice of the European Union and the European Court of Human Rights. The WTO also has a sophisticated adjudicatory system comprised of first-order panels and the Appellate Body. Besides dispute resolution, international bureaucracies (such as the WTO Secretariat) help implement treaties by clarifying agreed rules, coordinating policy discourse and administering enforcement.[20] Some international bureaucracies, such as the Codex Alimentarius Commission, established jointly by the World Health Organization (WHO) and the Food and Agricultural Organization (FAO), create a variety of soft norms in the form of recommendations and guidelines.[21] While delegation in general tends to elicit tensions with sovereign states, we still find collective commitment to highly centralized enforcement mechanisms in particular settings, as seen in the UN Security Council and the WTO Dispute Settlement Body (DSB).[22]

[18] *Id.* at 31–4. [19] *Id.* at 32. [20] *Id.* at 33. [21] *Id.* [22] *Id.* at 34.

Based on these three dimensions of legalization, Abbott and colleagues classify existing international organizations and other less institutionalized forms of international arrangements in accordance with eight ideal types: Type I (high degree of obligation, high degree of precision and high degree of delegation), Type II (high degree of obligation, low degree of precision and high degree of delegation); Type III (high degree of obligation, high degree of precision and low degree of delegation); Type IV (low degree of obligation, high degree of precision and high or moderate degree of delegation); Type V (high degree of obligation, low degree of precision and low degree of delegation); Type VI (low degree of obligation, low degree of precision and high or moderate degree of delegation); Type VII (low degree of obligation, high degree of precision and low degree of delegation); and Type VIII (low degree of obligation, low degree of precision and low degree of delegation).[23]

Using this model, the European Union treaties naturally fall under Type I, due to their sophisticated legal regimes that are close approximates to those of domestic governments. In the middle of that continuum, the 1987 Montreal Protocol on Substances that Deplete the Ozone Layer[24] belongs to Type III in that, despite clear binding obligations, it does not feature any delegation for implementation and adjudication. Further along the spectrum, the International Monetary Fund (IMF) falls under Type VI in that while delegation for policy coordination is conspicuous, legally binding obligation may

[23] *Id.* at 22.

[24] Montreal Protocol on Substances that Deplete the Ozone Layer, Sept. 16, 1987, 1522 U.N.T.S. 3.

be politically inconceivable in this issue area. Even further along, the G7 is categorized under Type VIII on account of its highly diplomatic nature, which is antithetical to legally binding obligation.

Turning to ASEAN, we will begin to see in this chapter, and the next chapter as well, that the AIR is generally characterized by a lower degree of legalization. According to the legalization indicators developed by Abbott and colleagues, the AIR's level of obligation may be considered "moderate" or "low" in the presence of a number of contingent obligations subject to various national reservations. Its level of precision may be deemed "low" due to the broad reservation of discretion left to member states. Its level of delegation may also be regarded as "low" on account of characteristically high jurisdictional thresholds that seriously impede the initiation of arbitration. Overall, the AIR appears to fall between Type V and VII in the Abbott and colleagues' scale of legalization and thus offers a far lower level of institutionalized protection for foreign investors than that extended by GIL.

Importantly, however, this "under"-legalization of the AIR does not necessarily exhaust the Western style of legalization as an evaluative benchmark. In fact, the AIR's "delegalization," which will be discussed in the next chapter, is an adaptive strategy informed by a critique of nomothetic assumptions of an orthodoxy of legalization. Ideational factors, such as identity and socialization, often punctuate a rationalist linearity of legalization. Here, it is essential first to chart a vital shift in orientation driven by a series of crises facing the ASEAN states by the mid- to late 1990s.

3.3 Identity Challenge: The Asian Financial Crisis and the Rise of China

According to Erickson, at the final stage of identity formation, adolescents suffer from serious role confusion as they become exposed to a new, broadened horizon (environment).[25] Their pre-established identification comes under question in the face of newly discovered challenges and opportunities. Only after they weather this "war within themselves,"[26] may adolescents build a genuine sense of direction and unearth their suitable place in the society that they belong to.[27] Erikson believed that this "identity crisis" is a rite of passage that is necessary for adolescents to develop a unique yet coherent whole (identity).[28] If we apply this notion of crisis to an ICR's identity formation, we may locate certain significant events or developments that compel a given Interstate Cooperative Regime (ICR) to rethink its earlier identification or organizational goal.

The AIR's expansionist reform in the 1980–1990s, albeit limited and incremental, attests to its neoliberal identity formation. In this period, the AIR's organizational identity is best described as a loosely knitted ICR that still retains an inter-governmental nature, albeit with common functional goals, such as expansion of scope of liberalization and reduction of transaction costs. A member of AIR tends to perceive another member as a rival, if not an enemy, in a potentially

[25] Erik H. Erikson, Childhood and Society, 163–64 (1950).

[26] Erik H. Erikson, Identity, Youth and Crisis 17 (1968).

[27] Erikson, *supra* note 25, at 161. [28] Erikson, *supra* note 26, at 16.

competitive relationship, rather than as a fellow in a highly integrated community.[29] Nonetheless, two colossal external shocks – the Asian financial crisis and the rise of China as a common threat – forced the AIR to rethink and modify its earlier identity toward deeper integration and community-building among its members.

First, over the course of 1997–1998, the Asian financial crisis wreaked havoc with the economies of some of the world's most successful performers.[30] Its massive shockwave dealt a blow to its main economies, in particular Thailand, Indonesia, Malaysia and the Philippines.[31] Capital inflows into the region had fueled rapid credit expansion, which lowered the quality of credit and led to asset price inflation. Highly leveraged corporate sectors and large, unhedged short-term debt made the crisis countries deeply vulnerable to changes in market sentiment. Weaknesses in bank and corporate governance exacerbated excessive risk-taking, as prudential regulations were limited or poorly enforced. The crisis was ultimately triggered by the floating of the Thai baht in July 1997. Changing expectations led to the

[29] Alexander Wendt, THE SOCIAL THEORY OF INTERNATIONAL POLITICS 250 (1999).

[30] For a comprehensive overview of the causes of and responses to the crisis, *see* Carl-Johan Lindgren, Tomas Balino, Charles Enock, Anne-Marie Gulde, Marc Quintyn & Leslie Teo, FINANCIAL SECTOR CRISIS AND RESTRUCTURING: LESSONS FROM ASIA (1999).

[31] Andrew McIntyre, *Institutions and Investors: The Politics of the Economic Crisis in Southeast Asia*, 55 INT'L ORG. 81 (2001); *see* Diane A. Desierto, *Investment Treaties: ASEAN*, in ASIA RISING: GROWTH AND RESILIENCE IN AN UNCERTAIN GLOBAL ECONOMY 184 (Hal Hill & Maria Socorro Gochoco-Bautista eds., 2012).

depreciation of most other currencies throughout the region, bank runs, rapid withdrawals of foreign private capital and dramatic economic downturns.

The shared priorities for the affected states were to stabilize financial systems and restore private sector confidence in economic management. Yet they employed boundedly different strategies to achieve these key goals. Three of the worst-affected countries – Thailand, South Korea and Indonesia – implemented orthodox adjustment policy as part of an IMF-supported program.[32] In return for financial assistance from the IMF (and other donors), those countries committed to float their exchange rates, raise interest rates, tighten fiscal policy, open up their financial markets to foreigners, close troubled banks and undertake a range of other structural reforms. Malaysia, however, took a radically different path, extending to the contentious practice of imposing controls of outflow of short-term capital.[33] Among other things, those capital controls blocked the repatriation of portfolio capital held by nonresidents in Malaysia for a period of 12 months, which was later replaced with a graduated system of exit levy on repatriation of portfolio investments (with the rate of levy decreasing with the duration of investment).[34] This triggered a hostile reaction from a range of commentators, including the IMF.[35] Yet economic analysis has now shown that compared to IMF-supported programs, the Malaysian strategy

[32] Ethan Kaplan & Dani Rodrik, *Did the Malaysian Capital Controls Work?*, CEPR Discussion Paper No. 2754 1 (2001).

[33] *Id.* [34] Lindgren et al., *supra* note 30, at 20.

[35] Kaplan & Rodrik, *supra* note 32, at 10–13.

produced faster economic recovery, smaller declines in employment and real wages, and a more rapid turnaround in the stock market.[36]

Paradoxically however, what has now been proven to be a sensible policy response runs immediately in conflict with the structure of many older Asian BITs and would indeed trigger an investment treaty claim against Malaysia.[37] Two elements are notable here. The scope of covered "investment" in most BITs extends far beyond "sticky" foreign direct investment (which had proven itself to be remarkably stable during the crisis) to also include unstable types of capital such as short-term debt and equity (whose rapid withdrawal had precipitated the crisis). Relatedly, the terms of older Asian BITs classically oblige states to enable free transfer of capital associated with *all* covered investments and do not – for the most part – allow for the imposition of restrictions for balance-of-payments reasons.

Ultimately, the collective nature of the crisis (a "regional" crisis) created a sense of bonding among ASEAN members as they suffered the crisis together.[38] Also, after the crisis they had to respond to a common demand from foreign investors – and the Bretton Woods institutions – including

[36] *Id.* at 26–8.

[37] *Philipp Gruslin* v. *Malaysia*, ICSID Case No. ARB/99/3, Award (Nov. 27, 2000).

[38] *See* Ralph Emmers, *Southeast Asia's New Security Institutions*, *in* Asia's New Institutional Architecture: Evolving Structures for Managing Trade, Financial, and Security Relations 201 (Vinod K. Aggarwal & Min Gyo Koo eds., 2008) (viewing that the Asian financial crisis revealed the ASEAN's institutional frailty).

invasive regulatory reform toward a more investor-friendly environment.[39] More importantly, however, the ASEAN economies advanced the AIR itself into a more integrative format so as to dramatically augment intra-ASEAN investment flow. In this line, the Second Informal ASEAN Summit, held in Kuala Lumpur in December 1997, decided to expedite the implementation of the ASEAN Free Trade Area (AFTA) as well as the formation of the ASEAN Investment Area (AIA).[40]

Second, the rise of China and the consequential threat it poses to the ASEAN region as a main competitor in the global export market also pushed the ASEAN members into deeper economic integration. As a striking example, consider the fact that for the past three decades the ASEAN region has been a popular investment destination for most computer component manufacturers, as it has become the world's second largest exporter of those components.[41] Recently, however, China, as the world's largest computer assembler, challenged ASEAN's hitherto dominant position in the production of computer components, as it benefited from competitive edges in labor, local suppliers and transportation.[42] As a result,

[39] Edmund R. Thompson, *ASEAN After the Financial Crisis*, ASEAN Econ. Bull. 1 (2000).

[40] Suthad Setboonsarng, *ASEAN Economic Cooperation: Adjusting to the Crisis*, Southeast Asian Aff. 35 (1998).

[41] United States International Trade Communication, Pub. No. 4176, ASEAN: Regional Trends in Economic Integration, Export Competitiveness, and Inbound Investment for Selected Industries 49 (2010).

[42] *Id.*

between 2004 and 2008 ASEAN's share of global computer parts export remained unchanged at 20 percent while China's share increased from 27 percent to 35 percent.[43] Likewise, China has surpassed ASEAN, by high margins, as a major FDI destination in Asia in the past decade. While FDI to ASEAN and FDI to China accounted for 66 percent and 16 percent, respectively, of total FDI to Asia in 1990, these two numbers were exactly reversed in 2003.[44]

With these significant external shocks, the AIR could no longer maintain its simple pre-crisis identity as a loose ICR. It was forced to adapt to the post-financial crisis environment and locate a new engine for regional economic development.[45] At the same time, the AIR needed to check the rise of China. The AIR identified its solution in the intensification of intra-ASEAN investment flow, allowing it to build sufficient scale and capacity to meet the new Chinese competitive threat. Obviously, this meant a dilemma over its longstanding legacy of the Lockean (mercantilist) competition among ASEAN economies. To the AIR, this was a central moment of identity crisis.

43 *Id.* at 51.

44 *See* David M. Jones & Michael L. R. Smith, *Making Process, Not Progress: ASEAN and the Evolving East Asian Regional Order,* 32 International Security 165 (2007).

45 *See* Robert J. R. Elliott & Kengo Ikemoto, *AFTA and the Asian Crisis: Help or Hindrance to ASEAN Intra-Regional Trade?,* 18 Asian Econ. J. 1, 17 (2004) (finding that the Asian financial crisis prompted a strong aspiration among ASEAN countries to increase *intra*-ASEAN trade).

3.4 1998 Framework Agreement on the ASEAN Investment Area: Measuring Community and Legalization

3.4.1 The Beginnings of an Investment Community

These dramatic environmental factors – the 1997–1998 Asian financial crisis and the rise of China – forced ASEAN and the AIR to search for a new integrationist identity. The shared challenge begot the shared response. The ASEAN economies realized that the erstwhile Lockean cooperation tinged with rivalry would no longer constitute a sustainable institutional arrangement governing their investment flows in and out of the ASEAN region. Instead, regional integration via an augmented intra-ASEAN investment foundation and attendant economic community-building surfaced as a new solution.[46] While the old identity of the AIR in the 1980–1990s may have operated as an agent of the ASEAN economies to help them achieve a limited functional goal of facilitating intra-ASEAN investment, the post-crisis AIR has begun to morph into a

[46] Consider the first preambular recital of the 1998 Framework Agreement on the ASEAN Investment Area: "Affirming the importance of sustaining economic growth and development in all Member States through joint efforts in liberalizing trade *and promoting intra-ASEAN trade and investment flows* enshrined in the Framework Agreement on Enhancing ASEAN Economic Co-operation signed in Singapore on 28 January 1992" (emphasis added). Framework Agreement on the ASEAN Investment Area, Recital 1, Oct. 7, 1998 http://agreement.asean.org/media/download/20140119040024.pdf (hereinafter 1998 Framework Agreement).

trustee role with a deeper integrationist *telos*.[47] As discussed in Chapter 2, a constructivist lens can capture this new identity.[48] A strong collective bond among ASEAN economies with a shared goal of building an ASEAN investment community has heralded an aspiration for a Kantian future in the ASEAN region.[49]

If we consider the construction of ASEAN investment rules in the post-crisis era, we can identify both internal and external influences that have shaped the contours of that developing project. As we have seen, at the internal level the preexisting BITs of individual ASEAN member states have continued to play a role in shaping collective treaty choice within ASEAN as a grouping. Given these foundations, it is perhaps understandable that the earliest stage of the ASEAN investment project – the 1987 ASEAN Agreement for Promotion and Protection of Investments – reflected a conservative BIT-style project of *only* delivering investment protection. Put differently, liberalization of restrictions on entry and operation of foreign investment was a marginal

47 *See* Anthea Roberts, *Power and Persuasion in Investment Treaty Interpretation: The Dual Role of States*, 104 Am. J. Int'l L. 179, 186 (2010).

48 *See* Amitav Acharya, *Regional Institutions and Asian Security Order: Norms, Power, and Prospects for Peaceful Change*, *in* Asian Security Order: Instrumental and Normative Features 211–12 (Muthiah Alagappa ed., 2003) (arguing that the ASEAN security community could be better understood from a constructivist perspective emphasizing ideational forces, rather than a realist one based on power and interest).

49 *But see* Jones & Smith, *supra* note 45, at 148 (holding a skeptical view on the "community" identity of ASEAN due mainly to its loose organization nature as an association that has remained unchanged since its inception).

element of early ASEAN investment rules. But with the late 1990s triggering external crises facing the ASEAN grouping, the normative direction of the ASEAN investment project had pointedly reversed. Now, under the 1998 ASEAN Investment Area, the ASEAN members had committed to strategically positioning the region as a single production base (as a means of countering the strategic threat posed by China), and foreign investment was a core component of that strategy. A single production base would supply ASEAN products for consumption not just in the region but also for export to elsewhere in the world. Foreign investment is a key driver of production networks that are so central to this vibrant aspect of the contemporary global economy. Large-scale foreign investment will locate different stages of a production process across different countries so as to achieve key efficiencies by minimizing overall production cost. Efficiency-seeking foreign investment "is by its very nature trade-creating" because "[b]y subdividing the production process in vertical stages between countries, trade is obviously created (compared to the situation where all stages are undertaken in one country)."[50] This is no minor or tangential economic fact. Approximately half of the world's trade today takes place between affiliates of multinational enterprises trading intermediate goods and services.[51] The potential benefits of using

[50] WTO, *The Relationship between Trade and Investment*, at 16, WTO Doc. WT/WGTI/W/7 (Sept. 8, 1997).

[51] European Commission, *Communication from the Commission to the Council, the European Parliament, the European Economic and Social Committee and the Committee of Regions; Towards a Comprehensive*

foreign investment to position ASEAN as an integrated production base are thus remarkably extensive, including the possibility of higher employment, higher wages and overall development throughout the region.

We can plainly trace these momentous shifts in legal framing and positioning in the new set of collective investment rules in ASEAN. A fundamental objective of the 1998 Framework Agreement is the establishment of "a competitive ASEAN Investment Area" (AIA),[52] indicating a strategic desire to position the region as an alternative host of foreign investment that would normally flow elsewhere (not least China). The means chosen to achieve this strategic goal are naturally different from the purely investment protective focus of the 1987 ASEAN Agreement. The AIR's new identity represented by the AIA now overcame Lockean limits under its old identity in the 1980s–1990s. Now member states would commit to a "more *liberal* and transparent investment environment" that would "substantially increase the flow of investments ... from *both* ASEAN and non-ASEAN sources."[53] This strong liberalization mandate was matched by an exceedingly ambitious time frame, whereby:

> (a) national treatment is extended to ASEAN investors by 2010, and to all investors by 2020, subject to the exceptions provided for under this Agreement;

European International Investment Policy, at 3, COM (2010) 343 final (July 7, 2010).

[52] 1998 Framework Agreement, *supra* note 47, art. 3(a).

[53] *Id.* art. 3(a)(i) (emphasis added).

> (b) all industries are opened for investment to ASEAN investors by 2010 and to all investors by 2020, subject to the exceptions provided for under this Agreement.[54]

The remaining substantive provisions operationalize the core commitment to investment liberalization of the ASEAN members, at least when it comes to flows of FDI within and among ASEAN states. Most fundamentally, each ASEAN member commits in Article 7(1) to:

> (a) [O]pen immediately all its industries for investments by ASEAN Investors;
> (b) [A]ccord immediately to ASEAN investors and their investments, in respect of all industries and measures affecting investment including but not limited to the admission, establishment, acquisition, expansion, management, operation and disposition of investments, treatment no less favourable than that it accords to its own like investors and investments ("national treatment").[55]

Compared to the conservative post-establishment orientation of the 1987 ASEAN Instrument (as well as almost all of the BITs of individual ASEAN members), the 1998 Framework Agreement now dramatically liberalizes restrictions on entry of foreign investment. The significant and valuable promise of market access in Article 7(1)(a) is especially remarkable as it precludes an ASEAN member from reserving any industry to participation only by that state or its state-owned entities. The promise of national treatment in Article 7(1)(b) also prevents

[54] *Id.* art. 4. [55] *Id.* art. 7(1).

an ASEAN member from restricting operation in a given industry to domestic private actors. Given the political challenges associated with this ambitious commitment to investment liberalization, it is unsurprising that the 1998 Framework Agreement provides for a degree of flexibility in meeting these obligations. ASEAN members are permitted to submit Temporary Exclusion Lists and Sensitive Lists, which specify the industries or sectors that would not be opened up to investment or for which the ASEAN member could not confer national treatment.[56] For most ASEAN members, the negative list exemptions (in the Temporary List) were to be reviewed biennially and phased out by 2010.[57]

Interestingly, it is at this point that we see the challenges faced by the newer, least-developed members of ASEAN find reflection as a matter of legal architecture. This, too, vividly illustrates the communal facets of the AIR. Vietnam and Laos are granted special and differential treatment in the form classically provided in the law of the WTO. These newer member states of ASEAN are given a staggered period of compliance with a progressive phase-out of their Temporary List to be concluded by 2015.[58] This is by no means a small or incidental change. Within investment law, the usual and strongly held assumption across most BITs is that developing states should be fully responsible for weaknesses in governance structures where these constitute wrongful harm to a foreign investor, rather than the WTO-based notion that development status might variegate the depth of a given international law commitment. It is also important to recall that the ASEAN

[56] *Id.* art. 7(2). [57] *Id.* art. 7(3). [58] *Id.*

members can submit an entirely separate Sensitive List (to the Temporary List) excluding themselves from the immediate obligation to open their economies to investment from other ASEAN members. And when it comes to such a Sensitive List, there is no hard phase-out contemplated, with the AIA simply providing that it "shall be reviewed by 1 January 2003 and at such subsequent periodic intervals as may be decided by the AIA Council."[59]

This hard promise of liberalization of entry restrictions to intra-ASEAN capital flows – even when accompanied by the possibility of negative list exemptions – has real potential to contribute to the key articulated goal of the construction of a competitive AIA that would "substantially increase the flow of investments into ASEAN."[60] In recent years, there have been multiple empirical studies that have sought to identify whether there is a causal relationship between state entry into BITs and an increase in inbound foreign investment.[61] This early empirical literature was characterized by methodological weakness in that investment treaties were treated as black boxes. More recent empirical research has however disaggregated treaties based on form and content. It

[59] *Id.* art. 7(4). [60] *Id.* art. 3(a)(i).

[61] For a comprehensive overview of the principal empirical studies, *see* Jason Webb Yackee, *Do Bilateral Investment Treaties Promote Foreign Direct Investment? Some Hints from Alternative Evidence*, 51 VIRG. J. INT'L L. 405–14 (2010). For one of the latest studies in this abundant stream of secondary literature (which post-dates Yackee's summary), *see* Todd Allee & Clint Peinhardt, *Contingent Credibility: The Impact of Investment Treaty Violations on Foreign Direct Investment*, 63 INT. ORG. 401 (2011).

now appears that the specific content of investment treaties matters a very great deal in attracting foreign investment. And of all the various provisions in investment treaties, pre-establishment market access (via national treatment) offers the greatest potential for increasing foreign investment flows. One study has estimated that a host country can increase its share in total FDI flows by almost 30 percent in the hypothetical case of switching from particular investment treaties without pre-establishment national treatment commitments to those with such provisions.[62]

The analysis so far has focused on the valuable, crystallized obligation of an ASEAN member in Article 7 to extend market access to FDI from another ASEAN member state. Yet, the broader articulated goal within the Framework Agreement was to "substantially increase the flow of investments into ASEAN *from both ASEAN and non-ASEAN sources.*"[63] On close observation however, there is a fundamental difference in treatment of investment from ASEAN states compared to investment from non-ASEAN, external sources. Article 7 of the 1998 Framework Agreement maps in some detail the "2010 promise" of free movement of capital *within* ASEAN. By contrast to this extended and nuanced treatment of investment flows *within* the ASEAN grouping, there are far fewer provisions directed at inflows of capital from sources *external* to the ASEAN members. For one thing,

[62] Axel Berger et al., *Do Trade and Investment Agreements Lead to More FDI? Accounting for Key Provisions Inside the Black Box*, 10 Int'l Econ. & Econ. Policy 247 (2013).

[63] 1998 Framework Agreement, *supra* note 47, art. 3 (emphasis added).

there is nothing within the actual text of the AIA designed to clearly crystallize the 2020 promise. Instead, Schedule III simply provides that member states shall implement "individual action plans" to meet that goal. Taken at face value (in the sense that the 2020 promise is formally structured as a hard legal obligation), this suggests a paradoxical distrust of intra-ASEAN investment compared to investment from other sources (given the abundant discretion to create exemption lists for the former). More realistically perhaps, the 2020 promise of opening up ASEAN to external capital might have been intended as an aspirational goal rather than a reflection of a fundamental sense of legal commitment.

That characterization is also confirmed by the manner in which the ASEAN members have sought to preserve the integrity of the valuable promise to *only* extend market access to investment from other ASEAN states. Before an economic actor can take the benefit of the newly liberalized ASEAN Investment Area (under the terms of the Framework Agreement), they must first meet the strict definition of an "ASEAN investor."[64] This encompasses a national or juridical person of any ASEAN member state, who makes "an investment in another Member State, the *effective ASEAN equity* of which taken cumulatively with all other ASEAN equities fulfills at least the minimum percentage required to meet the national equity requirement and other equity requirements of domestic laws and published national policies, if any, of the host country in respect of that investment."[65] "Effective ASEAN equity," in turn, is defined as the "ultimate holdings by nationals or

[64] *Id.* art. 4. [65] *Id.* art. 1 (emphasis added).

juridical persons of ASEAN Member States in that investment," without the treaty prescribing the legal test applicable to determine such "ultimate holdings." Instead, the 1998 Framework Agreement prioritizes the ASEAN member state's national rules and procedures for ascertaining such "effective equity." This positioning explicitly entitles an ASEAN host state to use its own laws to trace through the ownership structure of a given investment to guarantee that ultimate equity is held by ASEAN nationals or companies. Obviously, this emphasis on intra-ASEAN investment over extra-ASEAN investment prominently reverses the earlier trend (reverse open regionalism) typified by strategic considerations driven by neorealist suspicion or by neoliberal calculation.

3.4.2 *Investment Protection: Limitations on Legalization*

Measured against the benchmarks raised in Section 3.2 of this chapter however, the more advanced 1998 Framework Agreement is characterized by uneven indicia of legalization. It is important to recall the ambitious and expansive expansive mandate in the 1998 Framework Agreement to "substantially increase the flow of investments into ASEAN *from both ASEAN and non-ASEAN sources.*"[66] Yet in contrast to the detailed roadmap on liberalization of restrictions on flows of foreign investment (at least within ASEAN), the 1998 Framework Agreement makes no direct reference to the usual investment protection mechanisms found in most BITs, such as guarantees

[66] *Id.* art. 3 (emphasis added).

of fair and equitable treatment; full protection and security; and compensation in the event of direct or indirect expropriation.[67] On first view, this would seem to raise the paradoxical possibility that the ASEAN members are providing lower standards of investment protection among themselves compared to what is offered (via BITs) to foreign investors from non-ASEAN states. Yet on closer examination, the framers seem to have adopted a scaffolding strategy that would see the new liberalization guarantees (in the 1998 Framework Agreement) apply concurrently with the largely protective standards (in the 1987 ASEAN Agreement):

> Member States affirm their existing rights and obligations under the 1987 ASEAN Agreement for the Promotion and Protection of Investments and its 1996 Protocol. In the event that this Agreement provides for better or enhanced provisions over the said Agreement and its Protocol, then such provisions of this Agreement shall prevail.[68]

There are a number of problems with this general strategy, as well as with the particular framing of this clause. The strategy is certainly an opportunity lost for the ASEAN members. Many of the unqualified standards in the 1987 ASEAN Agreement reflect the high-water mark of investment protection as articulated in BITs entered into throughout the 1980s. By the mid-to-late 1990s (especially within NAFTA), a number of states had begun to calibrate those standards more carefully in an attempt to better balance investment protection with core components of regulatory autonomy. Of course, as we will see below, the

[67] *Id.* [68] *Id.* art. 12(1).

new 1998 Framework Agreement contains a range of very extensive exceptions that are designed to supply precisely such a recalibrated balance among the ASEAN members. Yet one can easily imagine a scenario whereby there is legal lacuna in how the two instruments relate to each other. For instance, the 1987 ASEAN Agreement provides for a largely unqualified obligation among member states to allow for free transfer of capital[69] and also provides for investor-state dispute resolution.[70] Yet the 1998 Framework Agreement inserts a range of exceptions that would enable an ASEAN member to impose capital restrictions. In a hypothetical dispute surrounding the imposition of capital controls, the question arises whether the ASEAN member can invoke the later exceptions to justify any prima facie breach of the earlier obligations. The framing of the loose conflict component in the formula above seems to suggest that the provisions of the 1998 Framework Agreement will prevail if they provide for "better or enhanced provisions."[71] Yet, this only begs the question of what evaluative criteria should be employed to identify whether the later 1998 Framework Agreement meets this standard. From a strict investor protection viewpoint, the earlier 1987 Agreement

[69] Agreement among the Government of Brunei Darussalam, the Republic of Indonesia, Malaysia, the Republic of the Philippines, the Republic of Singapore and the Kingdom of Thailand for the Promotion and Protection of Investments art. VII (Repatriation of Capital and Earnings), Dec. 15, 1987, https://asean.org/wp-content/uploads/2020/12/Agreement-for-the-ASEAN-Promotion-and-Protection-of-Investments-or-the-Investment-Guarantee-Agreement-ASEAN-IGA.pdf (hereinafter 1987 ASEAN Agreement).

[70] *Id.* art. X. [71] *Id.* art. III.

obviously provides a higher, and thus presumably "better," standard.[72] But one might also argue that the increased detail of the 1998 Agreement (especially on exceptions) necessarily constitutes "enhanced provisions" (and relatedly, to the extent they represent the new sovereign choice among ASEAN member states to recalibrate investment treaty exposure, also represent a "better" standard).

3.4.3 *Legal Innovation in Times of Crisis: Exceptions for Financial Stability*

The ASEAN members recalibrate their sovereign exposure under the 1998 Framework Agreement to prioritize broader social values over and above investment liberalization and protection under defined conditions. Like many states who are combining trade and investment rules in an FTA, they orientated their investment rules in line with trusted legal settings under international trade law by including a general exception clause modelled on different parts of the WTO.[73] Yet there is a more remarkable exceptions strategy on display

[72] This seems to be the position taken by the *Yaung Chi Oo* Tribunal: "[A]rticle 12(1) [of the 1998 Framework Agreement is] not [to] be interpreted as applying *de novo* the provisions of the 1987 ASEAN Agreement, including Article X, to ASEAN Investors. It simply makes it clear that in relation to any investment which is covered by both Agreements, the investor is entitled to the benefit of both and thus of the most beneficial treatment afforded by either." *Yaung Chi Oo Trading Pte Ltd.* v. *Gov't of the Union of Myanmar*, ASEAN I.D. Case No. ARB 01/1, ¶ 82 (Mar. 31, 2003), 42 ILM 540 (2003).

[73] 1998 Framework Agreement, *supra* note 47, art. 13.

in the 1998 Framework Agreement in its focus on the importance of preserving financial stability among the ASEAN member states. Indeed, as flagged above, the negotiations leading to the 1998 Framework were profoundly influenced by a desire to inject greater flexibility for state regulation of foreign investment driven by the causes and consequences of the 1997 Asian financial crisis. To that end, the negotiators have adopted two key innovations (measured against both the BITs of individual ASEAN member states and the 1987 ASEAN Investment Agreement).

First, there is a new provision (in Article 15) entitling ASEAN members to safeguard their balance of payments:

> 1. In the event of serious balance of payments and external financial difficulties or threat thereof, a Member State may adopt or maintain restrictions on investments on which it has undertaken specific commitments, including on payments or transfers for transactions related to such commitments. It is recognised that particular pressures on the balance of payments of a Member State in the process of economic development or economic transition may necessitate the use of restrictions to ensure, inter alia, the maintenance of a level of financial reserves adequate for the implementation of its programme of economic development or economic transition.
>
> 2. Where measures to safeguard balance of payments are taken pursuant to this Article notice of such measures shall be given to the AIA Council within 14 days from the date such measures are taken.
>
> 3. The measures referred to in paragraph (1):
>
> a. shall not discriminate among Member States;

b. shall be consistent with the Articles of Agreement of the International Monetary Fund;
c. shall avoid unnecessary damage to the commercial, economic and financial interests of any other Member State;
d. shall not exceed those necessary to deal with the circumstances described in paragraph I; and
e. shall be temporary and be phased out progressively as the situation specified in paragraph 1 improves.

4. The Member States adopting the balance of payments measures shall commence consultations with the AIA Council and other Member States within 90 days from the date of notification in order to review the balance of payment measures adopted by it.

5. The AIA Council shall determine the rules applicable to the procedures under this Article.

The ASEAN framers here have drawn on a notable influence in structuring this new exception: Article 15 is almost an exact copy of Article XII of the WTO *General Agreement on Trade in Services* (GATS).[74] On first view, this seems a logical baseline to delineate liberalization obligations and permitted flexibility to safeguard financial stability in highly exceptional circumstances. FDI is explicitly covered as one of four modes of supply of service (via "commercial presence" in Article 1(2)(c)) of the GATS. The provisions in the GATS can therefore potentially cover FDI in the financial services sector

[74] General Agreement on Trade in Services art. XII (Restrictions to Safeguard the Balance of Payments), Aor. 15, 1994, Marrakesh Agreement Establishing the World Trade Organization, Annex 1B, 1869 U.N.T.S. 401 (hereinafter GATS).

(which will almost always involve the periodic transfer of financial resources in and out of a host state).[75]

There is, however, an immediate problem in the way in which the ASEAN negotiators have drawn upon the GATS in framing Article 15 of the 1998 Framework Agreement. Under Article 15(1), restrictions on FDI may only target "specific commitments" of the ASEAN member states. That phrasing is taken directly from GATS Article XII(1) where it has a logical place given the architecture of that WTO agreement. The key obligations of both extending market access (under Article XVI) and national treatment (under Article XVII) in the GATS *only* apply where a WTO member has scheduled a specific commitment in a given sector (which can itself be subject to limitations and qualifications).[76] This method of scheduling commitments is commonly understood as a conservative *positive-list* mechanism, which affords WTO members enormous latitude to progressively liberalize and sequence different service sectors. But as we have already seen, the 1998 ASEAN Framework Agreement adopts a far more ambitious legal and economic strategy. The *negative-list* method begins from the premise that *all* economic sectors are subject to the discipline of national treatment under the

[75] Indeed, that very prospect is explicitly acknowledged in footnote 8 to article XVI (Market Access) in the GATS:

"If a Member undertakes a market-access commitment in relation to the supply of a service through the mode of supply referred to in subparagraph 2I of Article 1, it is thereby committed to allow related transfers of capital into its territory." *Id.* art. XVI, fn 8.

[76] *Id.* art. XX (Schedules of Specific Commitments).

Agreement unless specifically exempted through a Temporary Exclusion List or a Sensitive List. Strictly speaking then, the Framework Agreement does not contain a specific commitment (at least of the sort contemplated in the GATS) to which this dedicated exception would logically apply.

On the other hand, however, the ASEAN structure avoids some of the potential pitfalls inherent in the GATS. Under the latter, there are only two potential routes by which capital controls employed in the face of disruptive outflows are legally permitted. First, there is GATS Article XII (and – in the ASEAN context – its facsimile in Article 15) which *only* permits members to introduce restrictions on movement of capital in the event of "serious" balance-of-payments and external financial difficulties or when threatened by such difficulties. But there may well be a need for a WTO member to act in a precautionary manner for other key purposes and circumstances that are not explicitly contemplated in the wording of GATS Article XII, not least financial stability, high indebtedness and severe fiscal imbalances. Put simply, a respectable case can be made that countries should be allowed to counter disruptive capital flows even if a balance of payments crisis is not looming.[77] There is, however, a second mechanism by which such controls might be justified in the GATS and thus meet this broader systemic challenge. Exchange actions which are in conformity with the IMF's Articles of Agreement can also be employed "at the request

[77] Annamaria Viterbo, *How to Make the GATS a Code of Conduct for Capital Controls, in* Capital Account Regulations and the Trading System: A Compatibility Review 20 (Kevin Gallagher et al. ed., 2013).

of the Fund" under GATS Article XI.[78] Yet here too there are a number of controls that limit the feasibility of this second possibility. The IMF has not yet formally exerted its ability to request the introduction of capital controls under Article VI(1) of its Articles of Agreement.[79] Relatedly, the WTO Appellate Body has strongly indicated in *Argentina – Textiles* that a "legally binding commitment to the IMF" is a required pre-condition to any assessment of modifying a member's obligations under the WTO (where IMF intervention is contemplated by the terms of a given WTO provision).[80] Under this interpretation, policy pledges made by an IMF member in a letter of intent or in a memorandum of economic policy (of the sort at issue in *Argentina – Textiles*) would not be covered by GATS Article XI(2) even if part of an IMF lending program, as they could be understood to be implemented only on a voluntary basis.

When we turn to the 1998 ASEAN Framework Agreement, some of these pitfalls with the justificatory route of GATS Article XI(2) in the law of the WTO have been avoided. In fact, the negotiators break genuinely new ground in Article 14, which contemplates the novel implementation of "emergency safeguard measures" in an investment treaty context:

> 1. If, as a result of the implementation of the liberalisation programme under this Agreement, a Member state

[78] GATS, *supra* note 75, art. XI(2). [79] Viterbo, *supra* note 78, at 15.

[80] Appellate Body Report, *Argentina – Measures Affecting Imports of Footwear, Textiles, Apparel and Other Items*, ¶¶ 69–74, WTO Doc. WT/DS56/AB/R (adopted Mar. 27, 1998).

suffers or is threatened with any serious injury and threat, the Member State may take emergency safeguard measures to the extent and for such period as may be necessary to prevent or to remedy such injury. The measures taken shall be provisional and without discrimination.

2. Where emergency safeguard measures are taken pursuant to this Article, notice of such measure shall be given to the AIA Council within 14 days from the date such measures are taken.
3. The AIA Council shall determine the definition of serious injury and threat of serious injury and the procedures of instituting emergency safeguards measures pursuant to this Article.[81]

These provisions superficially resemble the ability of WTO members to take safeguard measures related to the entry of goods under GATT Article XIX. Safeguard measures are short-term emergency actions whereby WTO members depart from their GATT commitments if unforeseen developments, coupled with the effect of their GATT commitments, cause or threaten serious injury to domestic producers.[82] The flexibility to take safeguard action is an inherent recognition of the enormous political challenges faced by states when liberalizing trade barriers, which may require short-term breathing space (as a matter of shoring up political support for liberalization) and/or the ability to implement mechanisms to enable the

[81] 1998 Framework Agreement, *supra* note 47, art. 14.

[82] General Agreement on Tariffs and Trade, art XIX, Oct. 30, 1947, 61 Stat. A-11, 55 U.N.T.S. 194 (hereinafter GATT).

transition of affected industry and workers to more competitive sectors of the domestic economy.

The inclusion of such flexibility in the 1998 ASEAN instrument appears to be driven by a concern, embedded again by the very real experience of the Asian financial crisis, that an investment "liberalization programme" can be a direct cause of sudden and harmful downside effects. On one view, the achievements of the ASEAN members in inserting this novel clause are significant. The IMF, for instance, has fundamentally, albeit belatedly, shifted its position on flexibility for capital controls from its initial skeptical view of actions taken in the aftermath of the Asian financial crisis. In fact, it has now expressed concern that many FTAs and BITs lack adequate safeguards to put in place capital controls: "The limited flexibility afforded by some bilateral and regional agreements in respect to liberalization obligations may create challenges for management of capital flows."[83] Strikingly, in the recent context of providing financial support to Iceland, the IMF even welcomed that country's introduction of capital controls.[84] The General Assembly of the United Nations has also expressed its view that this is an option of critical importance to developing states in particular.[85] Against this

[83] IMF, *Liberalizing Capital Flows and Managing Outflows*, at 3, SM/12/55 (Mar. 13, 2012).

[84] Annamaria Viterbo, *Iceland's Capital Controls and the Constraints Imposed by the EEA Agreement*, 6 Cap. Mark. Law J. 214–37 (2011).

[85] "[D]eveloping countries facing an acute and severe shortage of foreign reserves because of the fallout of the crisis can use, as a measure of last resort, temporary capital account measures, in accordance with the

backdrop, the achievement of the ASEAN member states in anticipating the need for flexibility to employ such measures is significant. Indeed, that achievement is especially telling when it is viewed against key comparators. In particular, there are no firm disciplines on emergency safeguard measures in the GATS, with this subject remaining simply an ongoing topic of negotiation under Art. X(1).[86]

There are however two key problems with the structure and operation of the ASEAN safeguard mechanism. First, in order to be consistent with Article 14, an emergency safeguard measure must be "without discrimination." But at least when it comes to capital controls, these have now been understood (even by the IMF) as "measures affecting cross-border

relevant bilateral and multilateral agreements, in order to help mitigate the adverse impacts of the crisis." G.A. Res. A/RES/64/190, International Financial System and Development, at 12 (Dec. 21, 2009).

86 Members have on a number of occasions extended the deadline referred to in Article X:1 GATS. On March 15, 2004 in relation to the Fifth Decision on Negotiations on Emergency Safeguard Measures (S/L/159), Members decided the following: "1. The first sentence of paragraph 1 of Article X shall continue to apply. 2. Subject to the outcome of the mandate in paragraph 1, the results of such negotiations shall enter into effect on a date not later than the date of entry into force of the results of the current round of services negotiations. 3. Notwithstanding paragraph 3 of Article X, until the entry into effect of the results of the negotiations mandated under paragraph 1 of Article X, the provisions of paragraph 2 of that Article shall continue to apply." For a summary of the latest negotiations, *see* Working Party on GATS Rules, *Negotiations on Emergency Safeguard Measures: Report by the Chairperson of the Working Party on GATS Rules*, WTO Doc. S/WPGR/9 (Mar. 14, 2003).

financial activity that discriminate on the basis of residency,"[87] which was certainly a core component of Malaysia's controls imposed in the aftermath of the Asian financial crisis. Thus, the very obligation of non-discrimination could potentially preclude the use of these key controls in certain settings. Paradoxically perhaps, the second problem with this flexibility mechanism points in the opposite direction. The very architecture of the clause is questionable in that there are few restrictions on the obvious potential for ASEAN members to abuse the significant freedom inherent in this provision and practice raw protectionism in the guise of managing the challenges of investment liberalization. While somewhat ambiguous, the framing of the clause appears to prioritize the decision of the state on the necessity and form of safeguard measures, while relegating the AIA Council to the position of a loose supervisory organ. In particular, there are limited procedural checks on the commencement of safeguard measures compared to GATT Article XIX. And there is certainly no GATT Article XIX-like limit on abusive invocation such as the obligation to negotiate with affected partners with the end outcome of ensuring that appropriate "compensation" is paid to members subject to a safeguard response.

[87] IMF, "Recent Experiences in Managing Capital Inflows: Cross-Cutting Themes and Possible Policy Framework," SM/11/30 (2011). *See also* Annamaria Viterbo, *Tensions between International Investment Protection and Financial Stability*, in The Future of ICSID and the Place of Investment Treaties in International Law 192 (N. Jansen Calamita et al. eds., 2013).

3.4.4 The Fierce Pull of Sovereignty: Dispute Settlement

The dispute settlement provisions of the 1998 Framework Agreement are marked by a further pullback from earlier investment protection standards, further emphasising the uneven patter of legalization at this stage of the AIR's evolution. Specifically, the ASEAN members have confined dispute settlement to state-to-state procedures, revoking entirely the standing of foreign investors as private claimants to initiate investor-state arbitration (which continues to operate only under the 1987 ASEAN Agreement). The wisdom of this choice is questionable. The new treaty is characterized by both a limited scope of operation (in that it only extends to FDI) and a broad range of flexibilities (in the form of exemptions from investment treaty strictures for compelling state purposes). With this in mind, the likely concerns of unmeritorious instigation of investor-state arbitration, as well as the possibility of expansive pro-investor readings, seem to be countered (at least partly) by these treaty innovations. The costs of omission of investor-state arbitration are very real and significant. Affected foreign investors from a given ASEAN state are now left to the mercy of the discretion of their home governments to espouse their claim in the state-to-state forum.

This significant gap in legal protection is vividly illustrated by the *Yaung Chi Oo* dispute, where the Singaporean investor in Myanmar was denied protection under the 1987 ASEAN Agreement (for failure to show that Myanmar had "specifically approved" its investment for the purposes of that treaty), and, although falling within the scope of the later

1998 Framework Agreement, had no standing to commence a claim under that treaty.[88] In cases such as this –where the amount of invested capital is relatively small and the economic actor does not have political traction within the home state – the prospect of espousal under state-to-state dispute settlement process is remote at best. This weak intra-ASEAN investor protection is increasingly costly to ASEAN members and tends to necessarily impede further economic integration. In particular, considering the more liberal extra-ASEAN investment treaties, this asymmetry deters ASEAN members from fully taking advantage of synergies between intra- and extra-ASEAN investment treaties, tracking the inherent limitations of the "hub and spoke" model in regional trade agreements.[89]

3.5 Conclusion

In this next stage of the evolution of the AIR, the ASEAN member states have shifted dramatically from the start-point of the 1987 ASEAN Investment Agreement. As saw in Chapter 2, that start-point was marked by a remarkable degree of conservativism, with the member states unwilling to extend fundamental liberal and protective guarantees typically found

[88] *Yaung Chi Oo Trading Pte Ltd. v.'ov't of the Union of Myanmar*, ASEAN I.D. Case No. ARB 01/1, ¶ 23 (Mar. 31, 2003), 42 ILM 540 (2003).

[89] In the regional trade agreement setting, a hub (developed country) can get free access to multiple spokes (developing countries), while spokes do not usually offer the same access between each other unless they form a "rim" among themselves. Frank Garcia, *NAFTA and the Creation of the FTAA: A Critique of Piecemeal Accession*, 35 VA. J.'NT'L. L. 539, 557–8 (1995).

in their BITs with third countries among themselves. Yet by the late 1990s, a series of internal and external events would push those members to dramatically reshape their approach to investment rules. The combination of the disastrous effects of the 1997–1998 Asian financial crisis and the rise of China as a serious economic competitor would force those states to begin to develop a deeper level of integration. That identity crisis fundamentally shaped both the normative orientation and legal norms within the 1998 ASEAN Framework Agreement. Though limited when measured against conventional legalization indicators, any such critique ignores the vitality and creativity of the key choices made in this time of crisis.

Chapter 4

Positioning of the ASEAN Investment Regime

4.1 Introduction

In this chapter, we turn to the most recent (and current) iteration of investment rules in ASEAN being the 2009 ASEAN Comprehensive Agreement on Investment. Building on the conventional legalization indicators introduced in Chapter 3, we begin the process of assessing the shape and dimensions of legalization in the ACIA. Perhaps most strikingly, the ACIA continues the bold experiment of positioning the ASEAN region as an integrated production base. Yet, some of its underlying norms continue to exhibit a fairly low degree of legalization. However, these legalization indicators tend to represent, albeit implicitly, particular (Western) views on law and development.[1] Pointedly, Abbott and colleagues admit that "statutes or regulations in highly *developed* national legal systems are generally taken as prototypical of hard legalization."[2]

1 Tor Krever, *Quantifying Law: Legal Indicator Projects and the Reproduction of Neoliberal Common Sense*, 34 THIRD WORLD Q. 131, 132 (2013).

2 Kenneth W. Abbott, Robert O. Keohane, Andrew Moravcsik, Anne-Marie Slaughter & Duncan Snidal, *The Concept of Legalization*, *in* LEGALIZATION AND WORLD POLITICS 18 (Judith L. Goldstein, Miles Kahler, Robert O. Keohane & Anne-Marie Slaughter eds., 2001) (emphasis added).

Against this background, we aim to problematize this hidden nomothetic assumption behind the concept of legalization. Critiquing such assumption, we argue, will enable us to better understand the AIR's characteristically low degree of legalization from a non-functionalist perspective. In our view, it is both possible and desirable to construct the AIR's distinctively low degree of legalization as a *different* type of legalization, not necessarily as a failed or flawed model. After all, even Max Weber emphasized that the rational ideal embedded in legalization derives from a historically unique, particularly European, phenomenon. Our approach here departs from mainstream positivist comparisons. Nor do we frame our comparative research as "purely functional" in the manner advanced by Konrad Zweigert and Hein Kötz.[3] Our model instead reflects Werner Menski's critical work on comparative law in a globalizing world drawing on "a methodological approach that integrates the social and ethical elements of law in its various social contexts."[4]

Using that methodology, we make the following two arguments in this chapter. First, we argue that while ASEAN members subscribe to GIL in their own collective rules, they do so in a *selective* manner shaped fundamentally by key contextual dynamics. These encompass a complex combination of

[3] Konrad Zweigert & Hein Kötz, An Introduction to Comparative Law 40 (Tony Weir trans., 3rd ed. 1998). On the role of functionalism in comparative law, *see also* Ralf Michaels, *The Functional Method of Comparative Law*, *in* The Oxford Handbook of Comparative Law 339 (Mathias Reimann & Reinhard Zimmermann eds., 2008).

[4] Werner Menski, Comparative Law in a Global Context: The Legal Systems of Asia and Africa 7 (2nd ed. 2006).

ASEAN members' unique decision-making style (the "ASEAN Way") informed by their shared historical experience and collective memories, coupled with negative social learning from the vicarious experience of other nations' implementation of GIL. Second, we argue that the idiographic nature of legalization under the AIR compels us to rethink the conventional universal (nomothetic) concept of legalization and embrace a more nuanced one. Although the basic function of legalization to each economy should be "neither irrelevant nor unique,"[5] law's deeper, sociocultural dimension must not be hastily universalized.

This chapter is structured as follows. Section 4.2 traces the normative positioning and levels of legalization in the ACIA and finds that, even in this latest iteration, the AIR is generally characterized by a low degree of legalization. Section 4.3 then critiques nomothetic assumptions behind the conventional concept of legalization and sheds light on the idiographic nature of legalization in AIR from a comparativist standpoint. Based on critical observations made in section 4.3, section 4.4 identifies two main factors behind such a low degree of legalization under the AIR: the unique historical path of ASEAN members favoring informal structure of decision making, as well as effects from negative learning of ASEAN members from foreign investment practices of other countries. The chapter concludes that rethinking legalization

[5] Katharina Pistor & Philip A. Wellons, *The Role of Law and Legal Institutions in Asian Economic Development 1960–1995 (Executive Summary) – Prepared for the Asian Development Bank*, at 6 (1998), www.asianlii.org/asia/other/ADBLPRes/1998/3.pdf.

should be directed both to outside observers and ASEAN members themselves.

4.2 Legalization in the 2009 ASEAN Comprehensive Agreement on Investment

The ACIA, as the most advanced model of the AIR, is characterized by a fundamental normative shift in orientation coupled with thicker levels of legalization. While the 1987 and 1998 agreements focus on typical goals of most investment regimes, such as qualified investment liberalization and investor protection, the ACIA overtly embraces a deeper, integrationist *telos*. Under ACIA, ASEAN members have decided to achieve economic integration through "joint promotion of the region as an integrated investment area."[6] Strikingly, the 2007 AEC Blueprint on foreign investment had already sought to position ASEAN as an "integrated investment area and production network" by, for example, promoting "industrial complementation and production networks among MNCs in ASEAN" and "joint investment missions that focus on regional clusters and production networks."[7] That commitment is further emphasized in the later ASEAN Economic Community Blueprint 2025, with ASEAN members strategically positioning that integrationist commitment as a means to "enhance the region's

[6] ASEAN Comprehensive Investment Agreement art 1(d), Feb. 26, 2009, http://investasean.asean.org/files/upload/Doc%2005%20-%20ACIA.pdf [hereinafter ACIA].

[7] ASEAN, *ASEAN Economic Community Blueprint*, ¶ 29 (Jan. 2008) https://www.asean.org/wp-content/uploads/images/archive/5187-10.pdf.

participation in global value chains."[8] This core language finds express reflection as a distinct legal obligation in the ACIA.[9] What we have is now a deliberate focus on attracting one key type of foreign investment – efficiency-seeking FDI that would construct supply chains across the region – to achieve both a given level of economic integration and as a means of fulfilling the 1998 Framework Agreement's objective of developing a "competitive ASEAN Investment Area." As a body comprised mainly of developing countries, the unbundling of production facilities embedded in supply chains is a significant opportunity for the ASEAN members. Participation in a global value chain holds out the promise of development spillovers at a lower entry cost than past strategies, particularly those focused on industrialization.[10]

To that end, the ACIA's integrationist *telos* is accompanied by a considerable degree of both certainty and sophistication in the legal language. The old instruments from 1987 and 1998 are terminated on entry into force of the ACIA,[11] clearing any legal uncertainties that might have occurred due to the existence of multiple treaties on the same subject. Moreover, ACIA actively seeks to emulate global investment law ("comparable to international best practices") in the development of a "comprehensive

[8] ASEAN, *ASEAN Economic Community Blueprint 2025*, at 11 (Nov. 2015) https://www.asean.org/wp-content/uploads/2012/05/8.-March-2016-ASCC-Blueprint-2025.pdf.

[9] ACIA, *supra* note 6, art. 24(b) and (c).

[10] Richard Baldwin, The Great Convergence: Information Technology and the New Globalization, at chapter 9 (2016).

[11] ACIA, *supra* note 6, art. 47(1).

investment agreement."[12] Global investment law naturally connotes representative legal practices on international investment regulation demonstrated by the North American Free Trade Area (NAFTA) Chapter 11 and other model BITs created by the United States and other developed states. In the same line, ACIA now clarifies the previously undefined approval precondition to coverage ("covered investment") as investment in an ASEAN member "admitted according to its laws, regulations and national policies, and where applicable, specifically approved in writing by the competent authority of a Member State."[13] Now ASEAN members may no longer defer to domestic law conditions but are subject to an "approval in writing" requirement under ACIA, which provides "[f]or the purpose of protection, the procedures relating to specific approval in writing shall be specified in Annex 1 (Approval in Writing)."[14] This mandated approval in writing requirement is explicitly designed to secure "improvement of *transparency* and *predictability* of investment rules, regulations and procedures conducive to increased investment among Member States."[15]

Nonetheless, other aspects of the ACIA eclipse these enhanced levels of legalization. First, in terms of "obligation," the ACIA is littered with loopholes. The ACIA excludes *extra*-ASEAN investments, leaving them subject to BITs and investment chapters in FTAs. On the other hand, when it comes to facilitating intra-ASEAN capital flows, the ACIA seemingly breaks new ground in fostering liberalization. The twin-track system of temporary and sensitive reservations in the

[12] *Id.* recital 1. [13] *Id.* art. 4(a). [14] *Id.* art. 4(1) n.1.
[15] *Id.* art. 1(c) (emphasis added).

1998 Framework Agreement is now replaced with a single reservation list.[16] Yet even here, there are pointed indications of resistance to constraints on sovereignty. The market-access obligations in the ACIA are limited to a defined set of economic sectors.[17]

Moving from the nature of "obligations" to levels of "precision" as a second indicator of legalization, despite some efforts to enhance due process and transparency, the ACIA is still characterized by reservations of authority by states parties. In many other investment treaties, foreign investment may be permitted and thus protected if it satisfies the requirement that it contributes to economic development of a host country. Yet, the ACIA does not grant arbitrators the discretion to make this critical judgment as to contribution toward economic development. Arbitrators can only determine whether a given asset constitutes investment understood as, *inter alia*, "commitment of capital, the expectation of gain or profit, or the assumption of risk."[18] This aversion toward conferral of wide discretion on arbitrators originates from past experience by some ASEAN members in adjudication of the definition of "foreign investment" to be covered and

[16] *Id.* art. 9. For details on the reservation lists submitted by each member state, *see* Invest in ASEAN, *ASEAN Comprehensive Investment Agreement*, http://investasean.asean.org/index.php/page/view/asean-free-trade-area-agreements/view/757/newsid/871/the-asean-comprehensive-investment-agreement.html.

[17] ACIA, *supra* note 6, art. 3(3). For overview of the liberalization sectors in ACIA, *see* Julien Chaisse & Sufian Jusoh, The ASEAN Comprehensive Investment Agreement 69 (2016).

[18] ACIA, *supra* note 6, art. 4(c), n.2.

thus protected by BITs. In particular, a lone arbitrator in *Malaysian Salvors* v. *Malaysia* concocted various criteria necessary for a given investment (asset) to be covered by the ICSID Convention on the basis of whether (or not) it contributed to the economic development of the respondent state.[19] That award was ultimately overturned by an ICSID Annulment Committee, in large part because of the failure of the Arbitrator to apply the explicit terms of the BIT under review.[20] Despite that final outcome (which in any event post-dates the ACIA), given the plain terms of the definition of "covered investment" in the ACIA, most ASEAN members remain extremely reluctant to allow arbitrators to detail these developmental conditions when it comes to critical threshold questions on jurisdiction.

On "delegation," the ACIA surprisingly lacks one of the typical protections in modern investment treaties – an "umbrella clause" – which converts a breach of contract between a host country and a foreign investor into a treaty violation.[21] Here too, one can discern a fear of the potential

[19] *Malaysian Historical Salvors, SDN, BHD* v. *Malaysia*, ICSID Case No. ARB/05/10, Award on Jurisdiction ¶¶ 109–30 (May 17, 2007); Convention on the Settlement of Investment Disputes Between States and Nationals of Other States, Mar. 18, 1965, 575 U.N.T.S. 159 [hereinafter ICSID Convention].

[20] *Malaysian Historical Salvors SDN BHD* v. *The Government of Malaysia*, ICSID Case No. ARB/05/10, Decision on the Application for Annulment, ¶ 61 (Apr. 16, 2009).

[21] *Cf.* Agreement among the Government of Brunei Darussalam, the Republic of Indonesia, Malaysia, the Republic of the Philippines, the Republic of Singapore and the Kingdom of Thailand for the Promotion and Protection of Investments art III(3), Dec. 15, 1987, https://asean.org/

for broad interpretations of that clause, in a way that might unduly prevent host countries from exercising their regulatory policies. The Philippines' specific experience in *SGS* v. *Philippines* seems to have influenced this conspicuous omission. In this case, a foreign investor sued the Philippines for a breach of contract turned treaty violation under an umbrella clause in the Switzerland – Philippines BIT.[22] However, the contract in question explicitly required that any dispute arising under the contract should be adjudicated in the courts of the Philippines, raising the charged question of why the Tribunal would disrupt this specifically negotiated choice. Although the Philippines eventually prevailed in the case – with the Tribunal declaring the claim inadmissible – the Tribunal's broad interpretation that the umbrella clause could *potentially* apply to contractual bargains seemed to prompt the ACIA negotiators to eliminate the controversial clause.

There is further evidence of a tight feedback loop between key investor–state arbitral cases and particular negotiation choices that push toward less delegation of authority to third-party adjudicators in the ACIA.[23] When it comes to the obligation to accord most-favoured-nation (MFN) treatment,

wp-content/uploads/2020/12/Agreement-for-the-ASEAN-Promotion-and-Protection-of-Investments-or-the-Investment-Guarantee-Agreement-ASEAN-IGA.pdf (including an umbrella clause).

22 *SGS Société Générale de Surveillance S.A.* v. *Republic of the Phil.*, ICSID Case No. ARB/02/6, Decision of the Tribunal on Objections to Jurisdiction (Jan. 29, 2004).

23 *Cf.* Joel Vander Kooi, *The ASEAN Enhanced Dispute Settlement Mechanism: Doing It the "ASEAN Way,"* 20 N.Y. Int'l L. Rev. 1, 23

some arbitral tribunals have ruled that this obligation can be used by a foreign claimant to import dispute settlement mechanisms from another treaty entered into by the respondent host state. In that way, claimants have been able to avoid preconditions to the commencement of investor–state arbitration in the primary treaty such as a mandatory period of litigation in the domestic courts of the host state. In the first ruling of this jurisprudential line, the *Maffezini* v. *Spain* tribunal relied on a comparative methodology (drawing on different formulations within the universe of BITs) to justify its broad interpretation of the MFN obligation, pointing out that where states parties have decided to confine the obligation to substantive rather than procedural differences, they have done so explicitly in a given clause.[24] The ACIA negotiators in turn have provided future tribunals with precisely that sort of explicit direction in footnote 4, which provides that "[f]or greater certainty ... this Article shall not apply to investor–State dispute settlement procedures that are available in other agreements to which Member States are party."[25]

In sum, according to the legalization indicators developed by Abbott and colleagues, the AIR's level of obligation may be considered "moderate" or "low" in the presence of a number of contingent obligations subject to various national reservations. Its level of precision may be deemed

(2007) (observing that ASEAN states have traditionally avoided bestowing great power on the dispute resolution bodies).

[24] *Emilio Agustín Maffezini* v. *The Kingdom of Spain*, ICSID Case No. ARB/97/7, Decision of the Tribunal on Objections to Jurisdiction, ¶¶ 51–4 (Jan. 25, 2000).

[25] ACIA, *supra* note 6, art. 6, n.4(a).

"low" due to the broad reservation of discretion left to member states. Its level of delegation may also be regarded as "low" on account of characteristically high jurisdictional thresholds that seriously impede the initiation of arbitration. Overall, the AIR appears to fall between Type V and VII in the Abbott and colleagues' scale of legalization and thus offers a far lower level of institutionalized protection for foreign investors than that extended by GIL.[26]

4.3 Critiquing the Nomothetic Assumptions Underlying Legalization

4.3.1 Revisiting Legalization in the ASEAN Investment Regime

The aforementioned glaring gap between GIL and AIR appears perplexing. On the one hand, a legalization drive in the AIR originated *from within* for a functional purpose, driven by an urgent need for deeper integration and interstate cooperation to reduce uncertainty and transactions costs in administering complex international relations in the investment area.[27] From this perspective, the AIR's characteristically

[26] Abbott et al., *supra* note 2, at 22.

[27] *Cf.* Frederick M. Abbott, *NAFTA and the Legalization of World Politics: A Case Study*, *in* Legalization and World Politics 135–6 (Judith L. Goldstein, Miles Kahler, Robert O. Keohane & Anne-Marie Slaughter eds., 2001) (observing that legalization (using hard law) under NAFTA contributes to the reduction of interstate transaction cost and risk premiums borne by private businesses); Terence C. Halliday & Pavel Osinsky, *Globalization of Law*, 32 Ann. Rev. Soc. 447, 453 (2006).

low degree of legalization may demonstrate a deep-seated failure of cooperation in the area of intra-ASEAN investment.[28] On the other hand, however, legalization does not seem to be fully internalized among ASEAN members. It has not become their true internal operational language in public decision making, while they may still use legalization as an instrument for facilitating interstate cooperation with non-ASEAN members. ASEAN members may still fear that legalization in the AIR would somehow destroy or transmogrify ("decenter") their "imagined national essence[s]."[29]

Indeed, a number of scholars have vindicated these apprehensions against global law in general, particularly its Western version. Commentators have often put forward the proposition that law should be characterized beyond its mere manifestation as *lex scripta*, and appropriately represent dynamic, ever-changing reflections of distinct sociocultural lives.[30] At first glance, Abbott and colleagues seem to be

[28] *Cf.* Abbott, *supra* note 27, at 137 (viewing APEC as "a failed experiment in alternative legalization").

[29] Daniel C. Lynch, *International "Decentering" and Democratization: The Case of Thailand*, 48 INT'L STUD. Q. 339, 340 (2004).

[30] *Cf.* Robert M. Cover, *Nomos and Narrative*, 97 HARV. L. REV. 4, 9 (1982). ("A legal tradition is hence part and parcel of a complex normative world. The tradition includes not only a corpus juris, but also *a language and a mythos* – narratives in which the corpus juris is located by those whose wills act upon it. . . . These myths establish a repertoire of moves – a lexicon of normative action – that may be combined into *meaningful patterns culled from the meaningful patterns of the past.*" (emphasis added)).

By contrasting the traditional, formalist conception of rules with the Wittgensteinian social conception, Margaret Radin also elucidated the

cognizant of this concern. For example, they claim that they deliberately distance themselves from any evaluative use of the concept of legalization.[31] According to their claim, they simply employ this term purely for analytical and descriptive purposes, instead of advancing any explicit normative positions.

Nonetheless, despite the authors' disclaimer, the very gauging of the *degree* of legalization of representative international organizations in three main attributes (obligation, precision, and delegation) and *ranking* them (from I to VIII) cannot avoid being evaluative and therefore potentially normative. For example, the very fact that some of most advanced and sophisticated international entities, such as the European Union, are indeed ranked at the top of the list reveals certain normative traits underlying their legalization index. Or, a more accurate observation may be that it is the very experience and existence of those highly legalized (Western) organizations that tend to provide ideal types for legalization. This proposition appears to signify a certain causal relationship between legalization and socioeconomic development.[32] By the same token, it also seems to connote

same proposition. According to Radin, rules are a *social* conception determined essentially by social context, and therefore changeable and inseparable from mores and practices. *See* Margaret Jane Radin, *Reconsidering the Rule of Law*, 69 B.U. L. REV. 781, 797–10 (1989). *See also* Paul W. Kahn, *Freedom, Autonomy, and the Cultural Study of Law*, 13 YALE J.L. & HUMAN. 141, 141 (2001) (observing that "law is . . . constitutive of the self-understanding of individuals and communities").

[31] Abbott et al., *supra* note 2, at 19 (emphasizing that their concept of legalization is a "working definition, intended to frame the analytical and empirical" approaches).

[32] Krever, *supra* note 1, at 132.

the normative superiority of higher degrees of legalization, despite thoughtful disclaimers against any normative implications by the authors. Their legalization ranking system (from I to VIII) not only surveys legal reality but also highlights the "*gap* between reality and the ideal, between performance and the standard."[33]

Importantly, those numerical indicators may privilege the traditional Western type of legal function, which emphasizes an economic role of legalization such as a deregulatory (*laissez-faire*) function, and eventually reproduce such types in other regions in the name of governance.[34] The Western tradition of idealizing legalization dates back to Max Weber. The critical place of law and legalization in Max Weber's celebrated categorization of rationality lends credence to such observation. The capitalist obsession to "master all things by calculation,"[35] coupled with the market's inherent zeal toward predictability, naturally constructed an ideal of legalization as a symbol of formal rationality.[36] David Schneiderman observes that international investment law tends to demonstrate Weberian legalization in that it is "an ensemble of impersonal rules that must be administered

[33] *Id.* at 144 (emphasis added). [34] *Id.* at 142.

[35] Max Weber, *Science as a Vocation*, *in* FROM MAX WEBER: ESSAYS IN SOCIOLOGY 139 (Hans Heinrich Gerth & Charles Wright Mills trans. & eds., 1946).

[36] David Schneiderman, *International Investment Law as Formally Rational Law: A Weberian Analysis*, *in* RESEARCH HANDBOOK ON THE SOCIOLOGY OF INTERNATIONAL LAW (Moshe Hirsch & Andrew Lang eds., 2020).

impartially."[37] On this account, the legal protection provided by international investment law is said to simply allow investors to rationally calculate their risks when operating abroad.[38] The Weberian legalization is oft accompanied by the "inevitability" thesis, suggesting that it is "a natural, normal, and even inevitable process that all states everywhere would undergo if only certain pesky barriers were removed."[39]

Legalization as the Weberian ideal type has recently been reincarnated as a "global culture" of legalization[40] or "neoliberal legal globalization."[41] "World polity theory" aptly captures such trends, in particular the rise of GIL. Based on the thesis of global convergence of law,[42] world polity theorists would highlight the fact that ASEAN members voluntarily accepted GIL as they interacted with "rationalized others,"[43] including developed countries and international organizations. While ASEAN members may have been somehow

[37] *Id.* at 3.

[38] Zachary Douglas, The International Law of Investment Claims 1–2 (2009).

[39] *Cf.* Lynch, *supra* note 29, at 341 (discussing the inevitability thesis behind "democratization").

[40] *Id.* at 344.

[41] Boaventura de Sousa Santos, Toward a New Legal Common Sense: Law, Globalization and Emancipation 314 (2002).

[42] John W. Meyer et al., *World Society and the Nation-State*, 103 Am. J. Soc. 144, 146 (1997) ("Our forecast would be imprecise because of the complexity of the interplay among various world models and local traditions, but the likely range of outcomes would be quite limited.").

[43] John Boli & George M. Thomas, World Polity Formation since 1875: World Culture and International Non-Governmental Organizations (1997).

socialized to "want" GIL,[44] world polity theorists would not treat this socialization process as a forced one.[45] World polity theorists may instead represent GIL as an ideal (rationalized) form of economic governance and therefore adopting GIL actually legitimizes the AIR.[46] It is in this sense that legalization indicators adopted by Abbott and colleagues may translate into a tool for "global governance."[47] For Davis and colleagues, it is those social indicators that can shape the governance topology ("where, by whom, and in relation to whom governance takes place"), standard-setting processes, regulatory decision-making processes, and how the exercise of power is regulated and contested.[48]

4.3.2 *Perils of Blinded Legalization*

Notably, Max Weber himself observed that the rise of legalism in Western society resulted from the *unique* history of the

[44] Martha Finnemore, NATIONAL INTERESTS IN INTERNATIONAL SOCIETY 2 (1996).

[45] "World system theory" views that a world system is made up of core and periphery states in accordance with global division of labor based on their political-economic power. *See generally*, IMMANUEL WALLERSTEIN, THE MODERN WORLD SYSTEM (1974); CHRISTOPHER CHASE-DUNN, GLOBAL FORMATION: STRUCTURES OF THE WORLD ECONOMY (1989).

[46] Meyer et al., *supra* note 42, at 148.

[47] Kevin E. Davis et al., *Indicators as a Technology of Global Governance*, 46 LAW & SOC'Y REV. 71 (2012).

[48] *Id.* at 80. *See also* Sally Engel Merry, *Measuring the World: Indicators, Human Rights, and Global Governance*, 52 CURRENT ANTHROPOLOGY S83, S92 (2011) (observing that indicators may be a "form of knowledge production and governance").

West: the separation of religious and secular law allowing a "divorce" of legal and moral norms, "bureaucratization of the Catholic Church," "Roman law heritage," "European kings' alliance with rising bourgeois interests," and the existence of "highly specialized profession" handling law.[49] David Trubek insightfully observed that modern Western law thinkers, driven by their "core conception," which he referred to as a concept from their own society on the nature and function of law, might be led to believe that "measures to increase legal purposeness will both foster legal autonomy and strengthen liberal and democratic tendencies."[50] According to Trubek, this "ethnocentric" nature of the core conception derived from the Western culture and history is implicitly based on a "pluralist" political system under which law is a form of settlement out of competitive political struggle in a society.[51] For this reason, Trubek viewed that the Western legal *Idealtypus* highlighting an economic role of law should not be mechanically universalized.[52] In sum, tensions may rise when a nomothetic metric of legalization is applied through transplant to non-Western organizations that do not necessarily share the same genealogy, or its sociocultural and historical context.[53]

[49] David M. Trubek, *Max Weber on Law and the Rise of Capitalism*, 1972 WIS. L. REV. 720, 736–9 (1972).

[50] David M. Trubek, *Toward a Social Theory of Law: An Essay on the Study of Law and Development*, 82 YALE L.J. 1, 18–19 (1972).

[51] *See* LAWRENCE M. FRIEDMAN, THE REPUBLIC OF CHOICE: LAW, AUTHORITY AND CULTURE 201 (1990).

[52] Trubek, *supra* note 49, at 751–2.

[53] *Cf.* William P. Alford, *Tasselled Loafers for Barefoot Lawyers: Transformation and Tension in the World of Chinese Legal Workers*, 144

Admittedly, it might be unavoidable for Western observers to retain their own "rules of logic"[54] when investigating non-Western norms and institutions and thereby to lose sight of non-Western societies' own "accumulated body of interpretive constructs . . . that may appear in the form of proverbs, precepts, moral tales or myths."[55] However, if Western observers "impose," explicitly or implicitly, their own categories of legalization to judge non-Western legal systems, they might "blind" themselves to the potency of non-Western versions of legalization.[56] In other words, a universal and deracinated invocation of legalization tends to generate a static and commodified notion of law that can be transported across different social contexts.[57] According to John Ohnesorge, such prescriptive rhetoric of legalization is driven too often by international business lobbies which vehemently pursue a deregulatory agenda which limits the discretion of government officials.[58] In an emphatic objection to such a functional agenda of legalization, Ohnesorge disproves the relationship between law and development by highlighting economic development in the Northeast Asian countries, such as South Korea, Taiwan, and Japan. Economic

CHINA Q. 22 (1995) (criticizing the tendency of some foreign observers of China to "mistake appearances for substance" under the rhetoric of the "tasseled loafers" phenomenon).

[54] Bryan R. Wilson, *A Sociologist's Introduction*, *in* RATIONALITY x (Bryan R. Wilson ed., 1970).

[55] *Id.* at xi. [56] *Id.* at xvi. [57] *See* Trubek, *supra* note 49, at 751–2.

[58] John K.M. Ohnesorge, *The Rule of Law, Economic Development, and Developmental States of Northeast Asia*, in LAW AND DEVELOPMENT IN EAST AND SOUTHEAST ASIA 70, 97 (Christoph Antons ed., 2003).

successes of these countries, which share strong Confucian values, are not attributable to any salient role of law or rule of law.[59]

Concomitantly, this universalistic invocation of legalization is vulnerable to "attribution errors" in social psychology: Western observers might too easily attribute failures or suboptimal outcomes in foreign countries simply to lack of legalization. They tend to underestimate the contributions from non-legal factors, such as limited capacity and resources.[60] As a charged example, those observers often ascribe African countries' underdevelopment to their alleged lack of legalization. However, their poverty and government failures may be more reflective of extralegal factors, such as colonialist legacies and other complex geopolitical settings.

These attribution errors tend to dismiss the status quo too unreservedly and jump to "reflexive" prescriptions.[61] Many (Western) policy makers and international organizations still believe that legalization, as both a beacon and a metric, is a *sine*

[59] *Id. See also* Robert Wade, Governing the Market: Economic Theory and the Role of Government in East Asian Industrialization (1990) (emphasizing the role of government in East Asian economic development).

[60] *See generally* Ronald Inglehart, Modernization and Postmodernization: Cultural, Economic, and Political Change in 43 Societies (1997). *See also* Michael W. Dowdle, *Heretical Laments: China and the Fallacies of "Rule of Law,"* 11 Cultural Dynamics 287, 300–1 (1999).

[61] Dowdle, *supra* note 60, at 308. Regarding this type of prescriptions, *see, e.g.*, Paul Gewirtz, *The U.S.—China Rule of Law Initiative*, 11 Wm. & Mary Bill Rts. J. 603 (2003).

qua non for development.[62] Legalization or its alter ego of "good governance" is an important condition on the basis of which international organizations, such as the International Monetary Fund and the World Bank, determine the eligibility of funding to needy countries.[63] Recently, the "law optimists" have claimed a "methodological superiority" over those who are skeptical of the role of law in development by providing empirical studies to support their position.[64] For example, in the 1990s economists such as Robert Barro and Daniel Kaufmann began to analyze cross-country data to identify any causal relations between the existence of legal institutions and socioeconomic development.[65] In a similar vein, the so-called measurement movement has flourished, as is seen in various projects such as the "Contract Intensive Money" (CIM) measuring the degree of contract enforcement in a country,[66] the World Bank's "Worldwide Governance

[62] Kenneth W. Dam, THE LAW–GROWTH NEXUS: THE RULE OF LAW AND ECONOMIC DEVELOPMENT 2 (2006).

[63] Ohnesorge, *supra* note 58, at 97.

[64] Kevin E. Davis, *What Can the Rule of Law Variables Tell Us about Rule of Law Reforms*, 26 MICH. J. INT'L L. 141, 143 (2004) (emphasis added).

[65] *Id.* at 144 (citing Robert J. Barro, DETERMINANTS OF ECONOMIC GROWTH: A CROSS-COUNTRY EMPIRICAL STUDY (1997)); Daniel Kaufmann et al., *Governance Matters*, WORLD BANK POLICY RESEARCH WORKING PAPER NO. 2196 (1999); Christopher Clague et al., *Institutions and Economic Performance: Property Rights and Contract Enforcement*, in INSTITUTIONS AND ECONOMIC DEVELOPMENT: GROWTH AND GOVERNANCE IN LESS-DEVELOPED AND POST-SOCIALIST COUNTRIES 67 (Christopher Clague ed., 1997).

[66] Christopher Clague et al., *Contract-Intensive Money*, 4 J. ECON. GROWTH 185, 205 (1999).

Indicators,"[67] and the "Lex Mundi" project surveying lawyers on certain questions allegedly related to law and legalization.[68]

However, these quantitative studies involving indicators tend to amalgamate variables measuring legal and non-legal factors, such as the wealth of societies,[69] thereby exaggerating the attributive force of legalization to economic development. For example, some rule of law indices include such parameters as crime rate, number of judicial review cases, and number of lawyers per 100,000 persons, which may be related more to resources than purely *legal* factors.[70] Similarly, the World Bank has measured the level of good governance based on the quality of contract enforcement, the police, and the courts, as well as the likelihood of crime and violence. According to that measure, the United States is at the 90th percentile, while China is at less than the 50th percentile. Yet, as discussed above, all these (functional) criteria have originated from Western experiences and have failed to consider the unique context which might produce incommensurable consequences as to these functions. Those reformers and donors, albeit well intended, are so often

[67] World Bank, *Worldwide Governance Indicators*, http://info.worldbank.org/governance/wgi/.

[68] Simeon Djankov et al., *Courts: The Lex Mundi Project*, NAT'L BUREAU OF ECON. RESEARCH WORKING PAPER NO. 8890 (2002) www.nber.org/papers/w8890.

[69] Davis, *supra* note 64, at 146.

[70] Benny Y.T. Tai, *Developing an Index of the Rule of Law: Sharing the Experience of Hong Kong*, 2 ASIAN J. COMP. L. 1, 7 (2007).

oblivious to the fact that "law is rooted in a social context that may well vary among nations."[71]

In sum, the concept of legalization, as far as ASEAN is concerned, should not be defined as detached from the Southeast Asian sociocultural context. It must be "contextualized" by taking into due consideration ASEAN's unique culture, history, and tradition, such as the ASEAN Way,[72] which we now turn to.

4.4 Contextualizing Legalization in the ASEAN Investment Regime

4.4.1 Path Dependency ("ASEAN Way")

As discussed above, given the ASEAN members' explicit neoliberal commitments to intra-ASEAN investment liberalization, the characteristically low degree of legalization in the AIR may seem puzzling. Moreover, one might reasonably suspect that even this limited ex ante legal design (law on the books) would never be implemented ex post as it was originally anticipated (law in action).[73] Here, unique sociocultural attributes shared by ASEAN members tend to offer a key

[71] William P. Alford, *Exporting the "Pursuit of Happiness,"* 113 Harv. L. Rev. 1677, 1690 (2000) (reviewing Thomas Carothers, Aiding Democracy Abroad: The Learning Curve (1999)).

[72] Xin Ren, Tradition of the Law and Law of the Tradition: Law, State, and Social Control in China 4 (1997).

[73] *See, for example*, Watson, Alan, Law in Books, Law in Action and Society (Apr. 12, 2006) (paper presented as part of the Faculty Colloquium Series, School of Law, Univ. of Georgia, Apr. 12, 2006, Paper No. 1), https://digitalcommons.law.uga.edu/conf_coll_symp_colloquia/1/.

to solving the puzzle. In particular, one trait stands out that emphasizes informality, consultation, and consensus in collective decision making, often coined as the "ASEAN Way."[74] Once entrenched in the ASEAN structure at an earlier point in time, the ASEAN Way has since left an irreversible and indelible impact on subsequent institutional developments under the auspices of ASEAN, including the AIR.[75]

Peter Boyce aptly describes key operational terms of the ASEAN Way as follows:

> (1) A disposition to favour summit meetings . . . , (2) a recourse to *musyawarah* principles and concepts in the conduct of high level conferences, (3) a preference for concealed and often "unofficial" preliminary transactions

[74] The most conspicuous legal ground for the ASEAN Way may be found in the Treaty of Amity and Cooperation in Southeast Asia art. 2, Feb. 24, 1976, 1025 U.N.T.S. 297, which spells out six fundamental principles (respect for sovereignty, freedom from external interference, noninterference in internal affairs, peaceful resolution of disputes, prohibition of the use of force, and cooperation) that guide ASEAN members' foreign policies. *See also* Amitav Acharya, Constructing a Security Community in Southeast Asia 62 (3rd ed. 2014) (quoting the former Singaporean Foreign Minister S. Jayakumar, who observed that "the ASEAN Way stresses informality, organization minimalism, inclusiveness, intensive consultations leading to consensus and peaceful resolution of disputes"). *See also* Lee Kim Chew, *ASEAN Unity Showing Signs of Fraying*, Strait Times (July 23, 1998), at 23.

[75] *Cf.* William H. Sewell Jr., *Three Temporalities: Toward an Eventful Sociology*, *in* The Historic Turn in the Human Sciences 245, 262–3 (Terrance J. McDonald ed., 1996); Margaret Levi, *A Model, a Method, and a Map: Rational Choice in Comparative and Historical Analysis*, in Comparative Politics: Rationality, Culture, and Structure 19, 28–9 (Mark I. Lichbach & Alan S. Zuckerman eds. 1997).

> by special agents prior to formal ministerial conferences, (4) a preference for *ad hoc* rather than institutionalized practices, (5) an avoidance of judicial or arbitration machinery for the settlement of disputes, (6) readiness to accept mediation or good offices from friendly third parties in the region . . . .[76]

From this unique ASEAN perspective, legalization may be "neither inevitable nor desirable."[77] Delegalized strategies, such as informal diplomacy or trans-governmental networks, may coexist with legalization. Indeed, the ASEAN's core ideology is comprised of two principles – *musyawarah* (consultation) and *mufakat* (consensus) – that originate from an anti-legal domestic decision- making culture of many ASEAN members.[78] Moreover, the creation of "Senior Officials Meetings" (SOM) in various sectors, such as economics, the environment, and science, as well as national secretariats in the foreign ministry of

[76] Peter Boyce, *The Machinery of Southeast Asian Regional Diplomacy*, *in* New Directions in the International Relations of Southeast Asia: Global Powers and Southeast Asia 175 (1973), *quoted in* Acharya, *supra* note 74, at 63. *See also* Geoffrey B. Cockerham, *Regional Integration in ASEAN: Institutional Design and the ASEAN Way*, 27 E. Asia 165 (2010). Admittedly, the intensity of the ASEAN Way has not always been consistent, depending on various factors, such as expanded membership, formalistic needs due to ever-increasing intra-ASEAN interactions, and changes in the regional security situation (such as Vietnam's invasion of Cambodia in 1978). *See* Acharya, *supra* note 74, at 64, 69.

[77] Miles Kahler, *Conclusion: The Causes and Consequences of Legalization*, *in* Legalization and World Politics 299 (Judith L. Goldsteinet al. eds., 2001).

[78] Acharya, *supra* note 74, at 44.

each member, has prioritized trans-governmental cooperation in the ASEAN over more legalistic/judicial strategies.[79]

The informality of ASEAN is geared toward facilitating dialogue and cooperation among members, even on the most sensitive issues or under politically charged circumstances.[80] Miles Kahler aptly submits that:

> [T]hose regional institutions constructed with significant Asian participation remained highly informal and explicitly rejected legalization in their design. Formal rules and obligations were limited in number, codes of conduct or principles have been favored over precisely defined agreements; and disputes have been managed, if not resolved, without delegation to their-party adjudication.[81]

The ASEAN Way provides an "institutional point of reference" against which the opportunity costs of undermining sovereignty can be measured.[82] Viewed from the perspective of the ASEAN Way, legalization incurs "sovereignty costs,"[83]

[79] Miles Kahler, *Legalization as Strategy: The Asia-Pacific Case*, in Legalization and World Politics 169–70 (Judith L. Goldstein et al. eds., 2001).

[80] Vinod K. Aggarwal & Jonathan T. Chow, *The Perils of Consensus: How ASEAN's Meta-Regime Undermines Economic and Environmental Cooperation*, 17 Rev. Int'l Pol. Econ. 262, 269 (2010); Michael Leifer, ASEAN and the Security of South-East Asia 50 (1989); Tom Ginsberg, *The State of Sovereignty in Southeast Asia*, 99 Am. Soc'y Int'l L. Proc. 419, 421 (2005).

[81] Kahler, *supra* note 79, at 165.

[82] Leifer, *supra* note 80, at 151.

[83] Kahler, *supra* note 79, at 177; Carl J. Green, *APEC and Trans-Pacific Dispute Management*, 26 Law & Pol'y Int'l Bus. 719, 730–1 (1995).

which connotes the fear of "uncontrollability"[84] regarding "the potential for inferior outcomes, loss of authority, and diminution of sovereignty."[85] While sovereignty costs seem to be an inevitable and universal consequence from legalization,[86] their actual calculation tends to vary depending on the *context* in which such calculation is situated.[87] For example, ASEAN countries seem largely unconcerned with the sovereignty costs incurred by being members of the WTO, which is a fairly legalized organization. Indeed, it is telling that individual ASEAN members have a track record of challenging each other more via dispute settlement in the WTO than through processes in ASEAN.[88] Yet the AIR, with

[84] *See* Charles E. Lindblom, Politics and Markets: The World's Political–Economic Systems 24 (1977).

[85] Kenneth W. Abbott & Duncan Snidal, *Hard and Soft Law in International Governance*, in Legalization and World Politics 37, 53 (Judith L. Goldsteinet al. eds., 2001).

[86] The familiar criticism of "democratic deficiency" as well as the related appeal to the principle of "subsidiarity" has always accompanied the evolution of the European Union. In the United States, domestic politicians often express their umbrage toward unfavorable decisions of the WTO Tribunal, describing it as a "kangaroo court." *See* Gary G. Yerkey, *Sen. Baucus Calls WTO "Kangaroo Court" with Strong "Bias" Against the United States*, 19 Int'l Trade Rep. (BNA) 1679 (2002).

[87] Abbott & Snidal, *supra* note 85, at 57 (observing that sovereign costs may vary across states and temporal dimensions, even on the same issue).

[88] Panel Report, *Indonesia—Safeguard on Certain Iron or Steel Products*, WTO Doc. WT/DS496/R (adopted Aug. 18, 2007); Request for Consultations under Article XXIII.1 of the GATT 1994, *Malaysia—Prohibition of Imports of Polyethylene and Polypropylene*, WTO Doc. WT/DS1/R (adopted Jan. 13, 1995); Panel Report, *Thailand—Customs and Fiscal Measures on Cigarettes from the Philippines*, WTO Doc. WT/DS371/R (adopted Nov. 15, 2010).

its low degree of legalization *among* ASEAN members – across all three dimensions of obligation, precision, and delegation – clearly evidences the piercing priority and recognition given by those same states of sovereignty costs in that specific institutional context. This peculiar asymmetry in embracing legalization between an extra-ASEAN matter and an intra-ASEAN economic matter characterizes the ASEAN Way.

The ASEAN Way can be traced to the unique postwar history of this region.[89] All of the ASEAN states (except for Thailand) had been colonized (whether *de jure* or *de facto*) and thus held an existential angst on their sovereignty even after the political struggle to achieve independence. The desire for respect and recognition in the post-colonial era turned state sovereignty and nationalism into something of a moral agenda.[90] It is not surprising in this respect that the doctrine of non-interference, which is an essential element of the ASEAN Way, preceded the creation of the ASEAN and dates back to the famous 1955 Bandung Asian-African Conference.[91] In that same time period, exogenous anxiety was intertwined with their endogenous security concerns over insurgency brewed by economic deprivation prevalent across the region in the 1960s.[92] In sum, this prominent path-dependency as to a passionate defense of sovereignty, which Tom Ginsberg dubs

[89] For this part of discussion, we draw mainly on Aggarwal & Chow, *supra* note 80, and Leifer, *supra* note 80.

[90] *See also* Jürgen Haacke, ASEAN's Diplomatic and Security Culture: Origins, Development and Prospects 18–20, 31 (2003).

[91] *Id.* at 16; Acharya, *supra* note 74, at 56.

[92] Acharya, *supra* note 74, at 57.

"Eastphalia,"[93] tends to deter law, at least as it is understood in Western society, from playing a major role in the ASEAN integration process in general.

The ideological tensions of the Cold War further complicated this external–internal security dilemma as some governments, such as Indonesia, were directly challenged by communist-led revolutionary movements. After initial reconciliatory mechanisms, such as the "Association of Southeast Asia" (ASA) and "Maphilindo," bore no fruit, a critical incidence broke out. During the period from 1963 to 1966, Indonesia aggressively challenged – via both diplomatic and military interventions – Malaysia's new government (the Malaysian Federation). This destructive campaign, coined *Konfrontasi* ("Confrontation"),[94] has imprinted an indelible collective memory across the region characterized by strong appeal to the principles of sovereignty and non-interference. Shortly after the *Konfrontasi* ended, the Bangkok Declaration[95] established ASEAN in 1967 to forestall this type of destructive behavior by embedding security cooperation in the region among the five founding members (Indonesia, Malaysia, the Philippines, Thailand, and Singapore).

This distinct ASEAN history illustrates a reverse sequence in interstate cooperation from a traditional neofunctionalist perspective. Note that the origin of interstate

[93] Tom Ginsberg, *Eastphalia and Asian Regionalism*, 44 U.C. DAVIS L. REV. 859 (2011).

[94] *See generally* J.A.C. Mackie, KONFRONTASI: THE INDONESIA-MALAYSIA DISPUTE 1963–66 (1974).

[95] The ASEAN Declaration (Bangkok Declaration), Aug. 8, 1967, 6 I.L.M. 1233 (1967).

cooperation in the Southeast Asian region can be located not in the economic area but in the security area. Compare this ASEAN experience with the original architecture of European integration under which economic cooperation preceded political or security cooperation.[96] Given that the initial success of ASEAN security cooperation is attributable mainly to its informal structure centering on sovereignty and consensus, it would seem natural that the ASEAN Way would also set an enduring legacy in subsequent attempts to build economic cooperation in areas of trade and investment.[97]

Furthermore, these attributes of the ASEAN Way in shaping the strategic direction and level of economic cooperation among members is put into sharp perspective when ASEAN is compared with other international economic regimes. For example, in the case of the WTO, legalization has been a strong engine by which to accomplish a "meta-regime" of trade liberalization,[98] both functionally (such as reduction of uncertainty) and constitutionally (through the allocation of power between the WTO and its members). While ASEAN countries share, to some extent, this meta-regime of economic liberalization with the rest of the WTO

[96] Aggarwal & Chow, *supra* note 80, at 276.

[97] Of course, this is not an evaluative statement. In fact, some observers believe that the ASEAN Way has hindered economic cooperation in intra-ASEAN trade and investment. Vinod Aggarwal and Jonathan Chow argue that the principle of "non-interference," which constitutes the ASEAN Way, has severely hampered collective efforts in advancing regional interests, such as trade and investment. Aggarwal & Chow, *supra* note 80, at 276.

[98] *See generally* Vinod K. Aggarwal, Liberal Protectionism (1985).

members, those ASEAN states, among themselves, are subject to another, perhaps more strongly entrenched, meta-regime of "a preference for informal elite-based diplomacy, decision-making by mutual consultation and consensus, and a preference for incrementalism."[99] As a pointed example of the latter, ASEAN has developed unique legal tools that allow for variegation in the implementation of hard commitments. The "ASEAN-X" formula enables flexible participation in cases where member states are not able to commit to a specific initiative. For example, under the 2003 Protocol to Amend the ASEAN Framework Agreement on Services, two or more member states may proceed to liberalize a particular services sector (or subsector) without extending that promise to a member state that is not yet ready to do the same.[100] Variable geometry of this sort within ASEAN would be later enshrined in the 2007 ASEAN Charter.[101]

One might be tempted to simply equate the ASEAN Way with a visible anti-legal culture in the region, often attributed to so-called Asian values summarized as "less adversarial and litigious, less intent on demonstrating right and wrong, more concerned with avoiding conflict."[102] Critically, however, ASEAN countries are so culturally, ethnically, and religiously diverse that identifying common (lowest) denominators

[99] Aggarwal & Chow, *supra* note 80, at, 267.

[100] Protocol to Amend the ASEAN Framework Agreement on Services, art. 1, Sept. 2, 2003, http://investasean.asean.org/files/upload/Doc%2009%20-%20AFAS_Amendment_Protocol.pdf.

[101] Charter of the Association of Southeast Asian Nations art. 21(2), Nov. 20, 2007, 2624 U.N.T.S. 223 [hereinafter ASEAN Charter].

[102] Kahler, *supra* note 79, at 176.

necessary to form a formal organization with binding legal force has been daunting.[103] Their different languages, customs, moral systems, and stages in economic development[104] have been an impediment toward a strong degree of legalization that would in turn potentially limit each nation's exercise of its hard-won sovereignty. In this regard, Robert Scalapino observes that the "Asianization" which he defines as a "widening and deepening network of ties between and among Asian states of diverse political and cultural nature," remains unfinished.[105] Indeed, this unfinished Asianization also attests to the voluntary nature of another institution in the region made up of a majority of Asian states, the Asia Pacific Economic Cooperation (APEC). Member commitments under APEC also lack hard levels of legal binding.[106]

[103] *Id.* Paul M. Evans, *Regional Institutions, Regional Identities*, *in* Eastern Asia: An Introductory History 451, 451–8 (Colin Mackerras ed., 3rd ed. 2000); Harry Harding, *International Order and Organization in the Asia-Pacific Region*, in East Asia in Transition: Toward a New Regional Order 325, 327 (Robert S. Ross ed., 1995). The dearth of sociocultural commonalities among ASEAN members appears to be one of contributing factors to the ASEAN's characteristic "lowest common denominators" phenomenon, which tends to illuminate the yawning gap in the scope of investment liberalization between extra-ASEAN and intra-ASEAN FTAs. We owe this insight to an anonymous reviewer.

[104] *See* David Pilling, *The Fiction of a Unified, Harmonized ASEAN*, Fin. Times (Dec. 10, 2015), at 9. *See also* Mari Pangestu et al., *A New Look at Intra-ASEAN Economic Cooperation*, 8 ASEAN Econ. Bull. (1992).

[105] Robert A. Scalapino, *Regionalism in the Pacific: Prospects and Problems for the Pacific Basin*, 26 Atl. Cmty. Q. 174, 178 (1988).

[106] *See generally* Sungjoon Cho, *Rethinking APEC: A New Experiment for a Post-Modern Institutional Arrangement*, in WTO and East Asia 381 (Mitsuo Matushita & Dukgeun Ahn eds., 2004).

Granted, the enduring legacy of the ASEAN Way has not been without periodic challenge, such as with the launch of the "ASEAN Charter" in 2007. The Charter confers international legal personality on ASEAN[107] and implements a more legalized system, especially through the creation of formalized institutions.[108] Despite these challenges, the principles of non-interference, consultation, and consensus remain largely unscathed.[109] As a pointed example, consider the proposal for "flexible engagement" that emerged after the damaging 1997 Asian financial crisis. This would have modified the principle of non-interference and allowed ASEAN members to freely criticize each other's domestic policies under certain conditions. While Thailand and the Philippines supported this change,[110] most ASEAN members fiercely rejected it.[111]

[107] ASEAN Charter, *supra* note 101, art. 3. [108] *Id.* ch. IV (Organs).

[109] *Id.* art. 2(1)(2)(a) (affirming the principle of "respect for the independence, sovereignty, equality, territorial integrity of all ASEAN Member States"); *id.* art. 2(1)(2)(e) (affirming the principle of "non-interference in the internal affairs of ASEAN Member States"); *id.* art. 2 (1)(2)(g) (affirming the principle of "enhanced consultations on matters seriously affecting the common interest of ASEAN"). *See also* Aggarwal & Chow, *supra* note 80, at 274.

[110] Hiro Katsumata, *Why Is ASEAN Diplomacy Changing? From "Noninterference" to "Open and Frank Discussions,"* 44 ASIAN SURV. 237, 239 (2004).

[111] Jürgen Haacke, *"Enhanced Interaction" with Myanmar and the Project of a Security Community: Is ASEAN Refining or Breaking with Its Diplomatic and Security Culture?*, 27 CONTEMP. SE. ASIA 188, 189 (2005); Robin Ramcharan, *ASEAN and Non-interference: A Principle Maintained*, 22 CONTEMP. SE. ASIA 60 (2000). *Cf.* Diane A. Desierto, *Investment Treaties: ASEAN*, in ASIA RISING: GROWTH AND RESILIENCE IN AN UNCERTAIN GLOBAL ECONOMY 184, 197–9 (Hal Hill & Maria

4.4.2 *Negative Social Learning*

A social actor, whether human or state via anthropomorphic analogy,[112] learns through its social interactions. While it may learn through direct experience (such as learning by doing), it may also learn through *indirect* experience (learning by observation). Learning by observation takes place on a "vicarious" basis by witnessing others' behavior and its outcome.[113] This competence of learning by observation protects social actors from numerous trials and errors that they would have experienced themselves.[114] As Albert Bandura contends, "from observing others one forms an idea of how new behaviors

Socorro Gochoco-Bautista eds., 2013) (documenting a broad zone of discretion in some policy areas related to investment under ACIA).

112 Regarding anthropomorphism, see generally Sungjoon Cho, *An International Organization's Identity Crisis*, 34 Nw. J. Int'l L. & Bus. 359 (2014).

113 Albert Bandura, Social Learning Theory 12 (1977). While social scientists define and utilize social learning theory in various manners that may suit their particular research projects, one might still locate some coherent themes. For example, a specific process may translate into social learning only when it goes beyond an individual behavioral dimension and enters into a social unit or community of practice. Mark S. Reed et al., *What Is Social Learning?*, Eco. & Soc'y,. vol. 15, no. 4 (2010), www.ecologyandsociety.org/vol15/iss4/resp1/. Social learning theory has also been adopted to explain crimes and other socially deviant behaviors. *See, e.g.*, Travis C. Pratt et al., *The Empirical Status of Social Learning Theory: A Meta-Analysis*, 27 Justice Q. 765 (2010); Wesley Jennings & Brandy B. Henderson, *Social Learning Theory*, *in* The Encyclopedia of Theoretical Criminology 1 (J. Mitchell Miller ed., 2014). For the purpose of this Article, we draw mainly on the classical work by Albert Bandura.

114 Bandura, *supra* note 113, at 12.

are performed, and on later occasions this coded information serves as a guide for action."[115] Importantly, when a social actor builds its own behavioral model through observation, such modeling does not necessarily translate into mere mimicking or emulation of observed behaviors by others. Often, a social actor's modeling involves a creative path by departing, partially or entirely, from the conventional behavioral patterns of others.[116] Such negative social learning occurs when a social actor observes undesirable consequences that others may suffer due to the latter's adoption of particular strategies or policies. This "vicarious punishment" leads an observing actor to avoid the same path that others have trodden.[117]

This social learning theory offers a powerful analytical tool that can explain the AIR's selective adoption of GIL. Both emulation of *and* resistance to GIL demonstrate a complex manifestation of social learning by the AIR. ASEAN members did not merely imitate GIL *mutatis mutandis*; they made deliberate efforts to create a certain normative distance from the global legal culture, driven mainly by serious considerations of local conditions and capacities. By this concept of (negative) social learning, we intend to capture the AIR's conscious efforts to selectively limit model standards of legalization found in GIL comprised of NAFTA Chapter 11 and a dense web of bilateral BITs. Here, protections against "expropriation" and provision of rights to "dispute settlement" under the ACIA render excellent cases in point. Certain ACIA provisions on expropriation exhibit a decreased level of legalization in terms of "obligation," while other

[115] *Id.* at 22. [116] *Id.* at 48. [117] *Id.* at 119.

ACIA provisions on dispute settlement manifest the same trend in light of "delegation."

4.4.2.1 Indirect Expropriation

Like most investment treaties, the ACIA guarantees compensation for both direct and indirect expropriation of foreign investment. While the concept and identification of direct expropriation is clear, the real difficulty lies in understanding what comprises *indirect* expropriation. In older BITs – as well as NAFTA Chapter 11 – there is no real treaty guidance as to what criteria should be taken into account in assessing whether general regulation or taxation that causes economic harm to the foreign investor should be sanctioned as indirect expropriation, thereby triggering an obligation on the host state to compensate the foreign investor. In 2004, however, the United States in a post-NAFTA amendment elected to reorient its protections against indirect expropriation by reference to U.S. constitutional law,[118] specifically the U.S. Supreme Court's decision in *Penn Central Transportation Co.* v. *New York City.*[119] This strategy reflects the United

[118] U.S. Dep't of State, Model Bilateral Investment Treaty (2004), https://ustr.gov/sites/default/files/U.S.%20model%20BIT.pdf (hereinafter 2004 U.S. Model BIT), annex B(4) (requiring an adjudicator to consider the "character of the government action" along with its "economic impact" and interference with "reasonable investment-backed expectations" in determining whether a regulatory measure could constitute indirect expropriation).

[119] *Penn Central Transportation Co.* v. *New York City*, 438 U.S. 104 (1978). In engaging in these essentially ad hoc, factual inquiries, the Court's decisions have identified several factors that have particular significance. The economic impact of the regulation on the claimant and,

States' likely risk tolerance on the meta-question of compensation for general regulation that interferes with the profitability of foreign investment. Yet strangely, other states often simply replicate this American treaty innovation without any amendment or tailoring. This duplication is particularly puzzling from a country like Australia, whose constitutional position on compensation for government takings is much more conservative than that of the United States.[120]

Yet when it comes to the ACIA, the ASEAN states have avoided some of this problematic pathology. They have certainly drawn from the U.S. list of criteria that must be considered by an adjudicator in testing for indirect expropriation, but they have also modified it in one important respect. In particular, for example, Annex 2(3) of the ACIA provides that determining the existence of indirect expropriation requires "a case-by-case, fact-based inquiry" considering such factors as "whether the government action breaches the government's prior binding written commitment to the investor."[121]

particularly, the extent to which the regulation has interfered with distinct reasonable investment-backed expectations are, of course, relevant considerations. So, too, is the character of the governmental action. *Id.* at 124 (citation omitted).

[120] Under Australian constitutional doctrine, more is required than simple deprival of economic value in grounding a claim for breach of section 51 (xxxi) of the Commonwealth Constitution. Recently, the High Court of Australia ruled that an identifiable and clear "acquisition" of property (normally by the state) is a necessary condition of violation. *See ICM Agric. Pty, Ltd.* v. *Commonwealth,* [2009] HCA 51, 81–86 (French, C.J., Gummow, & Crennan, JJ.); *id.* at 142–54 (Hayne, Kiefel, & Bell, JJ.).

[121] ACIA, *supra* note 6, annex 2(3).

Note that in the U.S. version, it is enough that regulatory actions simply "interfere with distinct, reasonable, investment-backed expectations."[122] Compare this low threshold with the standard now set in the ACIA. Under the latter, it is the existence of a prior binding commitment that the state had specifically undertaken in writing which will be probative. The threshold is set significantly higher which, in turn, may better accommodate those ASEAN members with limited administrative capacity and internal clearing processes for dealing with prospective foreign investors.

4.4.2.2 Dispute Settlement

Claimants (foreign investors) have tended to appoint those who have extensive expertise in commercial arbitration to investor–state arbitral panels. Those legal professionals then come to the new construct with an existing set of habits and practices without always considering whether those methods are appropriate when resolving a dispute under a broadly worded treaty compared to an individually negotiated contract. There is, in short, a fundamental conceptual difference between commercial arbitration (based on a specifically negotiated contract between key parties) and investment arbitration (where the subject matter of the dispute will normally engage general legal regulation that is passed at some later stage after entry into the BIT). However, a certain set of arbitral awards have simply ignored the parameters of the

[122] 2004 US Model BIT, *supra* note 118, annex B(4)(a)(ii).

treaty bargain and instead created strained and largely implausible legal constructions.[123]

Under the ACIA, this concern about the contours of investor–state arbitration manifests itself in a range of provisions with various implications. In particular, the dispute settlement provisions of the ACIA confer significant authority on the ASEAN member states to impose their views on dispute settlement. For example, Article 40(3) of the ACIA confirms that any joint decision of the ASEAN member states shall not only be binding on a tribunal (using the language of NAFTA Article 1131(2)) but also that "any decision or award issued by a tribunal must be consistent with that decision."[124] There is then clear potential for the intervention of the "executive" into the activities of the "judiciary," both broadly described. The cause of this ex ante reservation of authority – which, by definition, constrains the zone of discretion afforded to adjudicators – is once again the growing state concern over the quality of reasoning and outcome in investor–state arbitration.

[123] *Compare Pope & Talbot* v. *The Government of Canada*, UNCITRAL Award on the Merits of Phase 2, ¶¶ 110–11 (Apr. 10, 2001), *and SD Myers* v. *The Government of Canada*, UNCITRAL Partial Award, ¶¶ 259–69 (Nov. 13, 2000) (both ruling that NAFTA Article 1105 adopts an additive component that extends beyond the scope of protection at customary international law), *with The United Mexican States* v. *Metalclad Corporation*, Supreme Court of British Columbia, Judgment of the Honourable Mr. Justice Tysoe, 2001 BCSC 664, ¶¶ 64–6 (May 2, 2001) (criticizing the Pope & Talbot and Myers awards on the interpretation of NAFTA Article 1105 as ignoring the plain text of that treaty provision).

[124] ACIA, *supra* note 6, art. 40(3).

The ACIA's negotiators have also been prudently mindful of the inevitable difficulties of reaching inter-governmental consensus in achieving a "joint interpretation," which are significantly higher in the ASEAN (with ten members) than in a typical bilateral treaty setting. Even if the ASEAN members fail to reach consensus, the individual interpretations submitted by any ASEAN member are to be forwarded to the tribunal giving it valuable (albeit partial) understanding of member state expectations of the legal orientation of the regime.[125]

4.5 Conclusion

One would certainly expect that the investment rules in ASEAN would rest on a foundation of the experience of the BITs entered into by individual ASEAN members. Relatedly, the arbitral claims brought against particular ASEAN states would be likely to shape the contour of their collective investment project. As we have seen in earlier chapters, both of these influences are clearly on display across the set of ASEAN investment treaties. But what is distinct about the ASEAN investment project – and potentially transformative – is the evolution in objectives surrounding the role of those treaty disciplines. By the time of the ACIA, those treaty constraints would no longer be used as part of a simple BIT-style project of delivering investment protection with the hope that this would somehow translate into greater flows of foreign investment. Instead, the ASEAN members now

[125] *Id.* art. 40(2).

seek to strategically position their region as an integrated production base for foreign investment, thereby leveraging one of the fastest and most dynamic aspects of the global economy. There is also a good degree of innovation at play in the expressed desire of the ASEAN members to construct an investment treaty representing world's best practice.

Yet clearly, the AIR as a whole exhibits a low degree of legalization measured against conventional benchmark indicators. We have sought to contextualize and explain this low degree of legalization through both the ASEAN Way and negative social learning. The adaptation and reimagination embedded into the AIR calls into question universalist assumptions underpinning the concept of legalization and highlights the idiographic nature of legalization from a comparative law perspective. Instead, delegalization can be an independent and entirely legitimate mode of legalization.

Rethinking legalization should be directed both toward outside observers and ASEAN members themselves. Outside observers should create within them a "critical space" in which they can acknowledge the provisional, not absolute, nature of assumptions underlying their contemporary beliefs that are susceptible to future changes.[126] ASEAN members should also realize that their strategic adoption of legalization might not bear the fruit expected, as they cannot reverse engineer the historical causal relationship between legalization and economic development that had originated from Europe. Looking to the future, it may well be that some

[126] Paul W. Kahn, *Speaking Law to Power: Popular Sovereignty, Human Rights, and the New International Order*, 1 Chi. J. Int'l L. 1, 8 (2000).

combination of collective political leadership,[127] alacritous bureaucracy, and enthusiastic private sector input can translate into greater intra-ASEAN investment flows, with or without relevant treaty texts.

[127] James V. Feinerman, *The Rule of Law Imposed from Outside: China's Foreign-Oriented Legal Regime since 1978*, *in* The Limits of the Rule of Law in China 305, 317–18 (Karen G. Turner et al. eds., 2015).

Chapter 5

Synthesis

5.1 Introduction: Revisiting the ASEAN Way

While the ASEAN Way is known to have contributed to the peaceful coexistence of ASEAN members for the past several decades, it often invites criticisms that the rigid "non-interference" principle undermines effective policy cooperation among ASEAN members.[1] Functional cooperation among ASEAN members is based on regulatory norms provided largely by the Western world. Yet, deeply rooted constitutive norms, such as non-interference, have been an inhibitive, rather than facilitative, force against institutionalized responses to collective regulatory challenges, as seen in the recent HIV/AIDS pandemic in the ASEAN region.[2] Some even lament the "habits of non-implementation"[3] among ASEAN members, as the lack of commitments opens a window for "negative social interaction" and subsequent realist strategies.[4]

[1] Vinod K. Aggarwal & Jonathan T. Chow, *The Perils of Consensus: How ASEAN's Meta-Regime Undermines Economic and Environmental Cooperation*, 17 Rev. Int'l Pol. Econ. 262, 283 (2010).

[2] Alan Collins, *Functional Cooperation and ASEAN Institutionalism: Responding to HIV/AIDS*, *in* ASEAN and the Institutionalization of East Asia 43, 48, 56 (Ralf Emmers ed., 2012).

[3] Takeshi Yuzawa, *The Fallacy of Socialization?: Rethinking the ASEAN Way of Institution-Building*, *in* ASEAN and the Institutionalization of East Asia 75, 81 (Ralf Emmers ed., 2012).

[4] *Id.* at 83, 85.

From this critical perspective, the relatively low level of *intra*-ASEAN investment liberalization, even after a serious evolution of the ASEAN Investment Regime (AIR) all the way to ACIA, can be said to be "a victim of the success of its security meta-regime,"[5] such as the ASEAN Way. The AIR can be said to suffer what Amitav Acharya dubs a "capability–legitimacy gap."[6] While the ASEAN Way informed by the ASEAN's unique "cognitive prior"[7] renders the AIR a symbolic, normative cover (legitimacy), such a cultural code entrenched in ASEAN legal instruments can be said to be responsible for the ASEAN's failure to deliver original policy goals, such as the promotion of *intra*-ASEAN investment liberalization (capability). For example, the AEC 2015 suffered serious "implementation shortfalls" and had a number of unfulfilled agendas carried forward into the AEC 2025.[8]

[5] Aggarwal & Chow, *supra* note 1, at 277.

[6] Amitav Acharya, *Foundations of Collective Action in Asia: Theory and Practice of Regional Cooperation* (Asian Dev. Bank Institute Working Paper Series, No. 344, 2012).

[7] Paruedee Nguitragool & Jürgen Rüland, ASEAN as an Actor in International Fora: Reality, Potential and Constraints (2015).

[8] *See* Siow Yue Chia, Presentation Delivered at the ASEAN Academy: Overview of AEC Progress and Evaluating AEC Blueprint 2025 (Aug. 16, 2019) (on file with author); Sanchita Basu Das, *Mind the Gap: Explaining Implementation Shortfalls in the ASEAN Economic Community* (ISEAS Econ., Working Paper No. 2017-7, 2017), www.iseas.edu.sg/images/pdf/ISEAS%20EWP%202017-07%20Sanchita.pdf; Somkiat Tangkitvanich & Saowaruj Rattanakhamfu, *The ASEAN Economic Community and the East Asian Agenda*, *in* Asian Economic Integration in an Era of Global Uncertainty 190, 199–200 (Shiro Armstrong & Tom Westland eds., 2018).

Importantly, this lack of capacity could undermine legitimacy, as seen in the ASEAN's collective impotence in tackling the East Asian financial crisis in 1997–98.[9] The fundamental principle of non-interference alone could neither avert an external financial risk nor fully take advantage of the force of globalization. Thus, ASEAN members need to recalibrate the balance between sovereignty envy (legitimacy) and economic cooperation (capability).

How to strike such a delicate balance depends on different theoretical lenses, which project different images of ASEAN economic integration. A neorealist approach focuses on the power structure within the ASEAN;[10] a neoliberal approach the ASEAN's function goal (such as overcoming collective problems);[11] and a constructivist approach its community spirit.[12]

For example, neorealists would argue that a hegemonic power equilibrium based on the Indonesia–Malaysia leadership is key to the success of ASEAN integration. A deep, cognitive root of the ASEAN Way is a Hindu-Brahmanic tradition of an extreme form of Realpolitik, as vividly

[9] Acharya, *supra* note 6, at 15.

[10] *See* M. Leifer, *The ASEAN Peace Process: A Category Mistake*, 12 The Pac. Rev. 25–38 (1999).

[11] *See* Jorn Dosch, *ASEAN's Reluctant Liberal Turn and the Thorny Road to Democracy Promotion*, 21 The Pac. Rev. 527–45 (2008); E. Solingen, *The Genesis, Design and Effects of Regional Institutions: Lessons from East Asia and the Middle East*, 52 Int'l Stud. Q. 261–94 (2008).

[12] *See* Amitav Acharya, Constructing a Security Community in Southeast Asia: ASEAN and the Problem of Regional Order (2014); Richard Higgott, *Ideas, Policy Networks and Policy Coordination in the Asia Pacific*, 7 Pac. Rev. 397–409 (1994).

documented in an ancient text such as Kautilya's *Arthasastra*. As a Machiavellian political guide to rulers, the *Arthasastra*, envisions symbolic concentric circles (*mandalas*), in which enemies are located in the immediate, neighboring circle and allies in the subsequent circle as the enemy of the enemy.[13] In this Hobbesian-like state of anarchy, an empire's survival is only secured by its persistent attack against its neighbor and vice versa.[14] The *Arthasastra* tradition has subsequently been reincarnated in the public minds through epics (*Mahabharata* and *Ramayana*), writings, and even media.[15] This old ASEAN Realpolitik tends to underscore "specific reciprocity"[16] informed by sovereignty envy. From this pessimistic perspective, ASEAN members are prone to an oversensitive perception of reciprocity or sovereignty cost.

Nonetheless, from a constructivist standpoint, free riders may still be tolerated to broaden shared normative grounds among members based on the notion of "diffuse reciprocity."[17] In this regard, Amitav Acharya observes that:

[13] *See generally* Roger Boesche, THE FIRST GREAT POLITICAL REALIST: KAUTILYA AND HIS ARTHASASTRA (2002).

[14] Anja Jetschke & Jürgen Rüland, *Decoupling Rhetoric and Practice: The Cultural Limits of ASEAN Cooperation*, 22 PAC. REV. 189 (2009).

[15] *Id.* at 191; Benedict R. O'G. Anderson, *The Idea of Power in Javanese Culture, in* CULTURE AND POLITICS IN INDONESIA 1–70 (Claire Holt ed., 1972); Andrew N. Weintraub, POWER PLAYS: WAYANG GOLEK PUPPET THEATRE OF WEST JAVA, SOUTHEAST ASIA SERIES, VOL. 110 (2004).

[16] Robert O. Keohane, *Reciprocity in International Relations*, 40 INT'L ORG. 1, 4 (1986).

[17] Acharya, *supra* note 6, at 3.

> The problem of free riding does not disappear, but is offset by the fact that incentive for a leading power or powers to provide public goods, (or lead in the collective provision of such goods) is based on communitarian rather than individualist thinking. Accepting a certain amount of free riding becomes key to legitimacy, and hence to justifying the inequities of power distribution. Thus, the stronger and more resource-rich actors voluntarily accept, or even encourage free riding.[18]

In pursuit of the AEC Blueprint 2025, ASEAN members need to form a new collective identity regarding their economic relationship by redefining their national interests beyond short-term sovereignty costs.[19] They will need to embrace long-term, systemic interests which can overcome parochial capture or sovereignty envy and envision a broadly-defined common prosperity in the region. Such a new collective identity among ASEAN members will be able to steer a more audacious level of investment liberalization among themselves than the status quo. It also constitutes the private businesses' social grammar for their actions.[20] Only with such a firm collective identity can ASEAN members achieve genuine cooperation, rather than merely projecting an "illusion of

[18] *Id.* at 4.

[19] *See* John H. Jackson, Sovereignty, the WTO and Changing Fundamentals of International Law 35–6 (2006) (criticizing a narrow version of self-interest in international law based on rational choice theories).

[20] Jacqueline Best, *Bringing Power Back In: The IMF's Constructivist Strategy in Critical Perspective, in* Constructing the International Economy 203 (Rawi E. Abdelal et al. eds., 2010).

cooperation."[21] Managing a tempestuous political process borne by disruptive competition[22] is a collective challenge that ASEAN leaders must tackle to achieve any meaningful intra-ASEAN economic integration.

In this regard, ASEAN members, especially traditionally outward-looking ones such as Singapore and Thailand, need to evoke a "rhetorical action"[23] to overcome parochial and inward-looking positions in larger economies, such as Indonesia and Malaysia, by appealing to the ASEAN's new normative foundations, such as "ASEAN Centrality," as well as its collective identity stipulated under the ASEAN Charter. In particular, the recent "development" focus of the ASEAN Charter, which sheds light on ASEAN's least-developed members, tends to call for a more integrationist ethos among ASEAN members. The ASEAN Centrality bolsters a case for the synthesis of *intra*-ASEAN and *extra*-ASEAN investment flows in tandem with regional and global value chains, thereby creating a new and expanded ASEAN economy, as discussed below.

[21] *See, e.g.*, David Martin Jones & Michael L.R. Smith, *Making Process, Not Progress. ASEAN and the Evolving East Asian Regional Order*, 32 Int'l Security 148–84 (2007).

[22] Lee Jones, *Explaining the Failure of the ASEAN Economic Community: The Primacy of Domestic Political Economy*, 29 Pac. Rev. 1, 5 (2015) (observing that vested domestic interests may subvert economic liberalization projects that threaten their rent bases).

[23] *See* Frank Schimmelfennig, *The Community Trap: Liberal Norms, Rhetorical Action, and the Eastern Enlargement of the European Union*, 55 Int'l Org. 47, 48 (2001).

The case for liberalizing FDI in the ASEAN region offers powerful microeconomic and macroeconomic benefits.[24] From a microeconomic perspective, local workers and managers can benefit from enormous learning effects as they are exposed to advanced operational and management skills and motivated to emulate them amid the ever-competitive environment. From a macroeconomic perspective, foreign capital inflows can compensate a deficiency in a host country's national saving level, boosting its potential for national income growth. ASEAN leaders should integrate these insights into a new cost–benefit analysis on political economy as their broader domestic constituencies, such as consumers, have recently demonstrated their robust support for free trade.[25] Their ultimate challenge is to defy constant political demands for protectionism to establish a stable foundation for economic growth as they harness the development potential within the ASEAN region.

5.2 Beyond Factory ASEAN: ASEAN Investment in the Global Context

In the past, ASEAN integration was driven largely by "production integration."[26] The Factory ASEAN mostly served

[24] *See* Tony Makin, *Advancing Foreign Investment in APEC*, Hinrich Foundation (Aug. 24, 2021) www.hinrichfoundation.com/research/article/fdi/advancing-foreign-investment-in-apec/.

[25] Andi Haswidi, *ASEAN Governments Out of Step on Free Trade*, Fin. Times (Feb. 12, 2019).

[26] Michael Ewing-Chow & Hsien-Li Tan, *The Role of the Rule of Law in ASEAN Integration*, EUI Working Paper RSCAS 2013/16 (2013), at 12.

assembly sites for foreign multinational enterprises, such as Sony and Panasonic. More recently, however, consistently rising growth rates and incomes in the region have spurred ASEAN market integration, as represented by the ASEAN Economic Community (AEC) agenda.[27] At the juncture, the critical correlation between trade and investment cannot be overemphasized for the sake of long-term growth and the development of ASEAN economies.

Empirical studies have demonstrated that trade flows and inward foreign direct investment (FDI) flows are mutually reinforcing each other, which suggests that transforming ASEAN into an integrated supply chain mega-hub in the Asia-Pacific region will tremendously increase both trade and FDI flows within the ASEAN region.[28] Richard Baldwin eloquently demonstrates this critical "nexus" between trade and investment in the operation of global value chains. Baldwin views that:

> Supply chain assurances address the necessity of connecting factories that cross borders. Twenty-first-century supply chains involve the whole trade-investment-service- intellectual-property "nexus," since bringing

[27] *See* Alan Boyd, *ASEAN Shines Bright in Foreign Investor Surveys*, Asia Times (Sept. 22, 2017).

[28] *See* Masahiro Kawai & Kanda Naknoi, *ASEAN Economic Integration through Trade and Foreign Direct Investment: Long-Term Challenges*, Asian Dev. Bank Institute Working Paper, No. 545 25 (2015). Regarding a similar empirical finding, see Kiki Verico, The Future of the ASEAN Economic Integration 106 (2017) (identifying "an endogenous relationship between intraregional trade (trade creation) and FDI inflows (investment creation) in ASEAN").

> high-quality, competitively priced goods to customers in a timely manner requires international coordination of production facilities via the continuous two-way flow of goods, people, ideas, and investments. Threats to any of these flows became barriers to global value chain participation and industrial development. This is why industrial protectionism became destructionism in the twenty-first century.[29]

Here, one may need to heed the external environment in which the recent Regional Comprehensive Economic Partnership (RCEP) was established. The recent trade war between the United States and China, as well as the subsequent outbreak of the pandemic, have pushed multinational enterprises (MNEs) to diversity their supply chains, especially from China to some ASEAN nations such as Vietnam. The United States–China trade war has pushed Chinese investors to move labor-intensive manufacturing facilities from China to ASEAN nations.[30] Even in the middle of the pandemic, FDI flows to Vietnam have remained relatively robust.[31] Likewise, the post-pandemic trend of "regionalization" of supply chains, which is to establish multiple regional sourcing hubs

[29] Richard Baldwin, The Great Convergence 217–18 (2016) (discussing the trade–investment "nexus" in global value chains).

[30] Alistair Gray, *US Retailers Accelerate Shift away from Chinese Suppliers*, Fin. Times (Sept. 10, 2019); Steve Johnson, *Trump's Trade War: Which of China's Neighbours Are Set to Profit?*, Fin. Times (Dec. 3, 2018).

[31] *See* John Reed, *Vietnam Prepares for Supply Chain Shift from China* Fin. Times (Dec. 28, 2020).

close to consumer markets, has emerged.[32] An empirical study has shown that positive welfare effects from the creation of the RCEP could help repair economic damages to ASEAN economies inflicted by the United States–China trade war.[33] Given that these trends are likely to continue in years to come, the inauguration of the RCEP provides a golden opportunity for ASEAN members to deepen trade and investment liberalization among themselves to maximize the RCEP's true potential; that is, the synthesis of *extra*-ASEAN and *intra*-ASEAN economic flows.

RCEP can be said to be a brainchild of "ASEAN Centrality"[34] or the "Global ASEAN" under the AEC Blueprint 2025.[35] First of all, RCEP, as a negotiation platform,

[32] *See* Mike Cherney, *Firms Want to Adjust Supply Chains Post-Pandemic, but Changes Take Time,* Wall St. J. (Dec. 27, 2020).

[33] *See* Peter A. Petri & Michael G. Plummer, *Trade War, RECP and CPTPP: Will East Asia Decouple from the United States?,* at 11 (Nov. 28, 2020), https://papers.ssrn.com/sol3/papers.cfm?abstract_id=3630294.

[34] Peter A. Petri & Michael Plummer, *RCEP: A New Trade Agreement That Will Shape Global Economics and Politics*, Brookings (Nov. 16, 2020) (attributing the launch of RCEP to the notion of "ASEAN Centrality").

[35] "Create a deeply integrated and highly cohesive ASEAN economy"; "to increase ASEAN's competitive edge in moving the region up the global value chains (GVCs) into higher technology and knowledge-intensive manufacturing and services industries." ASEAN, *ASEAN Economic Community Blueprint 2025,* ¶ 6 (Nov. 2015) www.asean.org/wp-content/uploads/2012/05/8.-March-2016-ASCC-Blueprint-2025.pdf; "ASEAN is continuing to make steady progress towards integrating the region into the global economy through FTAs and comprehensive economic partnership agreements (CEPs) with China, Japan, Republic of Korea, India, Australia and New Zealand. Negotiations to conclude the Regional Comprehensive Economic Partnership (RCEP) and the ASEAN-Hong

is complementary to, and consistent with, preexisting ASEAN FTAs,[36] in particular ASEAN plus 1 treaties, such as the ASEAN–China, ASEAN–Korea, ASEAN–Japan, ASEAN–India and, ASEAN–Australia/New Zealand FTAs. Thus, the ASEAN, not China, has been a main driver of the RCEP negotiation.[37] Service sector liberalization under RCEP, in particular in areas such as telecommunication, professional services, and electronic commerce, is likely to facilitate

Kong FTA (AHKFTA) are also ongoing. These FTAs/CEPs have been strengthening ASEAN's position as an open and inclusive economic region, and lay the foundation for ASEAN to retain its centrality in global and regional engagements, where possible. ASEAN Member States are also engaged in FTAs and CEPs with their strategic trade partners to complement the regional FTAs/CEPs." ASEAN, *ASEAN Economic Community Blueprint 2025*, ¶ 79 (Nov. 2015). In contrast, the direct contribution to the ASEAN Centrality from the Comprehensive and Progressive Agreement for Trans-Pacific Partnership (CPTPP) appears to be limited, in comparison with RCEP, due mainly to the fact that only four ASEAN members (Brunei, Malaysia, Singapore, and Vietnam) joined the CPTPP. For a critique on the CPTPP and its attempts to impose top-down rules for the global economy, see Eyal Benvenisti, *Democracy Captured: The Mega-Regional Agreements and the Future of Global Public Law*, 23 (1) CONSTELLATIONS 58–70 (2016).

[36] ASEAN, *Joint Leaders' Statement on the Negotiations for the Regional Comprehensive Economic Partnership (RCEP)* ¶ 5 (Nov. 14, 2018), https://asean.org/asean2020/wp-content/uploads/2021/02/18.-RCEP-Summit-2_Joint-Leaders-Statement_FINAL2.pdf.

[37] *See* Pasha L. Hsieh, *Against Populist Isolationism: New Asian Regionalism and Global South Powers in International Economic Law*, 51 CORNELL INT'L L.J. 683, 693 (2018) (viewing that ASEAN plus 1 FTAs and the ASEAN Economic Community (AEC) constitute a legal and political foundation for RCEP).

cross-border investment into the ASEAN region in the long term.[38] Also note that the dire post-pandemic situation in which income inequalities have increased in major ASEAN economies, such as Indonesia, may push these economies to fall victim to a middle-income trap.[39] This post-virus situation tends to accentuate an economic logic of synthesis between *intra*-ASEAN and *extra*-ASEAN trade and investment flows underlying the theme of ASEAN Centrality.[40]

Markedly, one of the most critical economic impacts from RCEP originates from its ambitious cumulative rules of origin (ROO) that will mitigate the notorious "noodle bowl" effect.[41] As the Asian version of the "spaghetti bowl" effect, it refers to enormous transaction costs incurred to value chain operators due to multiple ROOs in different FTAs in the region. In this regard, lenient and accommodative implementation of

38 *See* Samuel Scoles, *15 Asia-Pacific Countries Sign World's Largest FTA; A Closer Look at RCEP's Key Outcomes and Implications*, White & Case (Nov. 25, 2020).

39 *See* Erwida Maulia & Ismi Damayanti, *Pandemic Stalls Indonesia's Push to Escape Middle-Income Trap*, Fin. Times (Dec. 22, 2020).

40 "[T]o maintain the centrality and proactive role of ASEAN as the primary driving force in its relations and cooperation with its external partners in a regional architecture that is open, transparent and inclusive" Charter of the Association of Southeast Asian Nations art. 1 (15), Nov. 20, 2007, 2624 U.N.T.S. 223 [hereinafter ASEAN Charter].

41 Rocky Intan, *What RCEP Can Tell Us about Geopolitics in Asia*, Lowly Inst. (Dec. 1, 2020). *But see* Masahiro Kawai & Ganeshan Wignaraja, *Conclusion, in* Asia's Free Trade Agreements: How Is Business Responding? 263 (Masahiro Kawai & Ganeshan Wignaraja eds., 2011) (observing that many small firms in the region tend to export to a single, rather than multiple, market, which exempts them from an economic burden – from the noodle bowl effect).

ROO is called for so as to facilitate ASEAN economic integration through the promotion of both *intra*-ASEAN and *extra*-ASEAN investment.

Suppose that a Singaporean shampoo producer attempts to broaden its export market across Asia.[42] As a bottle of shampoo may contain more than 20 different ingredients, this company needs to source most of these ingredients from other countries, except for ingredients originating from Singapore. Importantly, to be eligible for duty-free treatment, the company needs to source all non-Singaporean ingredients from those countries with which Singapore signed an FTA. Otherwise, this company must pay an average of a 10–20 percent tariff to an export destination.

However, navigating all the different rules of origin of those FTAs that Singapore signed to receive duty-free treatment is a tall order for the company. For example, if its final destination is Korea, it needs to add enough Korean ingredients to be eligible for duty-free treatment under the Singapore–Korea FTA; if it wants to ship the shampoo products to Japan, it needs to replace Korean ingredients with Japanese ingredients to be eligible for duty-free treatment under the Singapore–Japan FTA. If the Singapore company is a small or medium-sized enterprise (SME), complying with all these complicated ROOs in accordance with FTAs with

[42] In this example, we draw on Deborah Elm, *Using RCEP: Creating Products for Asia*, Asia Trade Ctr.: Talking Trade (Dec. 4, 2019), http://asiantradecentre.org/talkingtrade/using-rcep-creating-products-for-asia.

sourcing/export jurisdictions would be prohibitively costly. Yet, under RCEP, the company no longer encounters the aforementioned sourcing dilemma: "as long as the content in the bottle comes *from anywhere in the 15 markets in Asia meeting the ROOs for RCEP* – it can be shipped to any of the 15 markets in Asia *without any changes in formulation*."[43]

Truly, these cumulative ROOs under RCEP are revolutionary for ASEAN investors. Duty-free access to RCEP markets, enabled by such integrationist ROOs, will catalyze both the expansion and the deepening of ASEAN value chains by attracting ASEAN investment from both outside and within. For example, a European investor may want to set up a shampoo factory in Vietnam, as he or she plans on sourcing most ingredients from ASEAN nations and shipping final products to Japan or Korea. If successful, this shampoo producer may open its subsidiary in Thailand or Indonesia with different sourcing schemes. This is the very outcome that the motto of "ASEAN Centrality" idealizes; that is to say, the integration of *intra*-ASEAN and *extra*-ASEAN value chains through a synthesis of *intra*-ASEAN and *extra*-ASEAN trade and investment. Thus far, ASEAN economies have mainly endeavored to manufacture and ship products to *other* markets; however, RCEP may transform ASEAN as a "coherent" economic zone

[43] *Id.* (emphasis original). *See also* Robin Harding et al., *Asian Trade Deal Set to Be Signed after Years of Negotiations*, Fin. Times (Nov. 11, 2020) (reporting that "US multinationals will be able to benefit from the RCEP provisions through their subsidiaries operating within member countries").

in which both an internal and external economic integration can transpire in a symbiotic fashion.[44]

Indeed, Europe's own recent Asia Pivot warrants this expansionist-integrationist scenario under the banner of ASEAN Centrality. Betraying an original expectation of many, including the newly-minted Biden administration, the EU signed the Comprehensive Agreement on Investment (CAI) with China at the end of last year.[45] The EU's surprisingly swift move, defying internal political contentions due mainly to human rights issues in China, appears to target the broadly-defined Asia-Pacific market, spanning from China to the ASEAN region to Australia/New Zealand.[46] Yet not all of the EU's strong preferences on legalization, grounded in its own experience of integration through law, were evidently acceptable to China. The EU has recently proposed an international investment court for investor-state disputes and indeed successfully persuaded certain states (including Vietnam and Canada) to replace arbitration with that judicial model in their FTAs.[47] The CAI, however, starkly reveals the

[44] Robin Harding & John Reed, *Asia-Pacific Countries Sign One of the Largest Free Trade Deals in History*, FIN. TIMES (Nov. 15, 2020) (quoting Deborah Elm).

[45] Jürgen Kurtz & Gong Baihua, *The EU – China Comprehensive Agreement on Investment: A Model for Investment Coverage in the WTO?, in* REBOOTING MULTILATERAL TRADE COOPERATION: PERSPECTIVES FROM CHINA AND EUROPE 191–257 (Bernard M. Hoekman et al. eds., 2021).

[46] See David Hutt, *EU-China Deal May Give Biden's Team More Options*, ASIA TIMES (Dec. 31, 2020).

[47] Free Trade Agreement between the European Union and the Socialist Republic of Vietnam, 30 June 1029, 2020 O.J. (L 186) 3; Comprehensive

limits of the EU's capacity to act as a norm entrepreneur in this contested area as well as China's revealed preferences that clearly mirror some of the delegalization techniques of the ASEAN states. In the CAI, China has *only* agreed to state-to-state dispute settlement, thus departing even from the baseline of extending standard procedural rights to foreign investors.[48]

Skeptics have recently questioned the wisdom of global value chains (GVCs) against the background of "de-globalization."[49] It is true that most recent empirical studies demonstrate "shorter GVCs" with "fewer cross-border stages."[50] However, such a decrease of production fragmentation logically indicates an increasing level of regional integration, especially in the ASEAN region, in the post-financial crisis environment.[51] Regionalization of GVCs is not just a cyclical or political trend; it is a "structural" one that reflects digitalization, servitization, and mass customization.[52] All in all, GVCs augur well for the future of the AEC. In fact, this important trend – and its potential benefits for ASEAN

Economic and Trade Agreement (CETA) between Canada and the European Union, Oct. 30, 2016, 2017 O.J. (L 11) 23.

48 Kurtz & Gong, *supra* note 45, at 205.

49 Harold James, *Deglobalization: The Rise of Disembedded Unilateralism*, 10 Ann. Rev. Fin. Econ. 219–37 (2018).

50 Sébastien Miroudot & Håkan Nordström, *Made in the World?: Global Value Chains in the Midst of Rising Protectionism*, 57 Rev. Ind. Org. 195, 214 (2020).

51 *Id.* at 215. *See also* Richard Baldwin & Javier Lopez-Gonzalez, *Supply-Chain Trade: A Portrait of Global Patterns and Several Testable Hypotheses*, 38 World Econ. 1682–1721 (2015).

52 Miroudot & Nordström, *supra* note 50, at 221.

economic integration – has been given massive impetus by the legal and institutional structure of the RCEP Agreement. In terms of substantive obligations, the RCEP Agreement provides several improvements in comparison to preexisting international investment agreements and investment chapters under existing FTAs. For example, it prohibits the performance requirements more rigorously than the WTO Trade-Related Investment Measures (TRIMS) Agreement, such as the prohibition of the requirements "to transfer a particular technology, a production process, or other proprietary knowledge to a person in its territory" (Article 10.6); it also adopts a "negative-list" approach to reservations and non-conforming measures (Article 10.8); it simplifies investment approval procedures (Article 10.17); and it also provides advisory services (Article 10.17).

On one view, the procedural aspects of the RCEP Agreement paint a more complicated picture,[53] given the absence of an investor-state arbitration mechanism (Article 10.18).[54] Yet more deeply, it reflects many of the theses

[53] *See* Michael Ewing-Chow & Junianto James Losari, *The RCEP Investment Chapter: A State-to-State WTO Style System for Now*, Kluwer Arbitration Blog (Dec. 8, 2020), http://arbitrationblog.kluwerarbitration.com/2020/12/08/the-rcep-investment-chapter-a-state-to-state-wto-style-system-for-now/.

[54] ASEAN Secretariat, *The Legal Text of the Regional Comprehensive Economic Partnership Agreement*, at chapter 10, https://rcepsec.org/legal-text/ ("The Parties shall . . . enter into discussions on the settlement of investment disputes between a Party and an investor of another Party . . . no later than two years after the date of entry into force of this Agreement"). *See* Spenser Karr, *A Battle for Choice: Selecting Investor-State Arbitrators under the RCEP*, 90 Temp. L. Rev. 127, 146 (2017)

presented in this book. The RCEP's investment chapter (Chapter 17) adopts a "delegalization" approach, as it demonstrates RCEP members' collective reluctance to codify pro-investor biases prevalent in most BITs and investment chapters in FTAs. Defying a controversial set of rulings by some investor-state arbitration panels, Article 10.4:3 blocks the possibility of outsourcing an investor-state arbitration mechanism to another international investment agreement by relying on an MFN clause.[55] Moreover, under Article 17.11 a host country's "pre-establishment" rights its decision "whether or not to approve or admit a foreign investment proposal" as well as "the enforcement of any conditions or

(criticizing the lack of the investor-state arbitration mechanism in the RCEP because "it infuses the dispute resolution system with political considerations while shifting control of the process away from investors").

[55] Admittedly, this explicit blocking of the investor-state arbitration mechanism has been thrown into doubt, as Article 20.2:1(b) also permits the co-existence of preexisting international investment agreements that contain the investor-state arbitration mechanism. Article 20.2:1(b) reads that:

"Recognising the Parties' intention for this Agreement to coexist with their existing international agreements, each Party affirms . . . in relation to existing international agreements to which that Party and at least one other Party are party, its existing rights and obligations with respect to such other Party or Parties, as the case may be."

See also Alicia Nicholls, *RCEP Investment Rules: Help or Hindrances to A'ia's COVID-19 Recovery?*, AfronomicsLAW (Feb. 17, 2021), www.afronomicslaw.org/category/analysis/rcep-investment-rules-help-or-hindrances-asias-covid-19-recovery.

requirements that an approval or admission is subject to" – shall not be subject even to a state-to-state dispute settlement mechanism under Chapter 19. After all, given that ASEAN members took a leadership role in the RCEP negotiation process, this characteristic mark of the ASEAN Way should not at all be surprising.

While it is still early to evaluate its merits (without details on implementation), the RCEP Agreement is expected to complement, and even accelerate, ASEAN members' collective efforts in protecting foreign investors and promoting investment liberalization. To foreign investors within and outside of the ASEAN region, the RCEP Agreement holds a great "symbolic" value in that it expresses a collective will to incentivize FDI within the region and codifies such a political resolution in the form of treaty provisions. It helps foreign investors regain confidence by reducing the pandemic-driven uncertainties in the investment climate across the region. ASEAN members should utilize some of advanced obligations under the RCEP Agreement to further promote and liberalize *intra*-ASEAN investment, for example as a legal justification for dismantling preexisting government measures that restrict *intra*-ASEAN investment flows.

5.3 In the Shadow of European Integration?

As discussed in Chapter 3, the mainstream (Western) view is that legalization, through formal, binding instruments, is likely to contribute to trade and investment liberalization by incentivizing traders and investors into further economic activities due to an enhanced level of stability and predictability.[56] Based on this orthodoxy, scholars and policy makers often propose that ASEAN members should expand legalization in the current ASEAN investment treaties, such as ACIA, to increase investment flows within the ASEAN region. Surprisingly, this sometimes even extends to claims for greater legalization of dispute settlement in ASEAN (whether through reform of the existing arbitration model or acceptance of the EU's judicial initiative).[57] On the procedural front, this seems to ignore both ASEAN's complex history and its revealed preferences (in the form of the RCEP Agreement). In fact, there are significant variances in the commitments toward legalization in dispute settlement across a range of regional integration schemes.[58] On the substantive front also, the causality between entry into an investment treaty and increased investment flows remains controversial.[59] Ultimately,

[56] *See e.g.*, Kenneth Abbott & Duncan Snidal, *Hard and Soft Law in International Governance*, 54'NT'L ORG. 421, 423 (2000) (arguing that "international legalization in all its forms must be considered one of the most significant institutional features of international relations").

[57] Trinh Hai Yen, *Fragmented Approaches to Investor-State Dispute Settlement Mechanisms in Intra-ASEAN and Extra-ASEAN Investment Treaties*, *in* ASEAN LAW IN THE NEW REGIONAL ECONOMIC ORDER: GLOBAL TRENDS AND SHIFTING PARADIGMS 252–70 (Pasha Hsieh & Bryan Mercurio eds., 2019).

[58] *See generally*, Karen J. Alter & Liesbet Hooghe, *Regional Dispute Settlement*, *in* THE OXFORD HANDBOOK OF COMPARATIVE REGIONALISM (Tanja Börzel & Thomas Risse eds., 2016).

[59] *See* Jason Webb Yackee, *Do Bilateral Investment Treaties Promote Foreign Direct Investment? Some Hints from Alternative Evidence*, 51 VA. J. INT'L L. 405–14 (2010). That said, liberalization guarantees (compared to protective norms) do offer the greatest potential for increased investment flows. *See* Axel Berger, Matthias Busse, Peter Nunnenkamp

extra-ASEAN investment flow appears to be driven more by the enormous economic potential in the ASEAN region, rather than by (at least simply protective) investment treaties signed by ASEAN economies.[60]

While even a formal (legalized) institution, such as the WTO, cannot effectively operate without cultural support, it is hard to locate a prevailing culture of Western-style legalization, at least for now, among ASEAN members. The Western legalization thesis informed by the "liberal theory of international law" becomes suspect considering the fact that Western-style democracies and authoritarian regimes coexist in the ASEAN region.[61] The complex constellation of ASEAN investment treaties, comprised of *intra*-ASEAN BITs, *extra*-ASEAN BITs, the ACIA, and investment chapters in FTAs signed by ASEAN members, seems to be unfathomable. Such sheer complexity tends to make a prudent observer believe that those legal instruments are meant to be symbolic or aspirational, rather than purely regulative in any methodical fashion.

In this regard, as discussed in Chapter 4, any hasty generalization of European economic integration by *legal* means, and its uncritical application to the ASEAN context,

& Martin Roy, *Do Trade and Investment Agreements Lead to More FDI? Accounting for Key Provisions from Inside the Black Box*, 10(2) I'NT'L ECON. & ECON. POL. 247 (2013).

60 *See, for example*, Beth Simmons, *East Asia, Investment and International Law: Distinctive or Convergent?*, 13 KOR. J. INT'L STUD. 461 (2015).

61 José E. Alvarez, *Instituted Legalization and the Asia-Pacific "Region,"* 5 N.Z. J. PUB. & INT'L L. 15, 27 (2007).

would seriously undermine any efforts to both diagnose and prescribe on the ASEAN economic community.[62] Granted, in certain aspects of the ASEAN project one might locate an ambitious emulation from the European experience.[63] Nonetheless, ASEAN's "cross-civilizational contacts and cultural entanglements with the West" do not translate into the proposition that the former's pathway to modernity is identical with that of the latter.[64] Most of all, historical contexts of integration differ. Historically, the pre-modern social structure of the ASEAN region, such as the dearth of social mobility as well as its colonial past, lacked formative conditions for the Weberian state based on legalization.[65] Moreover, while European integration "consummated the declining legitimacy of nationalism blamed for two world wars," ASEAN integration was based on powerful "nationalist crosscurrents."[66]

Some scholars attribute the checkered record of *intra*-ASEAN investment liberalization to an inadequate level of legalization and therefore advocate further legalization as a

[62] *See notably*, Jetschke & Rüland, *supra* note 14, at 179.

[63] *See e.g.*, Thanat Khoman, *ASEAN: Conception and Evolution*, *in* The ASEAN Reader, Singapore: Institute of Southeast Asian Studies xix (S. Siddique, C. Jeshurun, J. L. H. Tan & P. Thambipillai eds., 1992) ("for many of us and for me in particular, our model has been and still is, the European Community").

[64] Jetschke & Rüland, *supra* note 14, at 188; Shalini Randeria, *The State of Globalization: Legal Plurality, Overlapping Sovereignties and Ambiguous Alliances between Civil Society and the Cunning State in India*, 24 Theory, Culture & Soc'y 1–34 (2007).

[65] Jetschke & Rüland *supra* note 14, at 188.

[66] Amitav Acharya, *The Emerging Regional Architecture of World Politics*, 59 World Pol. 629, 633 (2007).

therapeutic response.[67] Indeed, the ASEAN Charter and the new AEC Blueprint 2025 exhibit certain provisions that may warrant such a legalistic approach. Overall, however, the Charter did not go as far as creating provisions that "might have shifted the regional balance of power towards those states interested in maintaining a more legalized Southeast Asia."[68] As we have indicated, an enhanced level of legalization, especially in the form of a more legalized dispute resolution mechanism, might not be the *only* way to preserve the ASEAN's symbolic universe. The ASEAN Way would advise ASEAN members to avoid stigmatizing a sovereign nation by officially accusing it of violating rules. It is highly doubtful that a European or North American-style litigation and enforcement model would work in the ASEAN culture, in which any investment dispute might be politically sensitive, if not combustible. Even those scholars who advocate for the Western-style litigation and enforcement model acknowledge that a non-adjudicative discourse is preferred in these circumstances.[69]

Perhaps the original sin of legalization in the ASEAN region is that it was imposed by Western colonizers for an

[67] *See* Paul J. Davidson, *The ASEAN Way and the Role of Law in ASEAN Economic Cooperation*, 8 Sing. Y. B. Int'l L. 165 (2004) (observing that the ASEAN economic cooperation will be shifted from a traditional "relation-based" model to a new "rule-based" one in the future).

[68] Levither Lee, *The ASEAN Charter: ASEAN Failure or Member Failure*, 43 N.Y.U. J. Int'l L. Pol. 159, 20 (2010).

[69] *See* Karen J. Alter, *Resolving or Exacerbating Disputes?: The WTO's New Dispute Resolution System*, 79 Int'l Aff. 783, 788 (2003); José E. Alvarez, *How Not To Link: Institutional Conundrums of an Expanded Trade Regime*, 7 Widener L. Symp. J. 1, 15 (2001).

exploitive purpose. As Anja Jetschke and Jürgen Rüland aptly observe, "an alien legal system that unilaterally served foreign interests and during colonial rule was a source of profound social injustice and political discrimination could hardly acquire the normative power on which postcolonial inter-state relations could be built."[70] The limits of legalization in the ASEAN integration project[71] tend to set a different pathway to integration from the one adopted in Europe. It is in this context that some scholars question the eventual efficacy of the recent quasi-constitutional project, the ASEAN Charter,[72] which appears to depart from the ASEAN Way.[73]

Under the aforementioned cognitive, social, and historical conditions, pooling sovereignties of individual ASEAN members to create a supranational organization, similar to the EU, could be hardly conceived, even against the plausible backdrop of aspirational emulation.[74] Once initiated, new

[70] Jetschke & Rüland, *supra* note 14, at 188.

[71] *See* Stefano Inama & Edmund W. Sim, The Foundation of the ASEAN Economic Community: An Institutional and Legal Profile (2015) (observing that ASEAN legal instruments, such as treaties, would not provide an effective tool to achieve intra-ASEAN economic integration).

[72] ASEAN Charter, *supra* note 40, art. 3 ("ASEAN, as an inter-governmental organization, is hereby conferred legal personality."). *See* Pasha L. Hsieh & Bryan Mercurio, *An Introductory Roadmap to the ASEAN Economic Community*, *in* ASEAN Law in the New Regional Economic Order: Global Trends and Shifting Paradigms 3–6 (2019) (viewing the establishment of the ASEAN Charter as an important constitutional moment for the bloc).

[73] *See* Inama & Sim, *supra* note 71.

[74] *See* Lay Hong Tan, *Law and Policy in ASEAN Economic Integration*, 38 Asia Bus. L. Rev. 7–8 (2002).

political ideas, such as converting ASEAN into an EU-style, rule-based, supranational organization, must be validated by external events to become a sustainable orthodoxy and thus transform a preexisting society.[75] At the other extreme, such ideas could end up exerting no meaningful changes in society and could entrench old worldviews. In this spectrum of "transformation" and "inertia," a middle ground of "localization" might be found in the form of modest changes without substantially altering the essential tradition of old worldviews.[76] Amitav Acharya defined localization as "the active construction . . . of foreign ideas by local actors which results in the former developing significant congruence with local beliefs and practices."[77]

The ASEAN's collective response to the Asian financial crisis demonstrates the difficulty of normative changes (transformation) brought by new political ideas. The financial crisis triggered open criticism of the ASEAN Way, as ASEAN failed to address the crisis as a collectivity.[78] In response, some ASEAN leaders began to float new agendas departing from

[75] Jeffery W. Legro, *The Transformation of Policy Ideas*, 44 AM. J. POL. SCI. 419, 425 (2000).

[76] Claudio M. Radaelli, *Whither Europeanization? Concept Stretching and Substantive Change*, 4 EUR. INTEGRATION ONLINE PAPERS (2000); Tanja Börzel & Thomas Risse, *When Europe Hits Home: Europeanization and Domestic Change*, 4 EUR. INTEGRATION ONLINE PAPERS (2000); Amitav Acharya, *How Ideas Spread: Whose Norms Matter? Norm Localization and Institutional Change in Asian Regionalism*, 58 INT'L ORG. 239, 245 (2004).

[77] Acharya, *supra* note 66.

[78] Ilan Alon & Edmund Kellerman, *Internal Antecedents to the 1997 Asian Economic Crisis*, 7 MULTINATIONAL BUS. REV. 1, 5 (1999).

the conventional ASEAN Way, such as "constructive intervention" and "flexible engagement."[79] However, the progressive rhetoric of these new ideas failed to match subsequent practice, which caused the ASEAN Way to remain intact.[80] In particular, as for ASEAN integration, the ASEAN Charter launched the "ASEAN Economic Community" (AEC) whose European emulation still awaits its eventual materialization: the resilience of national sovereignty still prevails over a power shift to ASEAN as an autonomous organization.[81] All in all, the European ideal of economic integration failed to dent the conventional orthodoxy, only corroborating its inertia. At best, the AEC might be translated into a localization effort whose final outcome is yet to come.

The ASEAN Way, while not necessarily inconsistent with the conventional rule of law ideal,[82] may still signify another manifestation of legal rationality in the ASEAN context, as seen in the phenomenon of delegalization. As Clifford Geertz observes, "ideas of some local depth . . . can direct us toward some of the defining characteristics, however various and ill ordered, of . . . a *different sense of law*."[83] The ASEAN

[79] Jetschke & Rüland, *supra* note 14, at 197.

[80] *See* Jürgen Rüland, *Coping with Crisis: Southeast Asian Regionalism and the Ideational Constraints of Reform*, 16 Asia Eur. J. 155 (2018); Jürgen Rüland, The Indonesian Way: ASEAN, Europeanization and Foreign Policy Debates in a New Democracy (2018).

[81] Jetschke & Rüland, *supra* note 14, at 199.

[82] We owe this insight to Ambassador Tommy Koh. *See* Tommy Koh et al., 50 Years of ASEAN and Singapore (2017).

[83] Clifford Geertz, Local Knowledge: Further Essays in Interpretive Anthropology 187 (1983) (emphasis added).

Way overlaps, to a substantial extent, with the "*Asian* Way."[84] For example, '[f]or Asians, vague language is often necessary to ensure consensus on sensitive issues. Ambiguity is almost an art form; it is viewed as a useful device in mitigating conflict and building common positions and confidence."[85] In the same vein, ASEAN members may be advised to benchmark East Asian examples of foreign investment reform, from Japan and Korea, rather than those from the West. As Kevin Davis and Michael Trebilcock point out, ASEAN members might better emulate legal reforms from "insiders," locals sharing similar cultural and historical contexts, rather than from "outsiders."[86]

In sum, any rushed and radical treaty-making attempt to drive investment liberalization among ASEAN members would bear little fruit without due consideration of their historically-entrenched sensitivity toward sovereignty.[87] We may witness an enhanced level of legalization, in the form of an increased number of material obligations and a generally strengthened set of languages, in future ASEAN investment instruments. Yet, such heightened legalization would not necessarily represent an instrument for further

[84] *See* Paul J. Davidson, *The Role of Soft Law in the Governance of International Economic Relations in Asia*, 24 Chinese (Taiwan) Y.B. Int'l L. & Aff. 1 (2006).

[85] Shin-yi Peng, *The WTO Legalistic Approach and East Asia: From the Legal Culture Perspective*, 1 Asian-Pac. L. & Pol'y J. 13, 21 (2000).

[86] *See* Kevin E. Davis & Michael J. Trebilcock, *The Relationship between Law and Development: Optimists v. Skeptics*, 56 Am. J. Comp. L. 895, 946 (2008).

[87] *See* Mariana Mota Prado & Michael J. Trebilcock, *Path Dependence, Development, and the Dynamics of Institutional Reform*, Univ. Toronto L. J. (2009).

liberalization; rather, it could reflect an already achieved outcome, and confidence therefrom, of past liberalization efforts. Even so, ASEAN members would still desire to leave various safety valves, in the form of exceptions and overriding provisions, by which to regain their regulatory control. After all, to most ASEAN members, legal texts would remain more as a porous symbol than as a rigid controlling mechanism.

5.4 The Perils of *Reverse* Open Regionalism

The original version of "open regionalism" is characterized by a typical situation in which preferential treatment is accorded exclusively to internal members of a regional bloc to the detriment of outsiders; that is to say, open to insiders yet closed to outsiders. Hence, a call for sharing such preferential treatment with outsiders. In contrast, "*reverse* open regionalism" refers to a situation in which better treatment is accorded exclusively to external (non-ASEAN) members to the detriment of insiders (ASEAN members), thus open to outsiders yet closed to insiders. Hence, a call for sharing such better treatment with insiders (fellow ASEAN members) as well.

One could reasonably speculate that the ASEAN Way, as discussed in Chapter 4 (Positioning), explicates this puzzling reverse discrimination. A historically framed strong attachment to sovereign space tends to discourage ASEAN members from taking bolder steps in liberalizing investment *among themselves*.[88] Moreover, reverse open regionalism may

[88] For example, regulatory space, in terms of public policy exceptions, remains relatively limited in mega regional deals, such as RCEP and

be emblematic of the ASEAN region's strategic bias to outward-looking economic policies that attempt to harness globalization. For example, a preference margin (the WTO MFN tariff rates minus *intra*-ASEAN preferential tariffs) is zero in more than 90 percent of ASEAN economies' tariff lines.[89] Only 20 percent of total FDI into the ASEAN region originates from ASEAN economies.[90] Nonetheless, this phenomenon remains a serious obstacle to ASEAN economic integration. There are at least three policy justifications against reverse open regionalism in ASEAN investment regulation.

First, the gap between *intra*-ASEAN and *extra*-ASEAN investment liberalization undermines ASEAN's economic integration represented by the ASEAN Economic Community (AEC). Once exempted from liberalization, those politically sensitive sectors tend to solidify their resistance and make it even more difficult for ASEAN governments to discuss and negotiate liberalization in the future.[91] Thus, parochial

CPTPP, in comparison to ACIA. Here, foreign investors may be tempted to engage in "regulatory arbitrage," which could lead to an disuse of ACIA. *See* Diane A. Desierto, *ASEAN Investment Treaties, RCEP, and CPTPP: Regional Strengths, Norms, Institutions, and Politics*, 25 Wash. Int'l L. J. 349, 392–3 (2018).

89 Jayant Menon, *Assessing ASEAN's Economic Performance*, Asian Dev. Bank (2018), www.adb.org/news/op-ed/assessing-asean-s-economic-performance-jayant-menon.

90 *Id.*

91 *See* Sungjoon Cho, *Defragmenting World Trade*, 27 Nw. J.'nt'l L. & Bus. 39, 64 (2006).

protectionism or "embedded mercantilism" may perpetuate itself.[92] Indeed, given the increasing importance of small and medium-sized enterprises (SMEs) in the ASEAN, such economic parochialism must be questioned. While nearly all (96 percent) enterprises within ASEAN are SMEs, which generate up to 85 percent of local jobs and up to 53 percent of local GDPs (gross domestic products), they account for only 30 percent of ASEAN exports.[93] Investment liberalization among ASEAN members empowers local SMEs by providing them with access to regional capital and technology.

While a number of Chinese firms have recently moved their factories to some ASEAN states (such as Cambodia and Vietnam) due to ever-increasing labor costs, upper-middle-income ASEAN states (like Thailand and Malaysia) may also take advantage of such low labor inputs from their neighbors once *intra*-ASEAN investment liberalization gathers increasing traction.[94] Moreover, a United States subsidiary in Thailand may also invest in Cambodia, which not only helps establish regional value chains within the ASEAN but also helps expand GVCs via local

[92] Kanishka Jayasuriya, *The Crisis of Open Regionalism and the New Political Economy of the Asia-Pacific*, 24 Third World Q. (2003).

[93] Asian Development Bank, *Asian Development Outlook 2014 Update: Asia in Global Value Chains*, at 60–61 (2014) www.adb.org/publications/asian-development-outlook-2014-update-asia-global-value-chains.

[94] UNCTAD, *Global Value Chains and Development: Investment and Value-Added Trade in the Global Economy*, at 63, 65, U.N. Doc. UNCTAD/DIAE/2013/1 (2013).

subsidiaries.[95] In sum, ASEAN firms can diversity their exports by participating in both local and global value chains.[96]

According to a comprehensive East Asian business survey, firms tend to proactively exploit new opportunities from regional economic arrangements (such as FTAs) to broaden, deepen and consolidate their supply chains.[97] Given the indispensable nexus between trade (in both goods and services) and investment in supply chain developments, such studies shed critical light on the AIR. For example, both Japanese and Chinese firms proactively tap FTAs to upgrade their regional production networks and in doing so elicit various types of government support.[98] Many firms, especially large enterprises in the ASEAN region, are expected to emulate the same business practices and strategies in years to come, as implied in the experience of the Thai automotive sector.[99] Markedly, upgrading *intra*-ASEAN investment will lead to *extra*-ASEAN investment, which can boost both capital and technology transfer into the region and globalize the customer base.[100]

[95] *See* Chris Devonshire-Ellis, *How US Businesses Can Access the East Asian US$25 Trillion RCEP Free Trade Market Agreement via Existing Agreements*, ASEAN Briefing (July 30, 2021) www.aseanbriefing.com/news/how-us-businesses-can-access-the-east-asian-us25-trillion-rcep-free-trade-market-agreement-via-existing-agreements/.

[96] *Id.* at 1. [97] Kawai & Wignaraja, *supra* note 41, at 262.

[98] Masahiro Kawai & Ganeshan Wignaraja, *Main Findings and Policy Implications*, *in* Asia's Free Trade Agreements: How Is Business Responding? 35 (Masahiro Kawai & Ganeshan Wignaraja eds., 2011).

[99] *Id.* at 36. [100] *Id.*

Second, closing the *intra*-ASEAN and *extra*-ASEAN investment gap is also vital to maximize the "development" potential of investment liberalization. From a development perspective, the paradox of reverse open regionalism is not an entirely new phenomenon. It is widely documented in trade regionalism under the label of the "hub-and-spoke" model. This model eloquently demonstrates the developmentally pernicious effects of asymmetrical trade liberalization. Suppose developing countries (spokes) sign bilateral trade deals with a developed country (a hub). A hub may benefit from importing cheap raw materials from spokes, while at the same time exploiting new export markets there.

The hub-and-spoke model in trade regionalism sheds critical light on the reverse open regionalism paradox within the context of the ASEAN investment regime. Isolated economic benefits from external BITs between individual ASEAN members (spokes) and selected large economies (hubs), such as Japan or China, may only be shared among ASEAN members if they succeed in fully integrating their internal investment regime. For example, "Factory Asia" whose final export destinations are the United States and Europe heavily trades parts and components within the region,[101] which is inextricably linked with the extensive FDI network within the region.[102] Under the "hub effect" coined by Paul Krugman, a hub-and-spoke economic arrangement

[101] Lurong Chen & Philippe De Lombaerde, *ASEAN between Globalization and Regionalization*, 25 Asia Pac. Bus. Rev. 729, 741 (2019).

[102] Richard Baldwin, *The Spoke Trap: Hub-and-Spoke Bilateralism in East Asia* 3, NCCR TRADE Working Paper No. 2009/28 (2009).

favors investing in hub nations, such as Japan or China, at the expense of investing in spoke nations, such as ASEAN economies.[103]

Political economy may explain the hub effect.[104] Political support for market opening tends to be stronger when dealing with bigger markets (hubs), rather than smaller ones (spokes). Thus, FTAs with hub economies produce better market access than FTAs with spoke economies. Naturally, FDI tends to concentrate in hub economies. To make things worse, foreign investors in spoke economies may demand from the host government long-term import protection as an incentive. Individual spoke economies' "uncoordinated pandering" to foreign investors may proliferate trade barriers in the region, while leaving spoke economies "Balkanized."[105] The built-in competition among spoke economies toward signing FTAs and BITs with a hub economy for the fear of losing trade and investment opportunities (the "domino effect") tends to render these dismal scenarios more likely than not.[106]

In sum, the distribution of benefits in hub-and-spoke arrangements are generally skewed in favor of the hub on account of its strong bargaining power as well as investment due to its greater market size.[107] While the hub may prevail on

[103] Paul Krugman, *The Hub Effect: or Threeness in Interregional Trade*, *in* THEORY, POLICY AND DYNAMICS IN INTERNATIONAL TRADE (Wilfred J. Ethier, Elhanan Helpman & J. Peter Neary eds., 1993).

[104] Baldwin, *supra* note 29, at 8. [105] *Id.* at 8–9. [106] *Id.* at 9–10.

[107] Mari Pangestu & Sudarshan Gooptu, *New Regionalism: Options for East Asia*, *in* EAST ASIA INTEGRATES: A TRADE POLICY AGENDA FOR SHARED GROWTH 48 (Kathie Krumm & Homi Kharas eds., 2004).

contentious matter, the spokes tend to block new entrants for fear of dilution of the latter's existing preferential treatments.[108] This distributional asymmetry between the hub and the spokes leads to investment diversion from the latter to the former. Foreign investors tend to gravitate toward the hub because firms located in the hub can secure duty-free inputs from each and every spoke, while firms in a spoke country face discrimination in other spoke markets.[109]

The only way to avoid the aforementioned "self-inflicted peripherality"[110] is for spoke economies to either form a "rim" among themselves or *unilaterally* liberalize trade and investment to the rest of the world to offset investment diversion from the spokes to the hub.[111] Here, a classical example of the European Free Trade Association (EFTA) is a case in point.[112] When the United Kingdom left the EFTA to join the European Economic Community (EEC) in the 1970s, the EEC (hub) negotiated FTAs with all the remaining EFTA members (Austria, Switzerland, Norway, Sweden, Finland, and Iceland). Here, the remaining EFTA members could have fallen victim to disadvantaged spokes. However, since the

108 *See generally* Richard Snape, *Which Regional Trade Agreement?*, *in* Regional Integration and the Asia Pacific (Bijit Nora & Christopher Findlay eds. 1996).

109 *See* Ronald Wonnacott, *Trade and Investment in a Hub-and Spoke System versus a Free Trade Area*, 19 World Econ. 237 (1996).

110 Baldwin, *supra* note 29, at 6.

111 Mari Pangestu & Sudarshan Gooptu, *supra* note 107 49.

112 Baldwin, *supra* note 29, at 22–23. In reality, however, forming a rim remains a difficult, if not impossible, task. *See* Kym Anderson & Richard Snape, *European and American Regionalism: Effects on and Options for Asia*, 8 J. Japanese & Int'l Econ. 454 (1994).

EFTA members had already provided a "rim" among themselves, these economies could avoid the self-inflicted peripherality discussed above. This anecdote corroborates a case for an *intra*-ASEAN investment liberalization and integration to overcome reverse open regionalism.

Third, overcoming the reverse open regionalism paradox is also necessary to harness the emerging engine of global value chains. ASEAN value chains have already emerged and prospered. Most parts and components travel duty-free across the ASEAN territories due to a variety of arrangements, including the WTO Information Technology Agreement (which eliminates tariffs of most electronic parts and components), domestic duty drawback schemes, and other Special Economic Zone privileges.[113] Under these favorable circumstances, liberalizing *intra*-ASEAN investment flows can even further promote the ASEAN region's economic prosperity by accelerating, and deepening, an internal division of labor among ASEAN economies.

Moreover, ASEAN members must think beyond low unit labor costs, which are definite comparative advantages of certain members, such as Vietnam, Myanmar, Cambodia, and Laos. Other members, such as Thailand, Indonesia, and Malaysia, may want to upgrade their growth foundation from simple labor-intensive manufacturing to advanced manufacturing. To these economies, opening trade in services (finance, communication, transportation, etc.) and related

[113] Menon, *supra* note 89.

FDI is imperative to harness the enormous development potential embedded in global value chains.[114]

In this regard, Richard Baldwin observes that:

> As the servicification of manufacturing advances, the competitiveness of a nation's manufactured exports will increasingly depend on the local availability of a broad range of excellent, reasonably priced services. In a sense, excellent and diverse service sectors should be thought of as twenty-first-century industrial bases.[115]

Thus, local (*intra*-ASEAN) integration in services and investment may prepare domestic industries for upcoming competition from more advanced economies. Indeed, opening service industries is a good way of promoting deep integration.[116] While emerging manufacturing centers (such as Vietnam) seldom directly export services, still about 40 percent of their exports, in value added terms, originate from services.[117] Considering the organic relationship between services and investment in global value chains, *intra*-ASEAN investment liberalization can be a tremendous impetus for the creation of "Factory ASEAN."[118]

[114] World Bank Group, *Global Value Chain Development Report 2017: Measuring and Analyzing the Impact of GVCs on Economic Development,* at 12 (2017), https://openknowledge.worldbank.org/handle/10986/29593.

[115] Richard Baldwin, The Great Convergence: Information Technology and the New Globalization 233 (2016).

[116] World Bank Group, *supra* note 114, at 13. [117] *Id.* at 11.

[118] Asian Development Bank, *supra* note 93, at 23, 37.

5.5 Promoting ASEAN Investment along the ASEAN Way

While the ASEAN Way has been criticized, rightly or wrongly, as a hindrance to ASEAN investment, the Western style of legalization can hardly be an answer. Promoting *intra*-ASEAN investment flows should be pursued *along*, not against, the ASEAN Way. What seems essential in soliciting cooperation from ASEAN members is to gradually expand shared grounds and consolidate the ASEAN identity pronounced in the ASEAN Charter. By embracing a constructivist logic, ASEAN members need a new paradigm of integration based on trust and confidence in their common market project. Here, an earlier success of the APEC regime offers an illustrative case in point.[119]

Considering the critical space occupied by ASEAN within the APEC regime, it is no coincidence that the latter's merits, such as effective human agency (trans-governmental bureaucrats) and soft law instruments, correspond with the ASEAN Way. Indeed, the recent successful delivery of RCEP has also been attributed to a similar low-profile yet practical *modus operandi*, which may be labeled "quiet diplomacy."[120] Touting human agency and soft law, ASEAN leaders can rebalance domestic political economy and collective economic interests, thereby synthesizing global and regional

[119] *See generally* Sungjoon Cho, *Rethinking APEC: A New Experiment for a Post-Modern Institutional Arrangement*, *in* WTO AND EAST ASIA: NEW PERSPECTIVES 381 (Mitsuo Matsushita & Dukgeun Ahn eds., 2004).

[120] *See* Khairy Tourk, *Asia-Pacific Pact Is a Triumph for the Region's 'Quiet Diplomacy'*, FIN. TIMES (Nov. 19, 2020).

(ASEAN) value chains and linking a single ASEAN market to the global market. ASEAN leaders should promote and upgrade ASEAN investment in the same manner.

5.5.1 Human Agency

Undoubtedly, the goal of the AIR, for example the ACIA, is to liberalize *intra*-ASEAN investment among ASEAN members and facilitate ASEAN market integration, with open arms toward the global market. Various legal instruments under the AIR may translate into not only external instruments for but also internal commitments toward such a goal.[121] Rationalists tend to focus on the first dimension of the AIR related to exogenous factors, such as incentives, which make states comply with these legal instruments. For example, neorealists emphasize negative incentives, such as sanctions, while neoliberals emphasize positive ones, such as reduction of transaction costs.[122] In contrast, constructivists tend to focus on the second dimension of the AIR related to endogenous factors, which generate compliance pull from within and therefore

[121] *Cf.* Benedict Kingsbury, *The Concept of Compliance as a Function of Competing Conceptions of International Law*, 19 MICH. J. INT'L L. 345, 368 (1998) (trenchantly observing that different "theories" of international law tend to beget different views on compliance since these diverging theories have different accounts on the relationship of international law to state behaviors).

[122] Robert O. Keohane, AFTER HEGEMONY: COOPERATION AND DISCORD IN THE WORLD POLITICAL ECONOMY (1984) (viewing that international institutions facilitate decentralized cooperation among state actors).

make compliance a default pattern.[123] Here, norm internalization leads to an identity shift, which converts the notion of compliance from forced conformity to voluntary cooperation.

As discussed in Chapter 4, the ASEAN Way complicates an instrumental understanding of the AIR. Delegalized texts appear to be ineffective as an instrument, since legal loopholes in the ACIA are prone to a shallow level of treaty goal attainment in the absence of a robust level of commitments from most ASEAN members toward *intra*-ASEAN investment liberalization. The undeniable gap between the rhetoric and the practice of *intra*-ASEAN investment liberalization should be filled by "human agency," rather than by legalization.[124] Alongside the long-standing ASEAN tradition of consensus and consultation, ASEAN members, especially their working-level governmental officials, need to reorganize their conversational apparatus, such as peer review or monitoring sessions,[125] and engage imaginative dialogues to collectively generate a new investment culture among

[123] *See* Harold Hongju Koh, *Why Do Nations Obey International Law?*, 106 YALE L.J. 2599, 2655 (1997) (discussing how institutional habits lead nations to compliance).

[124] *But cf.* Desierto, *supra* note 88 (criticizing the absence of harmonization in regional investment protection standards in the ASEAN investment regime).

[125] *See* Robert Wolfe, *See you in Geneva! Legal (Mis)representations of the Trading system*, 11 EUR. J. INT'L REL. 339 (2005) (observing that dense interactions within the SPS Committee tend to function better in enhancing WTO members' understanding of, and thus compliance with, the SPS Agreement than adjudicated decisions which are often confusing and incomprehensible).

themselves.[126] Social actors are more inclined to change their original positions when they are exposed to regular opportunities in which they can examine and defend their original positions in the face of new information.[127]

Here, working-level government officials in ASEAN nations who take charge of investment regulation can be said to form a "trans-governmental regulatory network" (TRN).[128] Importantly, a TRN differs from a typical *inter*-national diplomacy or treaty-making process, informed by a plenipotentiary logic. As widely documented, a formal treaty-making process is rigid and rife with many disadvantages.[129] In contrast, "working-level" government officials share epistemic grounds[130]

[126] Peter L. Berger & Thomas Luckmann, THE SOCIAL CONSTRUCTION OF REALITY: A TREATISE IN THE SOCIOLOGY OF KNOWLEDGE 154, 159 (1966). *See also* Joel P. Trachtman, *The Constitutions of the WTO*, 17 EUR. J. INT'L L. 623, 645 (2006) (discussing "a dialogue of imagination and possibility").

[127] James L. Gibson, *A Sober Second Thought: An Experiment in Persuading Russians to Tolerate*, 42 AM. J. POL. SCI. 819 (1998).

[128] *See generally* Sungjoon Cho & Claire R. Kelly, *Promises and Perils of New Global Governance: A Case of the G20*, 12 CHI. J. INT'L L. 491 (2012).

[129] *See* John H. Jackson, *International Economic Law in Times That Are Interesting*, 3 J. INT'L ECON. L. 8 (2000) (viewing that "[t]reaties are often an awkward albeit necessary method of designing institutions needed in today's interdependent world, but they do not solve many problems"). *See also* Charles Lipson, *Why Are Some International Agreements Informal?*, 45 INT'L ORG. 495, 537–8 (1991) (highlighting benefits of informal agreements in comparison with treaties).

[130] Cho & Kelly, *supra* note 128, at 501 ("This common belief tends to originate from common knowledge and experience shared by participants of the network, in other words, professional working-level government officials.").

in a given issue area, such as foreign investment regulation, and can mobilize informal modes of communication on an everyday basis. These officials "share a common concern that spans geographical boundaries" and "speak the shared language of safety and soundness."[131] "Human institutions" can facilitate the successful operation of the market as well as redress its failure.[132] This idea is not new. Even in the 1970s, Robert Keohane and Joseph Nye identified the phenomenon of "informal ties between government elites" or "transgovernmental coalition building" against a broad background of "complex interdependence."[133]

Trans-governmental bonds, based on professional understanding and common aspirations, can be "stickier" than they might seem from the outside.[134] Obviously, government officials from different states might not agree on every item on the table all the time, even if they take charge of the same policy issues, such as regulating foreign investment. Nonetheless, the very fact that they still "hang together," despite the risk of marginalization due to an occasional disagreement,[135] demonstrates the resilience, and the potential,

[131] John E. Shockey, *Bank Regulatory Examination and Enforcement after Barings and Daiwa, in Financial Services Litigation*, 935 Corp. L. & Prac. Course Handbook 681, 708 (Practicing Law Institute 1996).

[132] Jackson, *supra* note 129, at 4–5.

[133] Robert O. Keohane & Joseph S. Nye, *Transgovernmental Relations and International Organizations*, 27 World Pol. 39, 44 (1974); Robert O. Keohane & Joseph S. Nye, Power and Interdependence 24–6 (1977).

[134] Koh, *supra* note 123, at 2602–3.

[135] Cho & Kelly, *supra* note 128, at 510 (discussing "willing marginalization" that refers to network members' willingness to participate despite their knowledge that their influence will be limited).

of human agency from the government network, such as the Senior Officials' Meeting (SOM) among ASEAN government officials. Indeed, close treaty monitoring by government officials can help ASEAN members can overcome particular collective action problems.[136] Patterns of deep international regulation cooperation – in diverse domains such as food safety, civil aviation, and pharmaceuticals – offer enormous potential to substantially cut transaction costs for countries while offering a credible prospect of eventual multilateralization.[137] Effective coordination through practical insights at a microscopic level can help ASEAN leaders envision opportunities of mutual benefits from economic liberalization, which is often clouded by short-term political calculations.

The role of human agency in the AIR can be expanded to public–private partnership and engagement.[138] Historically, the building of Factory ASEAN was not a product of rule of law, as seen in Europe or North America. Rather, it was a business-driven *ad hoc* and spontaneous lobbying process. Business people prudently navigated around policy discretions of ASEAN government officials to overcome diverse barriers and organize *intra*-ASEAN

[136] Simon Chesterman, From Community to Compliance: The Evolution of Monitoring Obligations in ASEAN 102 (2015).

[137] Bernard Hoekman & Charles Sabel, *Open Plurilateral Agreements, International Regulatory Cooperation and the WTO*, EUI Working Paper RSCAS 2019/10 (2019).

[138] *See* Jayant Menon & Rodolfo Severino, *The ASEAN Community: An Overview, in* The ASEAN Economic Community: A Work in Progress (Sanchita Basu Das, Jayant Menon, Rodolfo Severino & Omkar Lal Shrestha eds., 2013).

production networks.[139] As the main architects and operators of GVCs, businesses, especially MNEs, hold enormous stakes in regulating foreign investment in and out of the ASEAN region.[140] Therefore, an operational emphasis on human agency enables ASEAN bureaucrats and investors to "negotiate over policy making, implementation, and enforcement" in the area of ASEAN investment policies.[141]

For example, from the standpoint of foreign investors, identifying the exact scope of "covered investments" that are amenable to local laws, regulations, and policies could be a daunting challenge given the pluralistic constellation of ASEAN investment law, comprised of both *intra*-ASEAN and *extra*-ASEAN investment treaties.[142] Here, a typical legalization strategy would advise toward enhancing precision by eliminating the admissibility requirement regarding local laws, regulations, and policies, as reflected in the Comprehensive and Progressive Agreement for Trans-Pacific Partnership (CPTPP) text.[143] However, this aggressive legalization under CPTPP appears largely impractical, at least within the context

[139] Chow & Tan, *supra* note 26, at 16–17. *See also* Abo Tetsuo, *Spontaneous Integration in Japan and East Asia: Development, Crisis, and Beyond*, *in* The Oxford Handbook of Economic Geography (Gordon L. Clark et al. eds., 2000); Richard Higgott, *De facto or De Jure Regionalism: The Double Discourse of Regionalisation in the Asia Pacific*, 11 Global Soc'y 166 (1997).

[140] *See* Grace A. Ballor & Aydin B. Yildirim, *Multinational Corporations and the Politics of International Trade in Multidisciplinary Perspective*, 22 Bus. & Pol. 573 (2020).

[141] *See* Jody Freeman, *The Private Role in Public Governance*, 75 N.Y.U. L. Rev. 543, 549 (2000).

[142] *See* Desierto, *supra* note 88, at 366–70.

[143] *Id.*

of AIR, such as ACIA. Rather, foreign investors would be better advised to communicate closely with ASEAN government officials, in the spirit of public–private partnership, and work out a pragmatic investment proposal tuned to local regulatory conditions. In this regard, public–private partnership, at least within the context of AIR, could be part of "due diligence" from legal counsel advising foreign investors.

A strong working relationship between the state and businesses, as well as an oft-blurred line between public and private domains, tends to make a direct application of Western legal categories to ASEAN policy questionable.[144] As seen in the example of the Pacific Economic Cooperation Council (PECC), past attempts to develop a formal regional organization under a legalistic institutional setting have failed in the ASEAN region. The vast cultural diversity in the region tends to lower the level of convergence necessary for any formal institutionalization among nations. Moreover, ASEAN nations fear that a formal organization spearheaded by the United States and/or Japan might replace the ASEAN and dominate the region.[145] Indeed, some scholars echo their fear that a neoliberal agenda implemented in the region in a sweeping manner might impair other important considerations, such as development.[146]

[144] *Cf.* William P. Alford, *Law, Law, What Law?: Why Western Scholars of Chinese History and Society Have Not Had More to Say about Its Law*, 23 Mod. China 398, 413 (1997).

[145] *See* Kenneth W. Abbott & Gregory W. Bowman, *Economic Integration for the Asian Century: An Early Look at New Approaches*, 4 Transnat'l L. & Contemp. Probs. 187, 207 (1994).

[146] *See* Mamiko Yukoi-Arai, *Regional Financial Institutionalization and the Creation of a Zone of Law: The Context of Financial Stability Regulation*

One of the key areas that has recently become increasingly pivotal in public–private cooperation is "logistics." Many scholars have long underscored the cardinal importance of equipping the ASEAN region with an efficient logistical infrastructure so as to induce private investment and enhanced competition. Given that ASEAN supply chains have recently dealt with relatively high-value products, there is a strategic need for advanced logistics capabilities in those basic services, including "freight forwarding, third-party logistics, warehousing, storage, packaging, e-business, and trucking."[147] In this regard, ASEAN members could consider tapping advanced private logistics industries for the capital, technology, and best practice necessary to create an environment favorable to foreign investment into the region.[148]

More generally, ASEAN governments need to adopt business-supportive policies in order to help firms actually utilize and exploit business opportunities from the AIR.[149] These policies may include knowledge transfer to the business sector, embracing greater business participation in monitoring

in East Asia, 35 INT'L L. 1627, 1649 (2001) (criticizing the APEC as a "tool to promote the neo-liberal deals, i.e., to liberalize the Asian markets, while on another hand this has contributed to the limitation of its development").

147 Robin Carruthers et al., *Trade and Logistics: An East Asian Perspective*, *in* EAST ASIA INTEGRATES: A TRADE POLICY AGENDA FOR SHARED GROWTH 90 (Kathie Krumm et al. eds., 2004).

148 *Id.*

149 Kawai and Wignaraja advance similar policy recommendations with regard to FTAs. Their recommendations can apply, *mutatis mutandis*, to different yet related types of international economic arrangements, such as the AIR. *Cf.* Kawai & Wignaraja, *supra* note 41, at 264.

and updating the AIR, and resolving business complaints incurred by the implementation of the AIR in advance.[150] For this purpose, a regional or country-based "advisory center" on the AIR, which can provide necessary training, capacity-building and other technical assistance, both to local businesses and to government officials from low-income nations in the region, must be seriously considered.[151]

The ultimate legitimacy of the AIR derives not from technical legality itself but from voluntary observance from both state and business actors.[152] Even transparency can be attained through informal avenues, such as the ASEAN Business Forum, as a regularized avenue for business–government consultation inspired by the ASEAN Way.[153] Such a delegalized form of transparency enables government officials to collaborate closely with businesses in a constructive manner to solve or manage practical issues, such as regulatory problems. For example, in a phenomenon that can be coined "centralized decentralization,"[154]ASEAN businesses may play a role in a public decision-making process

150 On the merits of investor-state dispute prevention (rather than resolution), see Lisa Johnson et al., *Investor-State Dispute Prevention: A Critical Reflection*, 75 (4) Disp. Resol. J. 107 (2021).

151 Kawai & Wignaraja, *supra* note 41, at 268–9.

152 *See* Pauline Westerman, Introduction in Outsourcing the Law: A Philosophical Perspective on Regulation 11 (2018).

153 Michael Ewing-Chow, *ASEAN Integration, the Rule of Law, and Investment Agreements*, 107 Am. Soc'y Int'l L. Proc. 284, 284–5 (2013) (observing that Asian businesses often work with Asian policymakers in an informal manner to reduce trade barriers).

154 Imelda Deinla, The Development of the Rule of Law in ASEAN: The State and Regional Integration 140 (2017).

but cannot replace the public authority itself. Such delegation with ASEAN characteristics is not necessarily identical with the Western liberal, bottom-up governance model. This "soft regionalism"[155] can eventually enhance both the legitimacy and effectiveness of the ASEAN investment regime.[156]

A renewed emphasis on human agency within the ASEAN context also evokes "bureaucratic empowerment," which is critical to maintain the "vitality" of the ASEAN economic integration project.[157] Therefore, ASEAN members must bolster the role of the ASEAN Secretariat[158] beyond the traditional role of logistical support to more proactive roles, including research, agenda-setting,[159] and compliance monitoring, as seen in the recent innovation of the "ASEAN Economic Community Scorecard."[160]

This call for bureaucratic empowerment within the ASEAN hearkens back to the highly elitist nature of public bureaucracy in the history of most East Asian countries.

[155] Robert A. Scalapino, *Regionalism in the Pacific: Prospects ad Problems for the Pacific Basin*, 26 ATL. COMMUNITY Q. 174, 179 (1988). *See also* Norman D. Palmer, THE NEW REGIONALISM IN ASIA AND THE PACIFIC 187 (1991).

[156] Chesterman, *supra* note 136, at 96.

[157] *See* Julia Gray, *How International Organizations Survive* (unpublished manuscript) (on file with author).

[158] Tangkitvanich & Rattanakhamfu, *supra* note 8, at 203 (observing that The ASEAN Secretariat is the only unit to coordinate, attend and summarize the burgeoning number of meetings).

[159] Deinla, *supra* note 154, at 171

[160] ASEAN Secretariat, *ASEAN Economic Community Scorecard* (Mar. 2010), https://asean.org/wp-content/uploads/2021/09/AEC-Scorecard.pdf.

Insert the classic Confucian notion of "scholar-official" (士):[161] rigorously trained and equipped with high moral characters; recruited through an extremely competitive state exam; promoted in a merit-based system; professional, rather than political, accountability. In the same vein, the ideal combination of the "wise ruler – virtuous minister" runs deep throughout the ancient Chinese political culture.[162] For example, Xunzi (荀子) prioritizes human agency, based on merits and qualities, over institutions for the sake of good governance.[163] Xunzi states that:

> What possible reason could there be for the lord of men not to search wide and far without regard for consanguinity or nobility and rank, being concerned solely to seek out those who are genuinely able? If a man were like this, then his servants would consider official positions less vital. They would yield to those who are more worthy and able and would be content to follow after them.[164]

In a contemporary manifestation of the aforementioned meritorious legacy of human agency within the government, Jon Quah and David Jones argue that:

> Sufficient number of qualified and competent personnel must be recruited and selected for the public bureaucracy

[161] *See* Su Li & Edmund Ryden, *Scholar-Officials, in* The Constitution of Ancient China 98 (Yongle Zhang & Daniel A. Bell eds. 2018).

[162] Yan Xuetong, *Xun Zi's Thoughts on International Politics and Their Implications*, 2 Chinese J. Int'l Pol. 135, 147 (2008).

[163] *Id.*

[164] John Knoblock, Xun Zi – A Translation and Study of the Complete Works, Vol. II 161 (1990).

> on the basis of merit and not patronage. They should be motivated to remain in the public bureaucracy and perform by providing them with relevant training opportunities, bonuses and other incentives.[165]

Admittedly, the constructive role of human agency, in terms of TRNs, is not without skeptics. Clearly, this construct is subject to the vital condition that developing states avoid payment of "capitulation wages," which essentially forces civil servants to engage in corruption.[166] Of course, we have evidence of this vital condition in the ASEAN context with Singapore's famous insistence on maintaining the high quality of its civil service, not least through the eventual choice of ensuring parity between public and private sector salaries.[167] Yet other accounts are critical of the very potential for human agency to act in such a fundamental role. Kenneth Anderson, for example, observes that government officials "are primarily fiduciaries acting on behalf of others whose values they represent, *not* seekers of reason or the truth as such, and they are not free to ignore the constituents they represent and to depart on their own searches for truth with their fellow

[165] Jon S.T. Quah & David Seth Jones, *Organising the Public Bureaucracy to Ensure Effective Implementation and Compliance with ASEAN Commitments* 33 (July 23, 2019) (unpublished manuscript) (on file with author).

[166] Caroline Van Rijckeghem & Beatrice Weder, *Corruption and the Role of Temptation: Do Law Wages in the Civil Service Cause Corruption?*, IMF WORKING PAPER WP/97/73 (1997).

[167] Jon Quah, *Why Singapore Works: Five Secrets of Singap're's Success*, 21(1) PUBL. ADMIN & POL. 5–21 (2018).

truth-seekers in an international forum."[168] However, these skeptics appear to predicate their evaluation of TRNs on their ideological (neorealist) tendencies, rather than on strict empirical data. One of the hidden assumptions behind these skeptics is positivism (state-centrism): states, *only* states, can, and should, negotiate, conclude, and enforce international projects. While this proposition still rings true to the extent that it signifies (domestic) democratic legitimacy involving ratification, it is oblivious to the microscopic operational dimension, i.e., ways and means through which government agencies or officials from different countries interact, cooperate, and produce meaningful regulatory changes.

It is these persistent, albeit uncelebrated, collaboration efforts at a practical level among working-level officials that pave the groundwork for a formal treaty. The point is that such a trans-governmental network, even if it may not necessarily lead to a formal legal document, *does* contribute to enhancing the level of regulatory cooperation.[169] In this regard, Sungjoon Cho and Claire Kelly observe that:

> [N]etworkers as regulators are subject to various domestic checks and pressures from not only their governments but also the media and the public. Yet they are neither "masterless ronin" nor mere mechanical tools of their government. They also "shape" their governments'

[168] Kenneth Anderson, *Squaring the Circle? Reconciling Sovereignty and Global Governance through Global Government Networks*, 118 Harv. L. Rev. 1255, 1292–3 (2005) (reviewing Anne-Marie Slaughter, A New World Order (2004)).

[169] Cho & Kelly, *supra* note 128, at 550.

policies. Most of them are not political appointees. On the contrary, many are career officials who sit on the same issue area for decades. Even politicians cannot ignore their judgments. Likewise, skeptics assume that the domestic power dynamics on a given regulatory issue are always linear and domestic constituencies' preferences unitary. The reality is far more complicated. There is simply more room for regulators, as norm-sponsors, to advocate and internalize network standards that enjoy professional (expert) legitimacy.[170]

5.5.2 *Soft Law*

Western political scientists often theorize that a low level of legalization leads to a low level of interstate cooperation.[171] In this vein, the increasing invocation of "law" or "rule of law" by politicians and elites in promoting ASEAN economic integration reveals a strong aspiration to "get things done" in *intra*-ASEAN market integration through trade and investment liberalization among ASEAN economies.[172] At a superficial level, there has indeed been a notable trend of legalization in recent treaties, especially in ACIA in 2009, subscribing to GIL for an instrumentalist purpose. Nonetheless, as discussed above, many loopholes, in the name of exceptions or reservations, hinder an ostensible functional operation of legalization in the implementation stage.

As seen in the ASEAN Way, ASEAN members are prone to interstate cooperation through an endogenous social

[170] *Id.* at 551. [171] *See* section 5.3 in this chapter.

[172] *See* John Shuhe Li, *Relation-based versus Rule-based Governance: An Explanation of the East Asian Miracle and Asian Crisis*, 11 REV. OF'NT'L ECON. 651, 657 (2003).

dynamic,[173] rather than exogenous pressure from enforceable legal instruments. ASEAN members prefer to be "evolutionary, cautious, and conservative, resting upon consensus building and peer pressure," rather than "operating under fixed schedules and time frames."[174] Driving *intra*-ASEAN investment liberalization through human agency, in lieu of the formal legalization-cum-compliance mechanism, countenances "soft law" instruments. Sharp economic, cultural, and institutional diversity among ASEAN members tend to warrant the reliance of soft law in regulating ASEAN investment.[175] Note that there has been no major regulatory harmonization in areas such as intellectual property law, consumer protection law, investment law, and finance among ASEAN members. Given plural values and diverse interests among ASEAN members,[176] legal pluralism is embedded in the minds of ASEAN practitioners and government officials.

173 *See* Alastair Iain Johnston, *Socialization in International Institutions: The ASEAN Way and International Relations Theory, in* International Relations Theory and the Asia-Pacific 107–8 (John G. Ikenberry & Michael Mastanduno eds., 2005). *See also* Takeshi Yuzawa, *The Fallacy of Socialization?: Rethinking the ASEAN Way of Institution-Building, in* ASEAN and Institutionalization of East Asia 75–76 (Ralf Emmers ed., 2011) (arguing that socialization facilitates cooperation).

174 Davidson, *supra* note 84, at 10–11.

175 *See* Iwan J. Azis, *Integration, Contagion, and Income Distribution, in* Regional Science Matters 131 (Peter Nijkamp et al. eds., 2014). *See also* Elodie Sellier, *The ASEAN Economic Community: The Force Awakens?*, The Diplomat (Jan. 12, 2016).

176 Paul Berman, *From International Law to Law and Globalization*, 43 Colum. J. Transnat'l L. 485 (2005).

They do not hold an allegiance to any particular "theory" of law. They "instead operate in an eclectic manner, choosing their arguments from wherever they can be found, irrespective of any theoretical starting points."[177]

In this regard, the soft law option could be well subsumed into a broader notion of "delegalization" in that it seriously neutralizes the traditional Weberian notion of formal legality represented by hard law, that is, binding treaties.[178] Importantly, soft law is not the lack of rules per se; rather, it is a codified record of past cooperative relationships among participants in a given regulatory regime. To the extent that such soft law guides states' future cooperation, it still holds a normative value despite the absence of technical bindingness.[179] In other words, soft law instruments can provide government officials with the operational flexibility necessary for smooth, and often incremental, execution, while still heralding clear regulatory directions. Soft law "fulfils a useful function in that it provides generally accepted manifestations of widespread and established views as to what is to be regarded as legal and just."[180]

177 Ulrich Fastenrath, *Relative Normativity in International Law*, 4 EUR. J. INT'L L. 305, 334 (1993).

178 Sungjoon Cho & Jürgen Kurtz, *Legalizing the ASEAN Way: Adapting and Reimagining the ASEAN Investment Regime*, 66 AM. J. COMP. L. 233, 251–7 (2018) (arguing that the ASEAN's historical and cultural traits, such as the "ASEAN Way," lead to "de-legalization" of the ASEAN investment regime).

179 *See* Davidson, *supra* note 84 (emphasizing an increasingly prominent role of soft law in the ASEAN's economic governance).

180 Fastenrath, *supra* note 177, at 323.

Ironically, soft law instruments, in the form of principles, guidelines, or aspirations with timelines, have already been "re-legalized" within the ASEAN context in the sense that they are legitimized as an important governance tool.[181] ASEAN members declare, officialize, and visualize them as an integral part of formal legal documents, such as treaties. Note that such re-legalization is not a "hardening" process, that is, simply converting originally non-binding norms into enforceable, binding ones.[182] Indeed, most legal obligations in AIR tend to fall within the rubric of these soft means in that they are subject to a number of exceptions and have nearly no chance of being exposed to litigation. Rather than enforceable obligations, most provisions are better understood as guidelines or best practices that effectively coordinate members' cooperative policy options based on mutual trust and respect.[183]

Naturally, soft law offers discursive baselines for trans-governmental peer review and consultation. Even

[181] Admittedly, any informal arrangements might be governance tools in and of themselves. *See* Commission on Global Governance, *Our Global Neighborhood: The Report of the Commission on Global Governance*, at 2 (1995) www.gdrc.org/u-gov/global-neighbourhood/. However, the notion of delegalization adopted here is still distinguished from such occasion in that delegalization does legalize such informal arrangements in a formal legal text without losing their soft nature.

[182] "Soft law is often seen as a stepping-stone to hard . . . law, permitting states to begin cooperation informally when they fear the impact of a fully legally binding commitment." Kal Raustiala, *The Architecture of International Cooperation: Transgovernmental Networks and the Future of International Law*, 43 VA. J. INT'L L. 1, 86 (2002).

[183] *See* Joseph Gold, *Strengthening the Soft International Law of Exchange Arrangements*, 77 AM. J.'NT'L L. 443, 443 (1983).

monitoring the implementation of ASEAN investment treaties may be of "symbolic" importance: "an expression of unity or of seriousness about an issue, rather than an intention to follow through on binding commitments."[184] The very *non*-binding nature of soft norms may incentivize those nations that adopt such norms to tolerate a robust monitoring mechanism.[185] Consequently, soft law may facilitate "learning" among members,[186] which explains why an increasing number of economic rules are shifting from rigid and formal to discretionary and informal.[187]

Given this processual and evolutionary nature of soft law instruments, their effectiveness must be evaluated in a dynamic fashion. They can function as useful policy references in gradually expanding the scope of *intra*-ASEAN investment liberalization by linking past instruments to future policy goals, "providing a framework for on-going dialogue and the development of common understanding and shared purposes."[188] They could eventually contribute to the cause of ASEAN Centrality, since they could readily draw third parties into a

[184] Chesterman, *supra* note 136, at 101.

[185] Dinah Shelton, *Introduction: Law, Non-Law and the Problem of Soft Law*, *in* COMMITMENT AND COMPLIANCE: THE ROLE OF NON-BINDING NORMS IN THE INTERNATIONAL LEGAL SYSTEM 1, 15 (Dinah Shelton ed., 2000).

[186] Kenneth Abbot & Duncan Snidal, *supra* note 56, 436, 447–8, 451–52.

[187] William Scheuerman, *Economic Globalization and the Rule of Law*, 6 CONSTELLATIONS 1, 6–19 (1999).

[188] Marise Cremona et al., ASEAN'S EXTERNAL AGREEMENTS: LAW, PRACTICE AND THE QUEST FOR COLLECTIVE ACTION (2015) (portraying this strategy as "omni-enmeshment").

"deeper involvement" in the ASEAN region and thus "plac[e] them within a web of sustained exchanges and relationships."[189]

Those soft law instruments, *qua* "regulatory prototypes,"[190] may be subject to a bold policy experimentation with a realistic option of reversal, such as a "snapback" clause for use in times of political exigency.[191] For this purpose, ASEAN members may consider mobilizing APEC as a laboratory for investment liberalization.[192] For example, ASEAN members may benchmark APEC's flexible liberalization plans based on voluntarism. The resilience of "soft institutionalism" in the ASEAN region has been empirically proven, as seen in the "Early Voluntary Sectoral Liberalization" (EVSL)

189 *Id.* 190 Sungjoon Cho, supra note 119, 403.

191 Indeed, this kind of flexibility is not unprecedented in the ASEAN experience. For example, under the ASEAN Free Trade Area (AFTA), a member may withdraw its prior tariff concessions under certain circumstance. *See* ASEAN Protocol Regarding the Implementation of the CEPT Scheme Temporary Exclusion List, Nov. 23, 2000, https://asean.org/protocol-regarding-the-implementation-of-the-cept-scheme-temporary-exclusion-list-singapore-23-november-2000/.

192 *See* Thomas C. Fischer, *A Commentary on Regional Institutions in the Pacific Rim: Do APEC and ASEAN Still Matter?*, 13 Duke J. Comp. & Int'l L. 337, 343 (2003) (emphasizing the APEC's role as a laboratory for the WTO due to the former's informal structure in which technical bureaucrats can communicate freely without political pressure); Martin Rudner, *Institutional Approaches to Regional Trade and Cooperation in the Asia Pacific Area*, 4 Transnat'l L. & Contemp. Probs. 159, 173–5 (1994) ("Consequently, unlike other formal international organizations, APEC retains a strong potential that regulatory challenges are duly 'managed,' rather than 'solved.'").

initiative.[193] In 1997, APEC members identified 15 sectors of early voluntary liberalization that is expected to have "a positive impact on trade, investment, and economic growth in the individual APEC economies as well as in the region": environmental goods and services; the energy sector; fish and fish products; the food sector; toys; natural and synthetic rubber; forest products; fertilizers; gems and jewelry; automotive; oilseeds and oilseed products; medical equipment and instruments; chemicals; civil aircraft; telecommunications mutual recognition arrangements (MRAs).[194]

ASEAN economies may initiate a similar voluntary "sectoral" investment liberalization scheme without the legal and political pressure of binding commitments. Such voluntary schemes can complement, in a constructive way, the ACIA. Initiating experimental investment liberalization among ASEAN economies may overcome the ACIA's restrictive scope of liberalization, characterized by the positive list and reservations. If such experimental investment liberalization proves successful and they gain confidence, ASEAN members may then codify such success by amending the ACIA.[195]

[193] David Capie, *Explaining ASEAN's Resilience, Institutions, Path Dependency, and Asia's Emerging Architecture*, *in* ASEAN AND THE INSTITUTIONALIZATION OF EAST ASIA 168, 168 (Ralf Emmers ed., 2012).

[194] Asia Pacific Economic Cooperation (APEC), *Annex – Early Voluntary Sectoral Liberalization* (Vancouver, Canada, Nov. 21, 1997), www.apec.org/Meeting-Papers/Annual-Ministerial-Meetings/1997/1997_amm/annex.

[195] *See* Chow & Tan, *supra* note 26, at 42–3.

Finally, soft law instruments shed critical light on the dispute settlement mechanism among ASEAN nations. Although the ASEAN Enhanced Dispute Settlement Mechanism emulates the WTO-style enforcement mechanism backed by the negative consensus rule,[196] it has rarely been invoked since members do not expect any serious enforcement when an actual occasion ever arises.[197] On the contrary, the AFTA Council experience demonstrates that the existence of a formal dispute resolution mechanism might not be a prerequisite for successful ASEAN economic integration: close consultations among government officials could effectively address a variety of practical problems.[198]

A formal investor-state dispute settlement (ISDS) is basically a "treaty" arrangement and its rigid, confrontational, and legalistic procedure has shunned many ASEAN members. More importantly, a number of investment disputes may be of a contractual nature and might be governed on a "commercial" basis. Here, the recently signed "UN Convention on International Settlement Agreements Resulting from Mediation" (2019) could be harnessed to help both ASEAN

[196] *See* Declaration of ASEAN Concord II (Bali Concord II), Oct. 7, 2003, 43 I.L.M. 18 (2004) ("[I]n moving towards the ASEAN Economic Community, ASEAN shall, inter alia strengthen the institutional mechanisms of ASEAN, including the improvement of the existing ASEAN Dispute Settlement Mechanism to ensure expeditious and legally binding resolution of any economic disputes").

[197] Deinla, *supra* note 154, at 155–6, 173; Joshua Karton, Lessons from International Uniform Law, in Reshaping the Investor-State Dispute Settlement System: Journeys for the 21st Century 48, 77 (2015).

[198] Chesterman, *supra* note 136, at 69.

investors and ASEAN host countries effectively resolve contractual investment disputes in a non-adversarial yet effective fashion, as a mediator provides disputing parties with full control in the settlement process.[199] In particular, the non-adversarial nature of mediation, that is, no "winner" or "loser" from the mediation, tends to help disputing parties prevent their working relationships from becoming toxic due to a legal dispute.[200]

[199] Nile Bowie, *Singapore Slings a Trade War Antidote*, ASIA TIMES (Aug. 8, 2019).
[200] *Id.*

Chapter 6

Conclusion: Economic Regionalism and ASEAN Investment

This book explores a key site of economic regionalism in ASEAN – its regulation of foreign investment. In a nutshell, economic regionalism in ASEAN features a dynamic legal interaction of centripetal force (represented by global economic norms) and its centrifugal counterpart (defined by ASEAN's unique historical and cultural traits). The main goal of this book is not to present and defend a narrowly articulated thesis that focuses on a single doctrinal or conceptual point or development within ASEAN. This book instead paints a broader canvass of evolution in law-making by uncovering unique patterns of innovation in legal tailoring while identifying also a central paradox – the wide gap in the degree of openness and commitments between the *intra*-ASEAN vis-à-vis *extra*-ASEAN sources of investment. This final chapter provides a summary and recount of the main observations and arguments in previous chapters from the standpoint of regionalist dynamics in ASEAN investment regulation. It also offers several policy proposals to harness the potential of the ASEAN Investment Regime (AIR) and achieve the mega-goal of "ASEAN Centrality."

6.1 A Dual Optic on ASEAN Investment Regulation

Despite its growing economic importance, there has been a surprising paucity of scholarship directed at the contours and patterns of regionalism in Asia. There are, to be sure, penetrating analyses by political scientists and economists directed at ASEAN, often with comparative orientations that seek to separate the drivers and components of regionalism in ASEAN vis-à-vis the EU.[1] Yet the legal academy has often been slow to recognize the richness and distinctiveness inherent in the normative facets of ASEAN.[2] International economic lawyers seem especially guilty of this sin of omission, at least when compared to the frenetic quality of writing directed at phenomena such as recalibration of investment treaty norms, procedural innovations championed by the EU,

[1] *E.g.*, ROUTLEDGE HANDBOOK OF ASIAN REGIONALISM (Mark Beeson & Richard Stubbs eds., 2012); INTEGRATING REGIONS: ASIA IN COMPARATIVE CONTEXT (Miles Kahler & Andrew MacIntyre eds., 2014); DRIVERS OF INTEGRATION AND REGIONALISM IN EUROPE AND ASIA (Louis Brennan & Philomena Murray eds., 2015).

[2] *Cf.* Julien Chaisse & Sufian Jusoh, THE ASEAN COMPREHENSIVE INVESTMENT AGREEMENT: THE REGIONALIZATION OF LAWS AND POLICY ON FOREIGN INVESTMENT (2016); Jean-Calude Piris & Walter Woon, TOWARDS A RULE-BASED COMMUNITY: AN ASEAN LEGAL SERVICE (2015); Simon Chesterman, FROM COMMUNITY TO COMPLIANCE? THE EVOLUTION OF MONITORING OBLIGATIONS IN ASEAN (2015); Jacques Pelkmans, THE ASEAN ECONOMIC COMMUNITY: A CONCEPTUAL APPROACH (2016). Regarding the distinctive legal dimension under the ASEAN investment regime, *see* Sungjoon Cho & Jürgen Kurtz, *Legalizing the ASEAN Way: Adapting and Reimagining the ASEAN Investment Regime,* 66 AM. J. COMP. L. 233 (2018).

the causes and consequences of Brexit, and the new trade politics of the United States.

On careful examination, however, the picture of economic regionalism in ASEAN is worthy of careful and extended legal consideration due to its ever-mounting prominence in the global economy.[3] In particular, a number of non-legal forms of cooperation and characteristic flexibilities in ASEAN's economic regulation provide both scholars and policy makers with new insights on the nature of law and legalization in global economic governance.[4] Therefore, understanding ASEAN's economic regulation necessitates a dual optic: an internal (synoptic) and external (panoptic) viewpoint. This final chapter seeks to make this case by focusing on the treatment of foreign investment in ASEAN countries.

This book begins by constructing a historical baseline for the establishment of regional rules covering foreign investment in ASEAN. It outlines the contours of "Global Investment Law" (GIL) which can be defined as a broad universe of bilateral investment treaties (BITs), investment chapters of regional trade agreements, and investment arbitration decisions derived from these primary sources.[5] GIL, especially BITs, predominantly regulates foreign investment in international law, much of which

[3] For example, by 2014 ASEAN had become the largest recipient of foreign direct investment in the developing world, surpassing China. ASEAN Secretariat & UNCTAD, *ASEAN Investment Report 2015*, at xv (Nov. 2015), https://perma.cc/W7YR-KJTB.

[4] *See* Sungjoon Cho & Jürgen Kurtz, *The Limits of Isomorphism: Global Investment Law and the ASEAN Investment Regime*, 17 Chi. J. Int'l L. 341 (2016).

[5] *Id.* at 343.

predates the formation of ASEAN. Individual ASEAN states joined the rest of the developing world in subscribing to GIL. They signed sovereignty-constraining investment pacts in the 1960s onwards under asymmetric political and economic bargaining conditions. The Washington Consensus and its neoliberal economic paradigm in the 1990s boosted GIL and left a strong pattern of path-dependence in treaty-making throughout much of the world (with unthinking replication of those early strong BITs).[6]

It then offers a synoptic charting of the creation of investment rules *within* ASEAN, seeking to identify internal patterns of attachment or diversion from the orientations of GIL. Here, it is presented with a remarkable set of primary sources developed incrementally in a stretch of more than two decades. The ASEAN member states have engaged in an evolutionary program of progressively reshaping their investment rules over a set of three formal iterations.[7] This itself is a striking development when compared to other similar regional instruments (such as the investment Chapter 11 of the North American Free Trade Agreement) that have typically been subject to a single set of negotiated outcomes. While early ASEAN instruments have closely modeled

[6] On the political economy of developing state entry into BITs, *see* Jonathan Bonnitcha, Lauge N. Skovgaard Poulsen & Michael Waibel, The Political Economy of the Investment Treaty Regime, at chapter 8 (2017).

[7] *See* Sungjoon Cho & Jürgen Kurtz, *International Cooperation and Organizational Identities: The Evolution of the ASEAN Investment Regime*, 36 Nw. J. Int'l L. & Bus. 173 (2017).

(albeit shifted across) the dominant purposes of the BIT movement ("protection" and/or "liberalization"), later manifestations have pushed toward a defined integrationist *telos* with distinct levels of innovation in legal tailoring. The tipping point in driving that change to deeper integration is, we argue, a complex, temporal combination of financial crisis, internalization of sovereignty costs, and the competitive threats and opportunities afforded by the rise of China.

This book then turns to the perplexing disparities between ASEAN (as a grouping) and non-ASEAN states in the treatment of foreign investment. At first glance, one might be tempted to assume that the evolution of the *intra*-ASEAN investment regime would conform to GIL norms. Interestingly, however, ASEAN members have been remarkably reticent in relinquishing their sovereignty in regulating *intra*-ASEAN investment flows, despite their collective integrationist zeal. ASEAN's own path-dependency, which can be epitomized by the "ASEAN Way" as well as its vicarious learning from other countries' negative experiences in adopting GIL, tend to explain the limit of conformity to GIL in establishing the *intra*-ASEAN investment regime.[8] Here, this book uncovers what appears to be a central paradox which might be dubbed "reverse open regionalism."[9] Select ASEAN member states offer better legal treatment for non-ASEAN partners (through individual FTAs) than they extend internally within the ASEAN collective. The main goal of this book is to go beyond the question of legal

[8] *See generally* Cho & Kurtz, *supra* note 2. [9] *Id.* at 195.

justification for that strategy to explore its inherent rationality measured against the specific integrationist vision of the ASEAN investment rules. In an attempt to address such paradox, this chapter concludes by suggesting some policy options based on human agency and soft law.

6.2 Global Investment Law: Legal and Conceptual Scaffolding

In the turbulent atmosphere of the post–Second World War period, BITs and their derivative legal products formed a general architecture of Global Investment Law (GIL). The obvious purpose of BITs was to promote foreign investment from the (capital-exporting) North to the (capital-importing) South, which explained the unique pro-investor bias embedded in GIL. Despite the pro-investor structure of prototypical BITs, however, post-colonial tensions were still at large, especially in the form of sovereignty envy from newly independent host countries. By the 1990s, the neoliberal zeitgeist suppressed, if not completely eliminated, such tensions. Signing a BIT, mostly between a developed and a developing country, had become part of global economic orthodoxy.[10]

[10] José Alvarez has observed that "[t]he 1990s, not the 1980s and certainly not the 1970s, were the era when the modern investment regime was born." José Alvarez, *The Once and Future Foreign Investment Regime, in* Looking to the Future: Essays on International Law in Honor of W. Michael Reisman 607 (Mahnoush H. Arasanjani et al. eds., 2010).

6.2.1 *The Post-Colonial Legacy of Global Investment Law*

Any inquiry into the creation of the collective rules governing foreign investment in ASEAN requires careful assessment of GIL, which predates the construction of the ASEAN investment treaties and thus operates as the legal and conceptual scaffolding for the construction of those dedicated collective rules. GIL, in particular a vast universe of BITs, is a product of a post-colonial dynamic between the North and the South. To the South, foreign investment could be seen as a continuing legacy of colonialism.[11] This anti-colonialist sentiment explains a whirlwind of nationalization (expropriation) movements immediately after the end of the Second World War.[12] The hard-fought political independence and sovereignty in the South translated promptly into a desire for economic sovereignty. Furthermore, the so-called import-substitution development strategy adopted in many former colonies naturally resisted foreign capital from former colonizers until the 1970s.[13] To the South, safeguarding their economic sovereignty meant seeking to wean themselves from foreign

[11] Louis T. Wells & Rafiq Ahmed, Making Foreign Investment Safe: Property Rights and National Sovereignty 38 (2007); *see* Amy Chua, World on Fire: How Exporting Free Market Democracy Breeds Ethnic Hatred and Global Instability 120–21 (2003) (on the parallel between colonialism and the modern phenomenon of "market-dominant minorities").

[12] *See* Thomas L. Brewer & Stephen Young, The Multilateral Investment System and Multinational Enterprises 52–3 (1998).

[13] For an overview of the influence of import substitution-based theory on development strategies throughout the 1950s and 1960s, *see* Michael

economic influence. As those developing countries attempted to nurture their own infant industries by preventing competition from foreign imports, foreign investment restriction also appeared as a complementary strategy.[14]

This post-colonial legacy – former colonies' apprehension of their former colonizers' continuing economic dominance – had become a development paradigm itself. Under this anti-North economic ideology, conventional international law governing foreign direct investments (FDIs) held little appeal to the South. Indeed, whether or to what extent customary international law should apply to post-war nationalization of foreign industry had quickly generated political and legal conflict between the North and the South.[15] Ironically, BITs emerged as a subtle compromise to mitigate the post-colonial tensions between the North and the South.

The North, in general, needed BITs to hedge downward shifts in the protection of foreign property under customary international law in the 1960s to 1970s.[16] The South

Trebilcock & Robert Howse, THE REGULATION OF INTERNATIONAL TRADE 486–8 (3rd ed. 2005).

14 The dominance of this view of development is even reflected in post-war efforts to multilateralize trade liberalization. The GATT 1947 countenances the use of trade barriers to nurse indigenous infant industry. *See* General Agreement on Tariffs and Trade art. XVIII(2), Oct. 30, 1947, 61 Stat. A-11, 55 U.N.T.S. 194.

15 *See, e.g.*, S.N. Guha Roy, *Is the Law of Responsibility of States for Injuries to Aliens a Part of Universal International Law?* 55 AM. J. INT'L L. 863, 866–86 (1961); C.F. Amerasinghe, STATE RESPONSIBILITY FOR INJURIES TO ALIENS 128–31 (1967).

16 Andrew Newcombe & Lluis Paradell, LAW AND PRACTICE OF INVESTMENT TREATIES – STANDARDS OF TREATMENT 18–44 (2009).

also could not completely excommunicate itself from Western capital, despite deep-rooted anti-colonialist sentiments. BITs provided both the North and the South with a reconciliatory mechanism that could defuse political tensions and manage diverging development models. By legally specifying a zone of protection for foreign investment and investors, BITs could depoliticize and de-escalate potential conflicts that might originate from nationalization or other forced taking of foreign property.[17] From the standpoint of newly independent states (including those in Asia), BITs would signal to the outside world their disaffiliation with Marxism despite the apparent post-colonial political dynamic. This signal had particular value in Asia given the Western preoccupation with the "domino theory" predicting contagion of communism in Southeast Asia in the 1960s and 1970s. The Western powers responded by tolerating, to some extent, non-liberal economic models adopted by developing countries, often in the name of "development."[18]

[17] For a similar account of the early BIT movement but one that focuses on "tribunalization" to manage interstate political and ideological conflict, *see* Ruti Teitel & Robert Howse, *Cross-Judging: Tribunalization in a Fragmented but Interconnected Global Order*, 41 N.Y.J. Int'l L. & Pol. 959 (2009).

[18] Such Western restraint was also demonstrated in the trade area, reflecting the zeitgeist of the 1960s and 1970s. For example, the GATT Contracting Parties passed the so-called Enabling Clause ("Differential and More Favourable Treatment, Reciprocity and Fuller Participation of Developing Countries") in 1979. *Decision on Differential and More Favourable Treatment, Reciprocity and Fuller Participation of Developing Countries*, L/4903 (Nov. 28, 1979), GATT B.I.S.D. 26S/203.

Nonetheless, these early, prototypical BITs could not completely erase antagonistic attitudes to foreign investors in host countries. The South, in particular developing countries in Southeast Asia, desired to retain their newly earned sovereignty even as they reluctantly opened to some foreign investment.[19] All in all, the post-colonial legacy embedded in early BITs militated against their proliferation. After the first BIT, signed by West Germany and Pakistan in 1959,[20] BIT growth throughout the 1960s to 1970s proceeded at a "largely desultory pace,"[21] with only 72 BITs being signed between 1959 and 1969 (half of which were concluded by Germany).[22]

6.2.2 The Triumphant Rise of Global Investment Law

The wind of change began to blow in the late 1980s in the developing world, including among the ASEAN members. The substandard outcomes of postwar development strategies (such as import-substitution) in Latin America and Sub-Saharan Africa forced many of those countries to recalibrate

[19] Simon Chesterman, *Asia's Ambivalence about International Law & Institutions: Past, Present and Futures*, 27 EUR. J. INT'L L. 945, 947–51 (2016).

[20] Newcombe & Paradell, *supra* note 16, at 42.

[21] Kenneth J. Vandevelde, *The Political Economy of a Bilateral Investment Treaty*, 92 AM. J. INT'L. L. 621, 627 (1998).

[22] UNCTAD, *International Investment Rule-Making: Stocktaking, Challenges and The Way Forward*, at 11, U.N. Doc. UNCTAD/ITE/IIT/2007/3 (Feb. 9, 2008).

their development path.[23] The dazzling success of East Asian nations in pursuing export-oriented policies added further momentum to legal and economic reform.[24] Nationalization as a historic source of friction had also sharply declined as developing countries largely gained the control of infrastructure and natural resources within their territories.[25] The sovereign debt crisis of the 1980s had blocked developing countries' access to private bank loans and compelled them to find alternative financial sources, such as FDI. Slowly but surely, a consensus emerged among developing countries to proactively attract FDI to finance their economic development.[26]

In embracing such a liberal, open investment policy, developing countries began to change their domestic laws and regulations in a way which would make their jurisdictions more attractive to FDI.[27] Often, they had to offer more

[23] For an overview of the policy failures associated with import substitution, see Trebilcock & Howse, *supra* note 13, at 486–7.

[24] These countries, though, did not by any means simply adopt policies of unconstrained market liberalization. Some of them offered a range of targeted industrial policies including export incentives to specific firms. South Korea, for instance, prominently used a range of subsidies and incentives to encourage private investment in strategic industries. *See generally* Alice Amsden, Asia's Next Giant: South Korea and Later Industrialization (1989).

[25] Michael S. Minor, *The Demise of Expropriation as an Instrument of LDC Policy 1980–1992*, 25 J. Int'l Bus. Stud. 177 (1994) (discussing the reduction of expropriations of foreign assets amongst developing countries).

[26] Kenneth Vandevelde, *Sustainable Liberalism and the International Investment Regime*, 19 Mich. J. Int'l L. 373, 390 (1998).

[27] *See generally* U.N. Conference on Trade and Development, Incentives and Foreign Direct Investment (1996).

favorable terms (such as tax breaks) to foreign investors than those accorded to domestic companies (reverse discrimination) to induce capital inflows into their markets.[28] For example, from 1991 to 2006, out of a total of 2,533 legal and regulatory changes related to foreign investment in developing countries, over 90 percent were devoted to forms of reverse discrimination.[29] Others had to involuntarily swallow a neoliberal pill of open investment policies as a condition of access to financial resources from the Bretton Woods institutions, such as the IMF and the World Bank.[30] As a result, the number of BITs skyrocketed throughout the 1990s. While 385 BITs were signed from 1959 to 1989,[31] a total of 1,857 BITs were concluded in the next ten years.[32] ASEAN member countries, too, joined this trend throughout the 1990s.[33]

The central *corpus juris* of GIL slowly took shape within this broad universe of BITs. Core legal disciplines

[28] Lisa Sachs & Karl Sauvant, *BITs, DTTs and FDI Flows: An Overview*, *in* The Effect of Treaties on Foreign Direct Investment: Bilateral Investment Treaties, Double Taxation Treaties and Investment Flows xlix (Karl P. Sauvant & Lisa E. Sachs eds., 2009).

[29] *Id.*

[30] Robert Gilpin, Global Political Economy: Understanding the International Economic Order 317–21 (2001).

[31] UNCTAD, *Bilateral Investment Treaties 1959–1999*, at 1, U.N. Doc. UNCTAD/ITE/IIA/2 (Dec. 2000).

[32] *Id.*

[33] Beth Simmons, *East Asia, Investment and International Law: Distinctive or Convergent?*, 13 Kor. J. Int'l. Stud. 461, 469–71 (2015) (outlining the "timing of Asia's [international investment agreements]"). *See also* Zachary Elkins et al., *Competing for Capital: The Diffusion of Bilateral Investment Treaties, 1960–2000*, 60 Int. Org. 811, 821 (2006).

appeared with regularity, including national and most-favoured-nation treatment, the nebulous guarantee of fair and equitable treatment, the obligation to compensate for direct and indirect expropriation, and investor-state arbitration. In the race to attract FDI through competitive entry into BITs, developing countries failed to systematically assess both costs and benefits of such sovereignty-constraining bargains.[34] The true sovereignty costs[35] incurred by these provisions would only materialize to the developing world by the early 2000s, when the onset of legal claims by foreign investors forced host countries to bear (internalize) such costs.

One of the most salient sovereign costs latent to developing countries can be found in provisions relevant to expropriation. Even if a host country needs to take a foreign property for a public purpose in a non-discriminatory manner, it will be required to pay compensation to a foreign owner of the expropriated property at a particular standard.[36]

[34] Lauge Poulsen, Bounded Rationality and Economic Diplomacy: The Politics of Investment Treaties in Developing Countries (2017).

[35] Regarding sovereignty costs incurred by legalization, such as BITs, see Miles Kahler, *Legalization as Strategy: The Asia-Pacific Case*, *in* Legalization and World Politics 165, 177 (Judith L. Goldstein et al. eds., 2001); Carl J. Green, *APEC and Trans-Pacific Dispute Management*, 26 L. & Pol'y Int'l Bus. 719, 730–1 (1995).

[36] For example, Article III of the model U.S. bilateral investment treaty provides: "Neither Party shall expropriate or nationalize a covered investment either directly or indirectly through measures tantamount to expropriation or nationalization . . . except for a public purpose; in a non-discriminatory manner; upon payment of prompt, adequate and

The original post-war customary standard of "appropriate" compensation had now been replaced with the more comprehensive requirement of "prompt, adequate and effective" compensation.[37] This heightened level of compensation goes beyond a typical and predictable case of direct expropriation. It can also be applied to so-called indirect expropriation that concerns regulatory or tax measures without any articulated criteria to determine illegality.[38] Likewise, the open-ended obligation of "fair and equitable treatment"[39] tends to burden host countries with uncertainty. In the absence of general exception clauses, this apparently one-sided, pro-investor provision leaves no trace of balancing investor protection with regulatory autonomy of host countries.

Sovereignty costs incurred by BITs go beyond the realm of substantive protection into procedural mechanisms. By the mid-1970s, BITs would accord private individuals (foreign investors) direct access to an arbitral panel for alleged treaty violations, usually without the requirement of domestic exhaustion. This radical model departs from conventional tenets of both public international law and commercial

effective compensation, and in accordance with due process of law and the general principles of treatment provided for in Article II(3)." UNCTAD, *International Investment Instruments: A Compendium, Vol. III*, at 198, U.N. Doc. UNCTAD/DTCI/30(Vol. III) (May 31, 1996). This type of provision is by no means limited to investment treaties concluded by the U.S. It is instead a feature of most post-war investment treaty regimes.

37 *Id.* 38 *Id.*

39 *See* UNCTAD, *International Investment Instruments: A Compendium Vol. I*, at 209–33, U.N. Doc. UNCTAD/DTCI/30 (Vol.I) (May 31, 1996).

arbitration. It departs from cardinal principles of public international law in that a private party may directly sue a sovereign state for a breach of a treaty (BIT), which classically denotes a state-to-state legal relationship. It even departs from basic tenets of commercial arbitration in that arbitral consents are institutionalized as a default pattern, rather than contracted in specific disputes (arbitration "without privity"[40]). Obviously, this investor-state arbitral mechanism generates a more far-reaching use of arbitration than what has been traditionally understood in the commercial context. Such an extraordinary remedial window has empowered foreign investors to take full advantage of those *pro*-investor substantive provisions in BITs themselves, shaped against a contingent and distinct historical background.

6.3 Synopsis: ASEAN Internal Evolution

This chapter now turns to an internal, synoptic account of *intra*-ASEAN investment regulation. As with other developing countries, individual ASEAN member countries concluded a great number of BITs with non-ASEAN members throughout the 1990s. In stark contrast to this proactive *extra*-ASEAN investment liberalization, the *intra*-ASEAN investment opening proceeded at a far slower pace, in a progressive evolution that spanned more than two decades. Even in its latest manifestations, one can still identify tenacious resistance to full conformation to GIL. Sovereignty envy, epitomized by the "ASEAN Way," tends to explain such limited

[40] Jan Paulsson, *Arbitration Without Privity*, 10 ICSID Rev. 232 (1995).

subscription to GIL, despite the official commitment to further economic integration among ASEAN economies.

6.3.1 *Ever More Open Yet Still Closed: Evolving Liberalization with Caveats*

By the mid-1980s, the ASEAN members began to seriously consider establishing a dedicated ASEAN treaty on foreign investment *within* the region. Naturally, GIL – to which individual ASEAN members had already subscribed in those BITs signed with non-ASEAN members – provided the "1987 ASEAN Agreement for Promotion and Protection of Investments"[41] (1987 ASEAN Agreement) with basic legal bricks and mortar. One of the most symbolic changes found in the 1987 ASEAN Agreement was a paradigm shift from state-driven capital control as part of industrial policy to market-driven investment flows. While "acceleration of industrialization of the region" remained as a core objective in the 1987 ASEAN Agreement, it now explicitly recognized that freer "flow of *private* investments" is a better alternative to the achievement of that goal.[42]

[41] Agreement among the Government of Brunei Darussalam, the Republic of Indonesia, Malaysia, the Republic of the Philippines, the Republic of Singapore and the Kingdom of Thailand for the Promotion and Protection of Investments, Dec. 15, 1987 [hereinafter 1987 ASEAN Agreement] https://asean.org/wp-content/uploads/2020/12/Agreement-for-the-ASEAN-Promotion-and-Protection-of-Investments-or-the-Investment-Guarantee-Agreement-ASEAN-IGA.pdf.

[42] *Id.* Preambular Recitals 2 and 3.

Yet this ambitious vision did not match actual substantive obligations within the 1987 ASEAN Agreement. The Agreement failed to stipulate an obligation of national treatment, which is one of the most fundamental liberalization disciplines in international economic law.[43] Obligations to protect foreign investment were accompanied by a variety of terms and conditions subject to sovereign determination. Most problematically, the general quality of those substantive obligations was questionable in that they would only apply on a *post*-approval basis. Therefore, whether or under what terms a host country ever approves an investment project would depend entirely on the host country's decision. For example, any substantive obligations would only apply if an ASEAN member had "specifically approved in writing" and "registered" an investment, upon which it can impose "such conditions as it deems fit for the purposes of this Agreement."[44]

Subsequently, these strict conditions proved to be prohibitive in practice, which severely undermined the original goal of the Agreement and "constitute[d] an artificial trap depriving investors of the very protection the BIT was intended to provide."[45] For example, an arbitral panel

43 Instead, the ASEAN members simply reserve the possibility for future bilateral or multilateral commitments on national treatment to be struck under the framework of the 1987 ASEAN Agreement: "Any two or more of the Contracting Parties may negotiate to accord national treatment within the framework of the Agreement." 1987 ASEAN Agreement, *supra* note 41, art. IV(4).

44 *Id.* art. II(1).

45 *Desert Line Projects LLC* v. *The Republic of Yemen,* ICSID Case No. ARB/05/17, Award, ¶ 106 (Feb. 6, 2008).

established under the Agreement denied jurisdiction because a Singaporean investor (Yaung Chi Oo) had failed to present the existence of a formal (written) approval from the host country (Myanmar).[46] Yet that was an impossible task for the investor, given the very absence of an approval mechanism under the law of the host state at the time of entry of investment. Given that Myanmar had already approved Yaung Chi Oo's investment, if not in writing, under the former's domestic law, such formalist mechanisms, when given adjudicatory force, proved a tremendous impediment to *intra*-ASEAN investment facilitation.

The anti-climactic contours of the 1987 ASEAN Agreement met a moment of forced innovation due to two subsequent incidences: the East Asian financial crisis (1997–98)[47] and the rise of China throughout the 1990s. First, the economic impact of the Asian financial crisis (1997–98), especially in Thailand, Indonesia, Malaysia, and the Philippines, was devastating.[48] Ironically, the collective (regional) nature of the crisis provided ASEAN members with a fresh moment of bonding as they suffered the crisis

[46] *Yaung Chi Oo Trading Pte Ltd.* v. *Gov't of the Union of Myanmar*, ASEAN I.D. Case No. ARB 01/1, ¶ 23 (Mar. 31, 2003), 42 ILM 540 (2003).

[47] For a comprehensive overview of the causes of and responses to the crisis, *see* Carl-Johan Lindgren et al., FINANCIAL SECTOR CRISIS AND RESTRUCTURING: LESSONS FROM ASIA (1999).

[48] Andrew McIntyre, *Institutions and Investors: The Politics of the Economic Crisis in Southeast Asia*, 55 INT'L ORG. 81 (2001); *see* Diane A. Desierto, *Investment Treaties: ASEAN*, *in* ASIA RISING: GROWTH AND RESILIENCE IN AN UNCERTAIN GLOBAL ECONOMY 184 (Hal Hill & Maria Socorro Gochoco-Bautista eds., 2012).

together.[49] Likewise, their responses to demands from those who bailed them out, including the Bretton Woods institutions, was a largely common (albeit flawed) strategy; drastic, neoliberal regulatory reform, including a more investor-friendly environment.[50] This *external* crisis drove ASEAN members to pursue *internal* integration among themselves.[51] Against this background, the Second Informal ASEAN Summit, held in Kuala Lumpur in December 1997, decided to expedite the implementation of the formation of the ASEAN Investment Area (AIA).[52]

Second, the rise of China as a global factory threatened the ASEAN region as a popular foreign investment destination, which also pushed ASEAN members into deeper economic integration. While FDI to ASEAN and to China accounted for 66 percent and 16 percent respectively, of total FDI to Asia in 1990, these two numbers were dramatically reversed a decade later.[53] In sectoral terms, ASEAN members

49 *See* Ralph Emmers, *Southeast Asia's New Security Institutions*, *in* ASIA'S NEW INSTITUTIONAL ARCHITECTURE: EVOLVING STRUCTURES FOR MANAGING TRADE, FINANCIAL, AND SECURITY RELATIONS 201 (Vinod K. Aggarwal & Min Gyo Koo eds., 2008) (viewing that the Asian financial crisis revealed the ASEAN's institutional frailty).

50 Edmund R. Thompson, *ASEAN after the Financial Crisis*, 17 ASEAN ECON. BULL. 1 (2000).

51 *See* Robert J.R. Elliott & Kengo Ikemoto, *AFTA and the Asian Crisis: Help or Hindrance to ASEAN Intra-Regional Trade?*, 18 ASIAN ECON. J. 1, 17 (2004) (finding that the Asian financial crisis prompted a strong aspiration among ASEAN countries to increase *intra*-ASEAN trade).

52 Suthad Setboonsarng, *ASEAN Economic Cooperation: Adjusting to the Crisis*, SOUTHEAST ASIAN AFF. 35 (1998).

53 David Martin Jones & Michael L.R. Smith, *Making Process, Not Progress: ASEAN and the Evolving East Asian Regional Order*, 32 INT'L SECURITY 148, 165 (2007).

had been leading producers of computer parts, due mainly to their competitive advantages in labor, local suppliers, and transportation.[54] Recently, however, China has surpassed the ASEAN members and secured its dominant position as a production hub for computer components. From 2004 to 2008, China's share of global computer parts export increased from 27 percent to 35 percent, while ASEAN's share remained unchanged at 20 percent.[55]

The confluence of these two factors brought an existential crisis to the *intra*-ASEAN investment regime left hollow by the 1987 ASEAN Agreement. The ASEAN members responded to this challenge by revamping the internal investment liberalization scheme under the "1998 Framework Agreement on the ASEAN Investment Area (AIA)."[56] In a conscious effort to counter the competitive threat from China as a global factory, the AIA vision represented an ambitious goal of establishing a single production base within the

[54] U.S. INT'L TRADE COMM'N, PUB. NO. 4176, ASEAN: REGIONAL TRENDS IN ECONOMIC INTEGRATION, EXPORT COMPETITIVENESS, AND INBOUND INVESTMENT FOR SELECTED INDUSTRIES 49 (2010).

[55] *Id.* at 51.

[56] Consider the first preambular recital of the 1998 Framework Agreement on the ASEAN Investment Area: "Affirming the importance of sustaining economic growth and development in all Member States through joint efforts in liberalising trade *and promoting intra-ASEAN trade and investment flows* enshrined in the Framework Agreement on Enhancing ASEAN Economic Co-operation signed in Singapore on 28 January 1992" (emphasis added). Framework Agreement on the ASEAN Investment Area, Recital 1, Oct. 7, 1998 [hereinafter 1998 Framework Agreement] http://agreement.asean.org/media/download/20140119040024.pdf.

region. The AIA attempted to appeal to multinational enterprises (MNE) whose increasingly prominent global supply chains would find in the ASEAN region an attractive investment destination.[57]

Obviously, facilitating *intra*-ASEAN investment flows would greatly benefit such global production networks, as the ASEAN region as a whole would turn into an integrated, mega-export base. This reflects the inherent synergy between trade and investment in the construction of global supply chains. Efficiency driven foreign investment "is by its very nature trade-creating" because "[b]y subdividing the production process in vertical stages between countries, trade is obviously created (compared to the situation where all stages are undertaken in one country)."[58] To ASEAN members, the AIA scheme would translate into vast development potential in the form of increased jobs and income across the region.

The 1998 Framework Agreement emphasizes this *open* nature of the AIA project. Unlike the 1987 ASEAN Agreement, ASEAN members would now commit to a "more *liberal* and transparent investment environment" that would "substantially increase the flow of investments ... from *both*

[57] Note that trade in intermediate goods (parts and components) between affiliates of MNEs accounts for nearly a half of the total world trade volume today. *Communication from the Commission to the Council, the European Parliament, the European Economic and Social Committee and the Committee of Regions; Towards a Comprehensive European International Investment Policy*, at 3, COM/2010/0343 (July 7, 2010).

[58] WTO, *The Relationship between Trade and Investment*, at 16, WTO Doc. WT/WGTI/W/7 (Sept. 8, 1997).

ASEAN and non-ASEAN sources."[59] Such a remarkable substantive commitment was matched by an extremely ambitious time frame, albeit with some exceptions, whereby "national treatment is extended to ASEAN investors by 2010, and to all investors by 2020" and "all industries are opened for investment to ASEAN investors by 2010 and to all investors by 2020."[60] Likewise, each ASEAN member commits in Article 7(1) to:

> [O]pen immediately all its industries for investments by ASEAN Investors;
>
> [A]ccord immediately to ASEAN investors and their investments, in respect of all industries and measures affecting investment including but not limited to the admission, establishment, acquisition, expansion, management, operation and disposition of investments, treatment no less favourable than that it accords to its own like investors and investments ("national treatment").[61]

Given the relatively poor quality of investment liberalization under the 1987 ASEAN Agreement, the 1998 Framework Agreement appears to be a significant step toward a full-scale, intra-ASEAN investment liberalization. As recent empirical studies have demonstrated, strong market access commitments of this sort tend to guarantee greater FDI flows.[62]

[59] 1998 Framework Agreement, *supra* note 56, art. 3(a)(i) (emphasis added).

[60] *Id.* art. 4. [61] *Id.* art. 7(1).

[62] *See* Axel Berger et al., *Do Trade and Investment Agreements Lead to More FDI? Accounting for Key Provisions Inside the Black Box*, 10 INT'L ECON. & ECON. POL'Y 247 (2013).

Nonetheless, even under this apparently strong AIA vision, ASEAN members retained significant autonomy for sovereign determination. For example, ASEAN members may submit "Temporary Exclusion Lists" and "Sensitive Lists," which exempt particular industries or sectors from being opened up to investment or from the national treatment obligation.[63] The negative list exemptions (in the Temporary List) were to be reviewed biennially and phased out by 2010 for most ASEAN members.[64]

The AIA vision under the 1998 Framework Agreement culminated in the 2009 "Comprehensive Investment Agreement" (ACIA).[65] What distinguishes the ACIA from the earlier (1987 and 1998) ASEAN instruments is the former's strong *community*-building *telos*.[66] The preamble of the ACIA highlights a "more integrated and interdependent future,"[67] which could be achieved by "joint promotion of the region as an integrated investment area."[68] Markedly, this language originates from the 2007 ASEAN Economic Community Blueprint ("AEC Blueprint 2007") to build "an ASEAN single market and production base."[69] Note that the AEC Blueprint promotes "industrial complementation and production *networks* among MNCs in ASEAN" and "joint investment missions that focus on regional clusters and

[63] 1998 Framework Agreement, *supra* note 56, art. 7(2). [64] *Id.* art. 7(3).

[65] ASEAN Comprehensive Investment Agreement, Feb. 26, 2009 [hereinafter ACIA] http://investasean.asean.org/files/upload/Doc%2005%20-%20ACIA.pdf.

[66] *Id.* art. 2(a). [67] *Id.* recital 2. [68] *Id.* art. 1(d).

[69] ASEAN, *ASEAN Economic Community Blueprint*, ¶ 9 (Jan. 2008) www.asean.org/wp-content/uploads/images/archive/5187-10.pdf.

production *networks.*"[70] Such core language has been recycled as a distinct legal obligation in the ACIA.[71] Indeed, this supply chain-oriented investment regime under the ACIA is a natural evolution from an earlier development project envisioned by the AIA under the 1998 Framework Agreement.

As the ACIA emphasizes the community-building goal, it takes "development" seriously in liberalizing and integrating the *intra*-ASEAN investment, especially considering ASEAN's least-developed members, such as Cambodia, Laos, and Myanmar. The ACIA explicitly states core development goals in a set of objectives[72] and guiding principles,[73] which supplement the general purpose of development in the ACIA Preamble. Recital 2 of the Preamble explicitly recognizes "the different levels of development within ASEAN especially the least developed Member States which require some flexibility including special and differential treatment as ASEAN moves towards a more integrated and interdependent future." The principle of "special and differential treatment," which originated from the WTO, is then explicitly repeated as one of the eight guiding principles in Article 2.[74] Given that the same notion is largely absent in GIL, this development clause in the ACIA eloquently demonstrates its collective identity. This saliency of the development agenda in the ACIA has brought the demise of the WTO Doha Development Round into sharp relief.[75]

[70] *Id.* at para. 29 (emphasis added).

[71] ACIA, *supra* note 65, art. 24(b)–(c). [72] *Id.* art. 1. [73] *Id.* art. 2.

[74] *Id.* art. 2(f).

[75] Masahiro Kawai & Ganeshan Wignaraja, *Conclusion*, *in* ASIA'S FREE TRADE AGREEMENTS: HOW IS BUSINESS RESPONDING? 261 (Masahiro Kawai & Ganeshan Wignaraja eds., 2011).

Concomitantly, the ACIA also endeavors to address legal uncertainties under earlier ASEAN investment treaties and further conform to CIL. One of goals of the ACIA is to develop an investment regime that is "comparable to international best practices."[76] First of all, the ACIA's entry into force terminates the earlier instruments (the 1987 ASEAN Agreement and the 1998 Framework Agreement).[77] Second, formerly burdensome approval preconditions are now subject to due process-style procedural disciplines. The previous "approval in writing" requirement now provides "[f]or the purpose of protection, the procedures relating to specific approval in writing shall be specified in Annex 1 (Approval in Writing)[78]." Annex 1 now requires each member:

> [w]here specific approval in writing is required for covered investments by a Member State's domestic laws, regulations and national policies, that Member State shall:
>
> a. inform all the other Member States through the ASEAN Secretariat of the contact details of its competent authority responsible for granting such approval;
> b. in the case of an incomplete application, identify and notify the applicant in writing within 1 month from the date of receipt of such application of all the additional information that is required;
> c. inform the applicant in writing that the investment has been specifically approved or denied within 4 months

[76] ACIA, *supra* note 65, recital 1.

[77] 1998 Framework Agreement, *supra* note 56, art. 12(1).

[78] *Id.* art. 4(1), n.1.

from the date of receipt of complete application by the competent authority; and

d. in the case an application is denied, inform the applicant in writing of the reasons for such denial. The applicant shall have the opportunity of submitting, at that applicant's discretion, a new application.[79]

Despite the ACIA's intended approximation to GIL through various exterior legal refinements, individual attachment to sovereignty remains. ASEAN states carved out a colossal space for sovereign decisions on the terms by which they may approve investment from their fellow ASEAN members. While the 1998 Framework Agreement is terminated upon the ACIA's entry into force, the former's Temporary Exclusion and Sensitive Lists still remain valid until the ACIA comes up with its own list of reservations.[80] Indeed, the ACIA's scope of liberalization regarding *intra*-ASEAN investment flows has shrunk from that of the 1998 Framework Agreement, which required a member state to "open immediately *all* its industries for investments by ASEAN investors," although subject to certain exemptions.[81] In contrast, the ACIA only provides:

> For the purpose of liberalization and subject to Article 9 (Reservations), this Agreement shall apply to the following sectors:
>
> (a) manufacturing;
> (b) agriculture;
> (c) fishery;

[79] *Id.* Annex 1. [80] ACIA, *supra* note 65, art. 47:2.

[81] 1998 Framework Agreement, *supra* note 56, art. 7(1)(a) (emphasis added).

(d) forestry;
(e) mining and quarrying;
(f) services incidental to manufacturing, agriculture, fishery, forestry, mining and quarrying; and
(g) any other sectors as may be agreed upon by all Member States.[82]

This is a significant backtrack from the earlier scope of liberalization, which brings into question the ACIA's strong integrationist *telos*. First of all, the list mostly covers primary industries, which would make only limited contributions to the ACIA's paramount goal of building an integrated production base within the region.[83] Granted, promoting the connectivity across supply chains via open investment on the manufacturing sector remains vital to ASEAN members.[84] Yet, merely listing manufacturing in such a positive list technique still allows member states to avoid necessary commitments by using the negative list reservation under Article 9.

6.3.2 *Caveats: The Vestige of the "ASEAN Way"*

A close investigation into the content of ASEAN investment treaties soon reveals a recurring mismatch between an official liberalization/integrationist goal and a deep-rooted

[82] ACIA, *supra* note 65, art. 3(3).
[83] UNCTAD, *Global Value Chains and Development: Investment and Value-Added Trade in the Global Economy*, at 6, U.N. Doc. UNCTAD/DIAE/2013/1 (2013).
[84] *Id.*

sovereignty-preserving sentiment. This mismatch also translates into a seemingly irreconcilable tension between conforming to, and departing from, GIL. Any functional or rationalist explanation would be futile in making sense of such a mismatch. Here, a historical account offers greater explanatory and analytical force.

The post-colonial legacy seems insufficient alone to explain the attachment to sovereignty so widely shared among ASEAN member states. Indeed, colonialism was not the sole historical trauma they shared. While colonialism was an external trauma, ASEAN members also suffered an *internal* schism in the 1960s, which has since left an indelible impact on ASEAN's political life. In the period between 1963 and 1966, Indonesia vehemently opposed the annexation of the Federation of Malaya, Singapore, and the crown colony/British protectorates of North Borneo and Sarawak.[85] Indonesia mobilized aggressive diplomacy to prevent the annexation, which eventually escalated into military operations leading to hundreds of casualties in the region.[86]

Shortly after the end of this violent conflict, coined "*Konfrontasi*," the Bangkok Declaration established ASEAN in 1967. Reflecting this trauma, ASEAN's original goal was broadly akin to that of the United Nations, especially the Security Council. It sought to institutionalize security cooperation among the five founding ASEAN members (Indonesia, Malaysia, the Philippines, Thailand, and Singapore) to prevent

[85] *See generally* J.A.C. Mackie, KONFRONTASI: THE INDONESIA – MALAYSIA DISPUTE 1963–6 (1974).

[86] *Id.*

this type of regional conflict. In this regard, the founding members all committed to respect each other's sovereignty and refrain from interfering in internal affairs. This political paradigm has been labeled the "ASEAN Way," which is given legal expression the 1976 Treaty of Amity and Cooperation in Southeast Asia. Article 2 spells out six fundamental principles of the "ASEAN Way," which are respect for sovereignty; freedom from external interference; non-interference in internal affairs; peaceful resolution of disputes; prohibition of the use of force; and cooperation.[87] Likewise, a former Singaporean Foreign Minister, S. Jayakumar, has observed that "the ASEAN Way stresses informality, organization minimalism, inclusiveness, intensive consultations leading to consensus and peaceful resolution of disputes."[88]

Notably, this political ideology has greatly influenced member states' cooperation in the economic sphere, including collective investment regulation. In tandem with such hypersensitivity to sovereignty, enduring tensions have run deep among key member states, which has further complicated collective efforts in economic cooperation. In its earliest manifestations, no ASEAN state was willing to give up its own industrial project that was duplicative to that of another ASEAN member and therefore highly inefficient from a

[87] Treaty of Amity and Cooperation in Southeast Asia art. 2, Feb. 24, 1976, 1025 U.N.T.S. 297.

[88] Amitav Acharya, Constructing a Security Community in Southeast Asia 62 (3rd ed. 2014).

collective perspective.[89] Interestingly, this is a reverse sequence from a conventional neo-functionalist proposition that economic cooperation among states tends to lead to political cooperation, as seen in the experience of European integration.[90] Reflecting the path dependence from the ASEAN Way and related historical experience, investment liberalization commitments throughout the 1987 ASEAN Agreement, the 1998 Framework Agreement, and the 2009 ACIA have always been accompanied by some type of sovereignty-preserving mechanism. In this regard, some scholars make a critical observation that the "ASEAN Way's" penetration into ASEAN's economic sphere has severely impeded collective cooperation in the area,[91] as so clearly evidenced in the form of *intra*-ASEAN investment regulation over the past two decades.

6.4 Panoptic Configuration and a Paradox of "Reverse Open Regionalism"

When we turn to a broader horizon that transcends the internal features of the ASEAN investment rules, there are immediate questions as to whether the choices made by the ASEAN members in the ACIA are likely to give effect to

89 Rodolfo C. Severino, Southeast Asia in Search of an ASEAN Community: Insights from the Former ASEAN Secretary-General 217 (2006).

90 *See* Vinod K. Aggarwal & Jonathan T. Chow, *The Perils of Consensus: How ASEAN's Meta-Regime Undermines Economic and Environmental Cooperation*, 17 Rev. Int'l Pol. Econ. 262, 276 (2010).

91 *Id.*

the critical normative goal of building a competitive and integrated production network within the region. As we have seen, the uncertainty inherent in a key part of the 1998 Framework Agreement has now been resolved. Yet the liberalization obligations in the ACIA apply *only* to questions of *intra*-ASEAN investment flows. Thus, the seemingly ambitious promise in 1998 to construct investment rules within ASEAN that would also extend to FDI from external sources has been jettisoned.

Therefore, ASEAN investment liberalization now proceeds on a dual-track basis with the ACIA only regulating *intra*-ASEAN capital flows, while the question of treatment afforded to external foreign investors remains subject to both treaties entered into by member states individually (including both BITs and investment chapters in preexisting FTAs) and the limited set of regional investment agreements entered into by ASEAN as a grouping with key partners such as China, Australia, and New Zealand, or the growing number of new FTAs concluded by individual ASEAN member states.[92]

Naturally, there is an immediate question as to the rationality of a strategy that allows the individual member states to enter FTAs whose investment provisions may well go beyond the core tenets of the internal ASEAN rules in terms of the degree of both liberalization and investor protection. On a strictly formal legal basis, there is nothing to prevent individual member states from acting in this unilateral fashion. Note that ASEAN is not a customs union and thus is not

92 For a listing of these treaties, see Diane A. Desierto, *Regulatory Freedom and Control in the New ASEAN Regional Investment Treaties*, 16 J. World Inv. & Trade 1018, 1018–24 (2015).

required to negotiate collectively with third-country partners.[93] With that in mind, it is remarkable that ASEAN as a collective grouping has even negotiated *some* third-country FTAs. That said, it still seems paradoxical that the ASEAN member states would easily (in their individual FTAs) go beyond the internal ASEAN *acquis* on investment, given the long development and careful tailoring in those ASEAN rules.

On one view, this paradox is endemic to ASEAN on account of its distinct path-dependency over internal affairs and negative social learning from other countries' adoptions of GIL.[94] Nonetheless, as discussed in Chapter 5, the paradox raises serious policy concerns given the powerful desire among the member states to build a competitive, integrated production base within the ASEAN region. For example, the gap between *intra*-ASEAN and *extra*-ASEAN investment liberalization undermines ASEAN's economic integration represented by the ASEAN Economic Community (AEC). The persistence of the *intra*-ASEAN and *extra*-ASEAN investment gap also prevents ASEAN members from maximizing the development potential of investment liberalization, as is often seen in the "hub-and-spoke" model. Finally, reverse open regionalism, if left unaddressed, will deter ASEAN economies from achieving the "ASEAN Centrality" goal as *intra*-ASEAN investment flows and *extra*-ASEAN investment flows remain separated and uncoordinated.

[93] Marise Cremona et al., ASEAN's External Agreements: Law, Practice and the Quest for Collective Action 23–51 (2015).

[94] *See* Cho & Kurtz, *supra* note 7, at 195; Cho & Kurtz, *supra* note 4, at 343–4.

6.5 Of Human Agency and Soft Law

The degree and orientation of future economic integration within ASEAN, as manifested in the AEC vision, will determine ASEAN's successful participation in global value chains.[95] Asian production networks exhibit more sophisticated and expansive webs of transactions between firms across the globe in comparison with those in North America and Europe.[96] This delicate configuration in Asia offers the ASEAN members a unique strategic advantage in their connectivity with both global producers and global consumers. But it also comes with a structural challenge. ASEAN members will need to engage more deeply in investment liberalization so as to form a "rim" that can integrate their local economies and allow for further and deeper penetration into global value chains. As seen in many African countries, the failure to upgrade industrial capacity in this manner has left them as "captive participants" in global value chains, forcing them to focus on low-value tasks or commodity exports.[97] Local integration and the resultant upgrading of industrial platforms is an imperative stepping stone for effective participation into global value chains. To fully harness the vast development potential of global value chains, ASEAN

[95] OECD, *Making Global Value Chains Work for ASEAN* (June 13, 2016), www.oecd.org/trade/events/making-global-value-chains-work-for-asean-13-june-2016.htm.

[96] *See* Mitsuyo Ando & Fukunari Kimura, *Fragmentation in East Asia: Further Evidence*, 20 Econ. Research Inst. for ASEAN and East Asia (2009).

[97] UNCTAD, *supra* note 83, at 77.

members must tackle the reverse open regionalism paradox by closing the gap between *intra*-ASEAN and *extra*-ASEAN investment liberalization. This mission necessitates revisiting ACIA as the current *intra*-ASEAN investment regime.

How then could ACIA be adapted in a way which might solve the reverse open regionalism paradox and thus conform to the grand vision of the AEC? One might be tempted to have recourse to conventional legal instruments such as treaty amendment.[98] However, reverting to binding legal avenues is not a viable option considering the "delegalized" nature, deeply entrenched in ACIA, which exhibits a number of reservations and exemptions despite its ostensibly legalized and evolved format in comparison to its precursors.[99] This delegalization undercurrent can be explained by a combination of factors, ranging from ASEAN's unique history to the vast economic, cultural, and political diversity among its members.[100] A better and more sustainable

98 The ACIA's general level of legalization can be said to be relatively low, given a number of exemptions in legal obligations. *See* Cho & Kurtz, *supra* note 2. *See also* Kenneth W. Abbott et al., *The Concept of Legalization*, *in* LEGALIZATION AND WORLD POLITICS (Judith L. Goldstein et al. eds., 2001). Regarding a position in favor of legally binding commitments for an enhanced level of economic integration in ASEAN, *see* Paul J. Davidson, *The ASEAN Way and the Role of Law in ASEAN Economic Cooperation*, 8 SING. Y. B. INT'L L. 165 (2004).

99 *See generally* Cho & Kurtz, *supra* note 2.

100 *Id. Cf.* Karen J. Alter & Laurence R. Helfer, TRANSPLANTING INTERNATIONAL COURTS: THE LAW AND POLITICS OF THE ANDEAN TRIBUNAL OF JUSTICE 277 (2017) (aptly observing that one "should look for evidence of judicial influence beyond case-specific compliance"). *See also* Luke Nottage & Sakda Thanitcul, *An Introduction, Special Issue:*

pathway to tackle the paradox is to draw on the "ASEAN Way," including human agency and the power of soft law.[101]

Critics tend to dismiss soft law as inherently limited, producing only shallow results due to its lack of binding force. This myopic view is misguided. A plethora of literature has explored soft law's unique role, both as supplementary and alternative to hard law (treaties), in inducing cooperative behavior from states.[102] As many have already been witnessed in the APEC experience,[103] soft law governance appears to be well received in the ASEAN/East Asian region.[104] Moreover,

International Investment Arbitration in Southeast Asia, 18 J. World Investment & Trade 767, 780 (2017) (observing that ASEAN treaties contain many legal mechanisms to preserve "regulatory space" of host countries).

101 *See* Iwan J. Azis, *Integration, Contagion, and Income Distribution, in* Regional Science Matters 131 (Peter Nijkamp et al. eds., 2014). *See also* Elodie Sellier, *The ASEAN Economic Community: The Force Awakens?*, The Diplomat (Jan. 12, 2016).

102 *See* Commitment and Compliance: The Role of Non-Binding Norms in International Legal System (Dinah Shelton ed., 2000) (observing that soft law mostly plays a supplementary role to treaties); Gregory C. Shaffer and Mark A. Pollack, *Hard vs. Soft Law: Alternatives, Complements, and Antagonists in International Governance*, 94 Minn. L. Rev. 706 (2010) (spotlighting an "antagonistic" relationship between soft law and hard law in international governance).

103 *See generally* Sungjoon Cho, *Rethinking APEC: A New Experiment for a Post-Modern Institutional Arrangement, in* WTO and East Asia 381 (Mitsuo Matushita & Dukgeun Ahn eds., 2004).

104 *See* Damian Chalmers & Julia Slupska, *The Governance of Regional Markets and Globalisation*, Paper Presented at the Regional Organizations and Regional Integration Workshop held at the National University of Singapore, 7–8 August 2017, at 29 (2017). *See also* ASEAN Secretariat, *ASEAN Economic Community 2015 – Progress and Key*

solid and effective government networks that already exist among working-level government officials of ASEAN members can play a critical role in mobilizing concerted efforts from ASEAN members toward voluntary liberalization in *intra*-ASEAN investment flows.[105] For example, ASEAN leaders can empower the "Coordinating Committee on Investment" (CCI) under the ASEAN Investment Area (AIA) Council,[106] comprised of senior government officials, by throwing their political support behind the Committee's recommendations in pertinent areas. Furthermore, given the increasing importance of public–private partnership in managing the connectivity of global value chains, the CCI must collaborate with private sector agencies (such as the "ASEAN Business & Investment Summit" under the auspices of the "ASEAN Business Advisory Council"[107]) in identifying

Achievement: A Blueprint for Growth, at 9 (2015), https://asean.org/wp-content/uploads/2021/09/1.-AEC-2015-Progress-and-Key-Achievements_04.11.2015.pdf; David Capie, *Explaining ASEAN's Resilience, Institutions, Path Dependency, and Asia's Emerging Architecture, in* ASEAN AND THE INSTITUTIONALIZATION OF EAST ASIA 168 (Ralf Emmers ed., 2012) (observing that the resilience of "soft institutionalism" in the ASEAN region has been empirically proven).

105 *Cf.* Luu Huong Ly, *Regional Harmonization of Competition Law and Policy: An ASEAN Approach,* 2 ASIAN J. INT'L L. 291 (2012) (discussing the soft law approach to the harmonization of competition law in the ASEAN region).

106 ASEAN, *ASEAN Investment Area (AIA) Council,* https://asean.org/asean-economic-community/asean-investment-area-aia-council/.

107 *See, e.g.,* Media Release, Malaysia Hosts World Leaders at ASEAN Business and Investment Summit 2015 (Nov. 21, 2015), http://aseanbac.com.my/2015/11/21/malaysia-host-world-leaders-at-asean-business-and-investment-summit-2015/.

priority points of liberalization and formulating workable programs to achieve those goals. Indeed, it has been an established tradition in the ASEAN that businesses rely on various levels of discretion vested in government officials, rather than turning to formal rules, in addressing particular non-tariff barriers.[108]

In closing, the challenge of redressing the paradox of reverse open regionalism is imperative to entrenching ASEAN's evolution from a mere Factory ASEAN to a more mature form of market integration.[109] Closing the gap between *intra*-ASEAN and *extra*-ASEAN investment liberalization will engender a dialectic relationship between these two dimensions of liberalization as envisioned in the launching of the AEC. Considering ASEAN's unique sociocultural characteristics, adequate mobilization of human agency through ASEAN government networks, rather than relying on a formal treaty-making process, is key to fulfilling this strategic vision.

108 Michael Ewing-Chow, *ASEAN Integration, the Rule of Law, and Investment Agreements*, 107 Am. Socy. Intl. L. Proc. 284, 284–5 (2013).

109 Michael Ewing-Chow & Tan Hsien-Li, *The Role of the Rule of Law in ASEAN Integration* 20, EUI Working Paper RSCAS 2013/16 (2013). *See also* Alan Boyd, *ASEAN Shines Bright in Foreign Investor Surveys*, Asia Times (Sept. 22, 2017).

BIBLIOGRAPHY

Abbott, Frederick M., *NAFTA and the Legalization of World Politics: A Case Study*, *in* LEGALIZATION AND WORLD POLITICS 13 (Judith L. Goldstein, Miles Kahler, Robert O. Keohane & Anne-Marie Slaughter eds., 2001).

Abbott, Kenneth W. & Duncan Snidal, *Hard and Soft Law in International Governance*, *in* LEGALIZATION AND WORLD POLITICS 37 (Judith L. Goldstein, Miles Kahler, Robert O. Keohane & Anne-Marie Slaughter eds., 2001).

Abbott, Kenneth W. & Gregory W. Bowman, *Economic Integration for the Asian Century: An Early Look at New Approaches*, 4 TRANSNAT'L L. & CONTEMP. PROBS. 187 (1994).

Abbott, Kenneth W., Robert O. Keohane, Andrew Moravcsik, Anne-Marie Slaughter & Duncan Snidal, *The Concept of Legalization*, *in* LEGALIZATION AND WORLD POLITICS 17 (Judith L. Goldstein, Miles Kahler, Robert O. Keohane & Anne-Marie Slaughter eds., 2001).

Acharya, Amitav, *Regional Institutions and Asian Security Order: Norms, Power, and Prospects for Peaceful Change*, *in* ASIAN SECURITY ORDER: INSTRUMENTAL AND NORMATIVE FEATURES 211 (Muthiah Alagappa ed., 2003).

How Ideas Spread: Whose Norms Matter? Norm Localization and Institutional Change in Asian Regionalism, 58 INT'L ORG. 239 (2004).

The Emerging Regional Architecture of World Politics, 59 WORLD POL. 629 (2007).

Foundations of Collective Action in Asia: Theory and Practice of Regional Cooperation (Asian Dev. Bank Institute Working Paper Series, No. 344, 2012).

Constructing a Security Community in South East Asia: ASEAN and the Problem of Regional Order. (3rd ed. 2014).

Aggarwal, Vinod K., Liberal Protectionism (1985).

Aggarwal, Vinod K. & Jonathan T. Chow, *The Perils of Consensus: How ASEAN's Meta-Regime Undermines Economic and Environmental Cooperation*, 17 Rev. Int'l Pol. Econ. 262 (2010).

Albert, Stuart & David A. Whetten, *Organizational Identity, in* 7 Research in Organizational Behavior 265 (Larry L. Cummings & Barry M. Staw eds., 1985).

Aldrich, Howard E., Organizations and Environments (1979).

Alford, William P., *Tasselled Loafers for Barefoot Lawyers: Transformation and Tension in the World of Chinese Legal Workers*, 144 China Q. 22 (1995).

What Law?: Why Western Scholars of Chinese History and Society Have Not Had More to Say about Its Law, 23 Mod. China 398 (1997).

Exporting the "Pursuit of Happiness," 113 Harv. L. Rev. 1677 (2000).

Allee, Todd & Clint Peinhardt, *Contingent Credibility: The Impact of Investment Treaty Violations on Foreign Direct Investment*, 63 Int. Org. 401 (2011).

Alon, Ilan & Edmund Kellerman, *Internal Antecedents to the 1997 Asian Economic Crisis*, 7 Multinational Bus. Rev. 1 (1999).

Alter, Karen J., *Resolving or Exacerbating Disputes?: The WTO's New Dispute Resolution System*, 79 Int'l Aff. 783 (2003).

Alter, Karen J. & Laurence R. Helfer, TRANSPLANTING INTERNATIONAL COURTS: THE LAW AND POLITICS OF THE ANDEAN TRIBUNAL OF JUSTICE (2017).

Alter, Karen J. & Liesbet Hooghe, *Regional Dispute Settlement, in* THE OXFORD HANDBOOK OF COMPARATIVE REGIONALISM (Tanja Börzel & Thomas Risse eds., 2016).

Alvarez, José, *How Not to Link: Institutional Conundrums of an Expanded Trade Regime,* 7 Widener L. Symp. J. 1 (2001).

Instituted Legalization and the Asia-Pacific "Region," 5 N.Z. J. PUB. & INT'L L. 15 (2007).

The Once and Future Foreign Investment Regime, in LOOKING TO THE FUTURE: ESSAYS ON INTERNATIONAL LAW IN HONOR OF W. MICHAEL REISMAN 15 (Mahnoush H. Arasanjani et al. eds., 2010).

Amerasinghe, Chittharanjan Felix, STATE RESPONSIBILITY FOR INJURIES TO ALIENS (1967).

American Society of International Law, LEGALIZATION OF INTERNATIONAL RELATIONS/INTERNATIONALIZATION OF INTERNATIONAL LAW, PROCEEDINGS OF THE 96TH ANNUAL MEETING (2002).

Amsden, Alice, ASIA'S NEXT GIANT: SOUTH KOREA AND LATER INDUSTRIALIZATION (1989).

Anderson, Benedict R. O'G., *The Idea of Power in Javanese Culture, in* CULTURE AND POLITICS IN INDONESIA 1 (Claire Holt ed., 1972).

Anderson, Kenneth, *Squaring the Circle? Reconciling Sovereignty and Global Governance through Global Government Networks,* 118 HARV. L. REV. 1255 (2005).

Anderson, Kym & Richard Snape, *European and American Regionalism: Effects on and Options for Asia,* 8 J. JAPANESE & INT'L ECON. 454 (1994).

Ando, Mitsuyo & Fukunari Kimura, *Fragmentation in East Asia: Further Evidence*, 20 ECON. RESEARCH INST. FOR ASEAN AND EAST ASIA (2009), https://www.eria.org/ERIA-DP-2009-20.pdf.

Asia Pacific Economic Cooperation (APEC), *Annex – Early Voluntary Sectoral Liberalization* (Vancouver, Canada, Nov. 21, 1997), www.apec.org/Meeting-Papers/Annual-Ministerial-Meetings/1997/1997_amm/annex.

Armstrong, Shiro (ed.), THE POLITICS AND ECONOMICS OF INTEGRATION IN ASIA AND THE PACIFIC (2011).

ASEAN, *ASEAN Economic Community Blueprint* (Jan. 2008) www.asean.org/wp-content/uploads/images/archive/5187-10.pdf.

ASEAN Economic Community Blueprint 2025 (Nov. 2015) www.asean.org/wp-content/uploads/2012/05/8.-March-2016-ASCC-Blueprint-2025.pdf.

Joint Leaders' Statement on the Negotiations for the Regional Comprehensive Economic Partnership (RCEP) (Nov. 14, 2018), https://asean.org/asean2020/wp-content/uploads/2021/02/18.-RCEP-Summit-2_Joint-Leaders-Statement_FINAL2.pdf.

ASEAN Secretariat, *ASEAN Economic Community Scorecard* (Mar. 2010), https://asean.org/wp-content/uploads/2021/09/AEC-Scorecard.pdf.

ASEAN Economic Community 2015 – Progress and Key Achievement: A Blueprint for Growth (2015), https://asean.org/wp-content/uploads/2021/09/1.-AEC-2015-Progress-and-Key-Achievements_04.11.2015.pdf.

ASEAN Secretariat & UNCTAD, *ASEAN Investment Report 2015* (Nov. 2015), https://perma.cc/W7YR-KJTB.

ASEAN Investment Report 2020-2021: Investing in Industry 4.0 (Sept. 2021), https://asean.org/wp-content/uploads/2021/09/AIR-2020-2021.pdf.

Asian Development Bank, *Asian Development Outlook 2014 Update: Asia in Global Value Chains* (2014) www.adb.org/publications/asian-development-outlook-2014-update-asia-global-value-chains.

The ASEAN Economic Integration Report 2021: Making Digital Platform Work for Asia and the Pacific (Feb. 4, 2021).

Azis, Iwan J., *Integration, Contagion, and Income Distribution*, *in* REGIONAL SCIENCE MATTERS (Peter Nijkamp et al. eds., 2014).

Babb, Sarah & Ariel Buira, *Mission Creep, Mission Push and Discretion in Sociological Perspective: The Case of IMF Conditionality* (Mar. 9, 2004), http://web.archive.org/web/20070719172319/http://www.g24.org/012gva04.pdf.

Baldwin, Richard, *The Spoke Trap: Hub-and-Spoke Bilateralism in East Asia* 3, NCCR TRADE WORKING PAPER NO. 2009/28 (2009).

THE GREAT CONVERGENCE: INFORMATION TECHNOLOGY AND THE NEW GLOBALIZATION (2016).

Baldwin, Richard & Javier Lopez-Gonzalez, *Supply-Chain Trade: A Portrait of Global Patterns and Several Testable Hypotheses*, 38 WORLD ECON. 1682 (2015).

Ballor, Grace A. & Aydin B. Yildirim, *Multinational Corporations and the Politics of International Trade in Multidisciplinary Perspective*, 22 BUS. & POL. 573 (2020).

Bandura, Albert, SOCIAL LEARNING THEORY (1977).

Barnett, Michael N. & Martha Finnemore, *The Politics, Power, and Pathologies of International Organizations*, 53 INT'L ORG. 699 (1999).

Basu Das, Sanchita, *Mind the Gap: Explaining Implementation Shortfalls in the ASEAN Economic Community* (ISEAS Econ., Working Paper No. 2017-7, 2017), www.iseas.edu.sg/images/pdf/ISEAS%20EWP%202017-07%20Sanchita.pdf.

Beeson, Mark, *What Does China's Rise Mean for the Developmental State Paradigm*, *in* ASIA AFTER DEVELOPMENTAL STATE: DISEMBEDDING AUTONOMY 192 (Toby Caroll & Darryl S. L. Jarvis eds., 2017).

Beeson, Mark & Richard Stubbs (eds.), ROUTLEDGE HANDBOOK OF ASIAN REGIONALISM (2012).

Benvenisti, Eyal, *Democracy Captured: The Mega-Regional Agreements and the Future of Global Public Law*, 23 (1) CONSTELLATIONS 58 (2016).

Berger, Axel, Matthias Busse, Peter Nunnenkamp & Martin Roy, *Do Trade and Investment Agreements Lead to More FDI? Accounting for Key Provisions Inside the Black Box*, 10 INT'L ECON. & ECON. POLICY 247 (2013).

Berger, Peter L. & Thomas Luckmann, THE SOCIAL CONSTRUCTION OF REALITY: A TREATISE IN THE SOCIOLOGY OF KNOWLEDGE (1966).

Berman, Paul, *From International Law to Law and Globalization*, 43 COLUM. J. TRANSNAT'L L. 485 (2005).

Best, Jacqueline, *Bringing Power Back In: The IMF's Constructivist Strategy in Critical Perspective*, *in* CONSTRUCTING THE INTERNATIONAL ECONOMY 203 (Rawi E. Abdelal et al. eds., 2010).

Boesche, Roger, THE FIRST GREAT POLITICAL REALIST: KAUTILYA AND HIS ARTHASASTRA (2002).

Boli, John & George M. Thomas, WORLD POLITY FORMATION SINCE 1875: WORLD CULTURE AND INTERNATIONAL NON-GOVERNMENTAL ORGANIZATIONS (1997).

Bonnitcha, Jonathan, Lauge N. Skovgaard Poulsen & Michael Waibel, THE POLITICAL ECONOMY OF THE INVESTMENT TREATY REGIME (2017).

Börzel, Tanja & Thomas Risse, *When Europe Hits Home: Europeanization and Domestic Change*, 4 EUR. INTEGRATION ONLINE PAPERS (2000), https://cadmus.eui.eu/handle/1814/1696.

Bowie, Nile, *Singapore Slings a Trade War Antidote*, ASIA TIMES (Aug. 8, 2019).

Boyce, Peter, *The Machinery of Southeast Asian Regional Diplomacy*, in NEW DIRECTIONS IN THE INTERNATIONAL RELATIONS OF SOUTHEAST ASIA: GLOBAL POWERS AND SOUTHEAST ASIA 175 (1973).

Boyd, Alan, *ASEAN Shines Bright in Foreign Investor Surveys*, ASIA TIMES (Sept. 22, 2017).

Brennan, Louis & Philomena Murray (eds.), DRIVERS OF INTEGRATION AND REGIONALISM IN EUROPE AND ASIA (2015).

Brewer, Thomas L. & Stephen Young, THE MULTILATERAL INVESTMENT SYSTEM AND MULTINATIONAL ENTERPRISES (1998).

Bromley, Dennis, *Relationships between Personal and Corporate Reputation*, 35 EUR. J. MARKETING 316 (2001).

Brown, Andrew D. & Ken Starkey, *Organizational Identity and Learning: A Psychodynamic Perspective*, 25 ACAD. MGMT. REV. 102 (2000).

Brütsch, Christian & Dirk Lehmkuhl, LAW AND LEGALIZATION IN TRANSNATIONAL RELATIONS (2007).

Buckley, Walter, SOCIOLOGY AND MODERN SYSTEMS THEORY (1967).

Capie, David, *Explaining ASEAN's Resilience, Institutions, Path Dependency, and Asia's Emerging Architecture, in* ASEAN AND THE INSTITUTIONALIZATION OF EAST ASIA 168 (Ralf Emmers ed., 2012).

Carroll, Toby & Darryl S. L. Jarvis, *Disembedding Autonomy: Asia after the Developmental State, in* ASIA AFTER DEVELOPMENTAL STATE: DISEMBEDDING AUTONOMY 7 (Toby Caroll & Darryl S. L. Jarvis eds., 2017).

Carruthers, Robin, et al., *Trade and Logistics: An East Asian Perspective, in* EAST ASIA INTEGRATES: A TRADE POLICY AGENDA FOR SHARED GROWTH 90 (Kathie Krumm et al. eds., 2004).

Cecil Abraham, Dato *State Approval in South East Asian Bilateral Investment Treaties*, *in* INVESTOR-STATE ARBITRATION: LESSONS FOR ASIA 123 (Michael J. Moser ed., 2008).

Chaisse, Julien, *The ACIA: Much More than a BIT of Protection for Foreign Investors*, *in* ASEAN LAW IN THE NEW REGIONAL ECONOMIC ORDER: GLOBAL TRENDS AND SHIFTING PARADIGMS 232 (Pasha Hsieh & Bryan Mercurio eds., 2019).

Chaisse, Julien & Sufian Jusoh, THE ASEAN COMPREHENSIVE INVESTMENT AGREEMENT: THE REGIONALIZATION OF LAWS AND POLICY ON FOREIGN INVESTMENT (2016).

Chalmers, Damien & Julia Slupska, *The Governance of Regional Markets and Globalisation*, Paper Presented at the Regional Organizations and Regional Integration Workshop held at the National University of Singapore, 7–8 August 2017 (2017).

The Regional Remaking of Trade and Investment Law, 30 (1) EUR. J. INT'L L. 169 (2019).

Chase-Dunn, Christopher, GLOBAL FORMATION: STRUCTURES OF THE WORLD ECONOMY (1989).

Chen, Lurong & Philippe De Lombaerde, *ASEAN between Globalization and Regionalization*, 25 ASIA PAC. BUS. REV. 729 (2019).

Cherney, Mike, *Firms Want to Adjust Supply Chains Post-Pandemic, but Changes Take Time*, WALL ST. J. (Dec. 27, 2020).

Chesterman, Simon, FROM COMMUNITY TO COMPLIANCE: THE EVOLUTION OF MONITORING OBLIGATIONS IN ASEAN (2015).

Asia's Ambivalence about International Law & Institutions: Past, Present and Futures, 27 EUR. J. INT'L L. 945 (2016).

Chew, Lee Kim, *ASEAN Unity Showing Signs of Fraying*, STRAIT TIMES (July 23, 1998).

Chia, Siow Yue, Presentation Delivered at the ASEAN Academy: Overview of AEC Progress and Evaluating AEC Blueprint 2025 (Aug. 16, 2019) (on file with author).

Chimni, B.S., *Capitalism, Imperialism, and International Law in the Twenty-First Century*, 14 Or. Rev. Int'l L. 17 (2012).

Cho, Sungjoon, Free Markets and Social Regulation: A Reform Agenda of the Global Trading System (2003).

Rethinking APEC: A New Experiment for a Post-Modern Institutional Arrangement, *in* WTO and East Asia: New Perspectives 381 (Mitsuo Matsushita & Dukgeun Ahn eds., 2004).

Defragmenting World Trade, 27 Nw. J. I'nt'l L. & Bus. 39 (2006).

Beyond Rationality: A Sociological Construction of the World Trade Organization, 52 Va. J. Int'l L. 321 (2012).

An International Organization's Identity Crisis, 34 Nw. J. Int'l L. & Bus. 359 (2014).

The Social Foundations of World Trade: Norms, Community and Constitution (2014).

Cho, Sungjoon & Claire R. Kelly, *Promises and Perils of New Global Governance: A Case of the G20*, 12 Chi. J. Int'l L. 491 (2012).

Cho, Sungjoon & Jürgen Kurtz, *The Limits of Isomorphism: Global Investment Law and the ASEAN Investment Regime*, 17 Chi. J. Int'l L. 341 (2016).

International Cooperation and Organizational Identities: The Evolution of the ASEAN Investment Regime, 36 Nw. J. Int'l L. & Bus. 173 (2017).

Legalizing the ASEAN Way: Adapting and Reimagining the ASEAN Investment Regime, 66 Am. J. Comp. L. 233 (2018).

Chua, Amy, World on Fire: How Exporting Free Market Democracy Breeds Ethnic Hatred and Global Instability (2003).

Clague, Christopher, et al., *Institutions and Economic Performance: Property Rights and Contract Enforcement*, *in* Institutions and Economic Development: Growth and

Governance in Less-Developed and Post-Socialist Countries 67 (Christopher Clague ed., 1997).

et al., *Contract-Intensive Money*, 4 J. Econ. Growth 185 (1999).

Cockerham, Geoffrey B., *Regional Integration in ASEAN: Institutional Design and the ASEAN Way*, 27 E. Asia 165 (2010).

Collins, Alan, *Functional Cooperation and ASEAN Institutionalism: Responding to HIV/AIDS*, *in* ASEAN and the Institutionalization of East Asia 43 (Ralf Emmers ed., 2012).

Commission on Global Governance, *Our Global Neighborhood: The Report of the Commission on Global Governance* (1995) www.gdrc.org/u-gov/global-neighbourhood/.

Cover, Robert M., *Nomos and Narrative*, 97 Harv. L. Rev. 4 (1982).

Cremona, Marise, et al., ASEAN'S External Agreements: Law, Practice and the Quest for Collective Action (2015).

Daly, Eoin, et al., *Reimagining Emerging ASEAN in the Wake of COVID-19*, McKinsey & Co. (Aug. 2020).

Dam, Kenneth W., The Law–Growth Nexus: The Rule of Law and Economic Development (2006).

Davidson, Paul J., *The ASEAN Way and the Role of Law in ASEAN Economic Cooperation*, 8 Sing. Y. B. Int'l L. 165 (2004).

The Role of Soft Law in the Governance of International Economic Relations in Asia, 24 Chinese (Taiwan) Y.B. Int'l L. & Aff. 1 (2006).

Davis, Kevin E., *What Can the Rule of Law Variables Tell Us about Rule of Law Reforms*, 26 Mich. J. Int'l L. 141 (2004).

Davis, Kevin E. & Michael J. Trebilcock, *The Relationship between Law and Development: Optimists v. Skeptics*, 56 Am. J. Comp. L. 895 (2008).

Davis, Kevin E., et al., *Indicators as a Technology of Global Governance*, 46 Law & Soc'y Rev. 71 (2012).

Deinla, Imelda, The Development of the Rule of Law in ASEAN: The State and Regional Integration (2017).

Desierto, Diane A., *Investment Treaties: ASEAN, in* Asia Rising: Growth and Resilience in an Uncertain Global Economy 184 (Hal Hill & Maria Socorro Gochoco-Bautista eds., 2012).

Investment Treaties: ASEAN, in Asia Rising: Growth and Resilience in an Uncertain Global Economy 184 (Hal Hill & Maria Socorro Gochoco-Bautista eds., 2013).

Regulatory Freedom and Control in the New ASEAN Regional Investment Treaties, 16 J. World Inv. & Trade 1018 (2015).

ASEAN Investment Treaties, RCEP, and CPTPP: Regional Strengths, Norms, Institutions, and Politics, 25 Wash. Int'l L. J. 349 (2018).

Devonshire-Ellis, Chris, *How US Businesses Can Access the East Asian US$25 Trillion RCEP Free Trade Market Agreement via Existing Agreements*, ASEAN Briefing (July 30, 2021) www.aseanbriefing.com/news/how-us-businesses-can-access-the-east-asian-us25-trillion-rcep-free-trade-market-agreement-via-existing-agreements/.

DiMaggio, Paul J. & Walter W. Powell, *The Iron Cage Revisited: Institutional Isomorphism and Collective Rationality in Organizational Fields*, 48 Am. Soc. Rev. 147 (1983).

Djankov, Simeon, et al., *Courts: The Lex Mundi Project*, Nat'l Bureau of Econ. Research Working Paper No. 8890 (2002) www.nber.org/papers/w8890.

Domke, Martin, *Indonesian Nationalization Measures before Foreign Courts*, 54 Am. J. Int'l L. 305 (1960).

Dosch, Jorn, *ASEAN's Reluctant Liberal Turn and the Thorny Road to Democracy Promotion*, 21 The Pac. Rev. 527 (2008).

Douglas, Zachary, The International Law of Investment Claims (2009).

Dowdle, Michael W., *Heretical Laments: China and the Fallacies of "Rule of Law,"* 11 CULTURAL DYNAMICS 287 (1999).

Einhorn, Jessica, *The World Bank's Mission Creep*, 80 FOREIGN AFF. 22 (2001).

Elkins, Zachary, Andrew Guzman & Beth Simmons, *Competing for Capital: The Diffusion of Bilateral Investment Treaties, 1960–2000*, 60 INTERNATIONAL ORGANIZATION 811 (2006).

Elliott, Robert J. R. & Kengo Ikemoto, *AFTA and the Asian Crisis: Help or Hindrance to ASEAN Intra-Regional Trade?*, 18 ASIAN ECON. J. 1 (2004).

Elm, Deborah, *Using RCEP: Creating Products for Asia*, ASIA TRADE CTR.: TALKING TRADE (Dec. 4, 2019), http://asiantradecentre.org/talkingtrade/using-rcep-creating-products-for-asia.

Emmers, Ralph, *Southeast Asia's New Security Institutions*, *in* ASIA'S NEW INSTITUTIONAL ARCHITECTURE: EVOLVING STRUCTURES FOR MANAGING TRADE, FINANCIAL, AND SECURITY RELATIONS 201 (Vinod K. Aggarwal & Min Gyo Koo eds., 2008).

Erikson, Erik H., CHILDHOOD AND SOCIETY, 156–65 (1950).

IDENTITY, YOUTH AND CRISIS (1968).

European Commission, *Communication from the Commission to the Council, the European Parliament, the European Economic and Social Committee and the Committee of Regions; Towards a Comprehensive European International Investment Policy*, COM (2010) 343 final (July 7, 2010).

Ewing-Chow, Michael, *ASEAN Integration, the Rule of Law, and Investment Agreements*, 107 AM. SOC'Y INT'L L. PROC. 284 (2013).

Ewing-Chow, Michael & Junianto James Losari, *The RCEP Investment Chapter: A State-to-State WTO Style System For Now*, KLUWER ARBITRATION BLOG (Dec. 8, 2020), http://arbitrationblog.kluwerarbitration.com/2020/12/08/the-rcep-investment-chapter-a-state-to-state-wto-style-system-for-now/.

Ewing-Chow, Michael & Hsien-Li Tan, *The Role of the Rule of Law in ASEAN Integration*, EUI Working Paper RSCAS 2013/16 (2013).

Evans, Paul M., *Regional Institutions, Regional Identities*, *in* Eastern Asia: An Introductory History 451 (Colin Mackerras ed., 3rd ed. 2000).

Fastenrath, Ulrich, *Relative Normativity in International Law*, 4 Eur. J. Int'l L. 305 (1993).

Feinerman, James V., *The Rule of Law Imposed from Outside: China's Foreign-Oriented Legal Regime since 1978*, *in* The Limits of the Rule of Law in China 305 (Karen G. Turner et al. eds., 2015).

Finger, Matthias & Bérangère Ruchat, *The Transformation of International Public Organizations: The Case of UNCTAD* (Institut de Hautes Etudes en Administration Publique, Working Paper No. 14/2000, 2000).

Finnemore, Martha, National Interests in International Society 128 (1996).

Norms, Culture, and World Politics: Insights from Sociology's Institutionalism, 50 Int'l Org. 325 (1996).

Fischer, Thomas C., *A Commentary on Regional Institutions in the Pacific Rim: Do APEC and ASEAN Still Matter?*, 13 Duke J. Comp. & Int'l L. 337 (2003).

Freeman, Jody, *The Private Role in Public Governance*, 75 N.Y.U. L. Rev. 543 (2000).

Friedman, Lawrence M., The Republic of Choice: Law, Authority and Culture (1990).

Garcia, Frank, *NAFTA and the Creation of the FTAA: A Critique of Piecemeal Accession*, 35 Va. J.'nt'l. L. 539 (1995).

Gathii, James Thuro, *The Neoliberal Turn in Regional Trade Agreements*, 86 Wash. L. Rev. 421 (2011).

Geertz, Clifford, Local Knowledge: Further Essays in Interpretive Anthropology (1983).

Gewirtz, Paul, *The U.S.—China Rule of Law Initiative*, 11 WM. & MARY BILL RTS. J. 603 (2003).

Gibson, James L., *A Sober Second Thought: An Experiment in Persuading Russians to Tolerate*, 42 AM. J. POL. SCI. 819 (1998).

Gilpin, Robert, GLOBAL POLITICAL ECONOMY: UNDERSTANDING THE INTERNATIONAL ECONOMIC ORDER (2001).

Ginsberg, Tom, *The State of Sovereignty in Southeast Asia*, 99 AM. SOC'Y INT'L L. PROC. 419 (2005).

Eastphalia and Asian Regionalism, 44 U.C. DAVIS L. REV. 859 (2011).

Gioia, Dennis A. et al., *Organizational Identity, Image, and Adaptive Instability*, 25 ACAD. MGMT. REV. 63 (2000).

Goh, Gillian, *The "ASEAN" Way: Non-Intervention and ASEAN's Role in Conflict Management*, 3 STAN. J. EAST ASIAN AFF. 113 (2003).

Gold, Joseph, *Strengthening the Soft International Law of Exchange Arrangements*, 77 AM. J.'NT'L L. 443 (1983).

Goldsmith, Jack L. & Eric A. Posner, THE LIMITS OF INTERNATIONAL LAW (2005).

Goldstein, Judith & Robert O. Keohane, *Ideas and Foreign Policy: An Analytical Framework*, in IDEAS AND FOREIGN POLICY: BELIEFS, INSTITUTIONS, AND POLITICAL CHANGE 3 (Judith Goldstein & Robert O. Keohane eds., 1993).

Gómez-Palacio, Ignacio & Peter Muchlinski, *Admission and Establishment*, *in* THE OXFORD HANDBOOK OF INTERNATIONAL INVESTMENT LAW 243 (Peter Muchlinski, Federico Ortino & Christoph Schreuer eds., 2008).

Gorb, Peter, *The Psychology of Corporate Identity*, 10 EUR. MGMT. J. 310 (1992).

Gouldner, Alvin W., *Organizational Analysis*, *in* SOCIOLOGY TODAY 404 (Robert K. Merton et al. eds., 1959).

Grandori, Anna, *Notes on the Use of Power and Efficiency Constructs in the Economics and Sociology of Organizations*, *in* INTERDISCIPLINARY PERSPECTIVES ON ORGANIZATION STUDIES 61 (Siegwart M. Lindenberg & Hein Schreuder eds., 1993).

Gray, Alistair, *US Retailers Accelerate Shift away from Chinese Suppliers*, FIN. TIMES (Sept. 10, 2019).

Gray, Julia, *How International Organizations Survive* (unpublished manuscript) (on file with author).

Green, Carl J., *APEC and Trans-Pacific Dispute Management*, 26 LAW & POL'Y INT'L BUS. 719 (1995).

Guha Roy, S.N., *Is the Law of Responsibility of States for Injuries to Aliens a Part of Universal International Law?* 55 AM. J. INT'L L. 866 (1961).

Guzman, Andrew T., HOW INTERNATIONAL LAW WORKS: A RATIONAL CHOICE THEORY (2008).

Haacke, Jürgen, ASEAN'S DIPLOMATIC AND SECURITY CULTURE: ORIGINS, DEVELOPMENT AND PROSPECTS (2003).

"Enhanced Interaction" with Myanmar and the Project of a Security Community: Is ASEAN Refining or Breaking with Its Diplomatic and Security Culture?, 27 CONTEMP. SE. ASIA 188 (2005).

Halliday, Terence C. & Pavel Osinsky, *Globalization of Law*, 32 ANN. REV. SOC. 447 (2006).

Harding, Harry, *International Order and Organization in the Asia-Pacific Region*, *in* EAST ASIA IN TRANSITION: TOWARD A NEW REGIONAL ORDER 325 (Robert S. Ross ed., 1995).

Harding, Robin & John Reed, *Asia-Pacific Countries Sign One of the Largest Free Trade Deals in History*, FIN. TIMES (Nov. 15, 2020).

Harding, Robin, et al., *Asian Trade Deal Set to Be Signed after Years of Negotiations*, FIN. TIMES (Nov. 11, 2020).

Haswidi, Andi, *ASEAN Governments Out of Step on Free Trade*, FIN. TIMES (Feb. 12, 2019).

Helfer, Laurence R., *Understanding Change in International Organizations: Globalization and Innovation in the ILO*, 59 VAND. L. REV. 662 (2006).

Higgott, Richard, *Ideas, Policy Networks and Policy Coordination in the Asia Pacific*, 7 PAC. REV. 397 (1994).

De facto or De Jure Regionalism: The Double Discourse of Regionalisation in the Asia Pacific, 11 GLOBAL SOC'Y 166 (1997).

Hoekman, Bernard & Charles Sabel, *Open Plurilateral Agreements, International Regulatory Cooperation and the WTO*, EUI WORKING PAPER RSCAS 2019/10 (2019).

Hsieh, Pasha L., *Against Populist Isolationism: New Asian Regionalism and Global South Powers in International Economic Law*, 51 CORNELL INT'L L.J. 683 (2018).

Hsieh NEW ASIAN REGIONALISM IN INTERNATIONAL ECONOMIC LAW (2021).

Hsieh, Pasha L. & Bryan Mercurio, *An Introductory Roadmap to the ASEAN Economic Community*, *in* ASEAN LAW IN THE NEW REGIONAL ECONOMIC ORDER: GLOBAL TRENDS AND SHIFTING PARADIGMS (2019).

Hutt, David, *EU–China Deal May Give Biden's Team More Options*, ASIA TIMES (Dec. 31, 2020).

IMF, "Recent Experiences in Managing Capital Inflows: Cross-Cutting Themes and Possible Policy Framework," SM/11/30 (2011).

Inama, Stefano & Edmund W. Sim, THE FOUNDATION OF THE ASEAN ECONOMIC COMMUNITY: AN INSTITUTIONAL AND LEGAL PROFILE (2015).

Inglehart, Ronald, MODERNIZATION AND POSTMODERNIZATION: CULTURAL, ECONOMIC, AND POLITICAL CHANGE IN 43 SOCIETIES (1997).

Intan, Rocky, *What RCEP Can Tell Us about Geopolitics in Asia*, LOWLY INST. (Dec. 1, 2020).

International Law Commission, *Draft Articles on the Responsibility of International Organizations* (2011), http://legal.un.org/ilc/texts/instruments/english/commentaries/9_11_2011.pdf.

Irwin, Douglas, AGAINST THE TIDE: AN INTELLECTUAL HISTORY OF FREE TRADE (1996).

Jackson, John H., *International Economic Law in Times That Are Interesting*, 3 J. INT'L ECON. L. 8 (2000).

SOVEREIGNTY, THE WTO AND CHANGING FUNDAMENTALS OF INTERNATIONAL LAW (2006).

James, Harold, *Deglobalization: The Rise of Disembedded Unilateralism*, 10 ANN. REV. FIN. ECON. 219 (2018).

Jayasuriya, Kanishka *The Crisis of Open Regionalism and the New Political Economy of the Asia-Pacific*, 20 POL'Y & SOC. 89 (2001).

Jennings, Wesley & Brandy B. Henderson, *Social Learning Theory*, *in* THE ENCYCLOPEDIA OF THEORETICAL CRIMINOLOGY 1 (J. Mitchell Miller ed., 2014).

Jetschke, Anja & Jürgen Rüland, *Decoupling Rhetoric and Practice: The Cultural Limits of ASEAN Cooperation*, 22 PAC. REV. 189 (2009).

Johnson, Lisa, et al., *Investor-State Dispute Prevention: A Critical Reflection*, 75 (4) DISP. RESOL. J. 107 (2021).

Johnson, Steve, *Trump's Trade War: Which of China's Neighbours Are Set to Profit?*, FIN. TIMES (Dec. 3, 2018).

Johnston, Alastair Iain, *Socialization in International Institutions: The ASEAN Way and International Relations Theory*, *in* INTERNATIONAL RELATIONS THEORY AND THE ASIA-PACIFIC (John G. Ikenberry & Michael Mastanduno eds., 2005).

Jones, David M. & Michael L. R. Smith, *Making Process, Not Progress: ASEAN and the Evolving East Asian Regional Order*, 32 INTERNATIONAL SECURITY 165 (2007).

Jones, Lee, *ASEAN and the Norm of Non-Interference in Southeast Asia: A Quest for Social Order*, Nuffield College Politics Group Working Paper (Mar. 2009).

Explaining the Failure of the ASEAN Economic Community: The Primacy of Domestic Political Economy, 29 PAC. REV. 1 (2015).

Jusoh, Sufian, *Investment Liberalization in ASEAN: Moving from Myths to Reality*, *in* ASEAN LAW IN THE NEW REGIONAL ECONOMIC ORDER: GLOBAL TRENDS AND SHIFTING PARADIGMS 209 (Pasha Hsieh & Bryan Mercurio eds., 2019).

Kahler, Miles, *Legalization as Strategy: The Asia-Pacific Case*, *in* LEGALIZATION AND WORLD POLITICS 169 (Judith L. Goldstein, Miles Kahler, Robert O. Keohane & Anne-Marie Slaughter eds., 2001).

Conclusion: The Causes and Consequences of Legalization, *in* LEGALIZATION AND WORLD POLITICS 299 (Judith L. Goldstein, Miles Kahler, Robert O. Keohane & Anne-Marie Slaughter eds., 2001).

Kahler, Miles & Andrew MacIntyre (eds.), INTEGRATING REGIONS: ASIA IN COMPARATIVE CONTEXT (2014).

Kahn, Paul W., *Speaking Law to Power: Popular Sovereignty, Human Rights, and the New International Order*, 1 CHI. J. INT'L L. 1 (2000).

Freedom, Autonomy, and the Cultural Study of Law, 13 YALE J.L. & HUMAN. 141 (2001).

Kaplan, Ethan & Dani Rodrik, *Did the Malaysian Capital Controls Work?*, CEPR DISCUSSION PAPER NO. 2754 (2001).

Karr, Spenser, *A Battle for Choice: Selecting Investor-State Arbitrators under the RCEP*, 90 TEMP. L. REV. 127 (2017).

Karton, Joshua, LESSONS FROM INTERNATIONAL UNIFORM LAW, IN RESHAPING THE INVESTOR-STATE DISPUTE SETTLEMENT SYSTEM: JOURNEYS FOR THE 21ST CENTURY (2015).

Katsumata, Hiro, *Why Is ASEAN Diplomacy Changing? From "Noninterference" to "Open and Frank Discussions,"* 44 ASIAN SURV. 237 (2004).

Kaufmann, Daniel, et al., *Governance Matters,* WORLD BANK POLICY RESEARCH WORKING PAPER NO. 2196 (1999).

Kawai, Masahiro & Kanda Naknoi, *ASEAN Economic Integration through Trade and Foreign Direct Investment: Long-Term Challenges,* ASIAN DEV. BANK INSTITUTE WORKING PAPER, No. 545 (2015).

Kawai, Masahiro & Ganeshan Wignaraja, *Main Findings and Policy Implications, in* ASIA'S FREE TRADE AGREEMENTS: HOW IS BUSINESS RESPONDING? 35 (Masahiro Kawai & Ganeshan Wignaraja eds., 2011).

Conclusion, in ASIA'S FREE TRADE AGREEMENTS: HOW IS BUSINESS RESPONDING? 261 (Masahiro Kawai & Ganeshan Wignaraja eds., 2011).

Kelly, Claire R., *The Value Vacuum: Self-Enforcing Regimes and the Dilution of the Normative Feedback Loop,* 22 MICH. J. INT'L L. 673 (2001).

Keohane, Robert O., AFTER HEGEMONY: COOPERATION AND DISCORD IN THE WORLD POLITICAL ECONOMY (1984).

Reciprocity in International Relations, 40 INT'L ORG. 1 (1986).

International Institutions: Two Approaches, 32 INT'L STUD. Q. 379 (1988).

Keohane, Robert O. & Joseph S. Nye, *Transgovernmental Relations and International Organizations,* 27 WORLD POL. 39 (1974).

POWER AND INTERDEPENDENCE (1977).

Khoman, Thanat, *ASEAN: Conception and Evolution, in* THE ASEAN READER, SINGAPORE: INSTITUTE OF

Southeast Asian Studies xix (S. Siddique, C. Jeshurun, J. L. H. Tan & P. Thambipillai eds., 1992).

Kingsbury, Benedict, *The Concept of Compliance as a Function of Competing Conceptions of International Law*, 19 Mich. J. Int'l L. 345 (1998).

Klotz, Audie, Norms in International Relations: The Struggle against Apartheid (1995).

Knoblock, John, Xun Zi – A Translation and Study of the Complete Works, Vol. II (1990).

Koh, Harold Hongju, *Why Do Nations Obey International Law?*, 106 Yale L.J. 2599 (1997).

Koh, Tommy, et al., 50 Years of ASEAN and Singapore (2017).

Krasner, Stephen D., *Structural Causes and Regime Consequences: Regimes as Intervening Variables*, *in* International Regimes 1 (Stephen D. Krasner ed., 1983).

Krever, Tor, *Quantifying Law: Legal Indicator Projects and the Reproduction of Neoliberal Common Sense*, 34 Third World Q. 131 (2013).

Krugman, Paul, *The Hub Effect: or Threeness in Interregional Trade*, *in* Theory, Policy and Dynamics in International Trade (Wilfred J. Ethier, Elhanan Helpman & J. Peter Neary eds., 1993).

Kurtz, Jürgen & Gong Baihua, *The EU–China Comprehensive Agreement on Investment: A Model for* Investment *Coverage in the WTO?*, *in* Rebooting Multilateral Trade Cooperation: Perspectives from China and Europe 191 (Bernard M. Hoekman, Tu Xinquan & Wang Dong eds., 2021).

Lee, Levither, *The ASEAN Charter: ASEAN Failure or Member Failure*, 43 N.Y.U. J. Int'l L. Pol. 159 (2010).

Legro, Jeffery W., *The Transformation of Policy Ideas*, 44 AM. J. POL. SCI. 419, 425 (2000).

Leifer, Michael, ASEAN AND THE SECURITY OF SOUTH-EAST ASIA (1989).

The ASEAN Peace Process: A Category Mistake, 12 THE PAC. REV. 25 (1999).

Levi, Margaret, *A Model, a Method, and a Map: Rational Choice in Comparative and Historical Analysis*, *in* COMPARATIVE POLITICS: RATIONALITY, CULTURE, AND STRUCTURE 19 (Mark I. Lichbach & Alan S. Zuckerman eds. 1997).

Li, John Shuhe, *Relation-Based versus Rule-based Governance: An Explanation of the East Asian Miracle and Asian Crisis*, 11 REV. OF'NT'L ECON. 651 (2003).

Li, Su & Edmund Ryden, *Scholar-Officials*, *in* THE CONSTITUTION OF ANCIENT CHINA 98 (Yongle Zhang & Daniel A. Bell eds. 2018).

Lindblom, Charles E., POLITICS AND MARKETS: THE WORLD'S POLITICAL–ECONOMIC SYSTEMS (1977).

Lindgren, Carl-Johan, Tomas Balino, Charles Enock, Anne-Marie Gulde, Marc Quintyn & Leslie Teo, FINANCIAL SECTOR CRISIS AND RESTRUCTURING: LESSONS FROM ASIA (1999).

Lipson, Charles, *Why Are Some International Agreements Informal?*, 45 INT'L ORG. 495 (1991).

Ly, Luu Huong, *Regional Harmonization of Competition Law and Policy: An ASEAN Approach*, 2 ASIAN J. INT'L L. 291 (2012)

Lynch, Daniel C., *International "Decentering" and Democratization: The Case of Thailand*, 48 INT'L STUD. Q. 339 (2004).

Mackie, J.A.C., KONFRONTASI: THE INDONESIA–MALAYSIA DISPUTE 1963–66 (1974).

Maduro, Miguel, WE THE COURT: THE EUROPEAN COURT OF JUSTICE AND THE EUROPEAN ECONOMIC CONSTITUTION (1998).

Makin, Tony, *Advancing Foreign Investment in APEC*, HINRICH FOUNDATION (Aug. 24, 2021) www.hinrichfoundation.com/research/article/fdi/advancing-foreign-investment-in-apec/.

Marchegiano, Giuseppe, *The Juristic Character of the International Commission of Cape Spartel Lighthouse*, 25 AM. J. INT'L L. 339 (1931).

Maulia, Erwida & Ismi Damayanti, *Pandemic Stalls Indonesia's Push to Escape Middle-Income Trap*, FIN. TIMES (Dec. 22, 2020).

McIntyre, Andrew, *Institutions and Investors: The Politics of the Economic Crisis in Southeast Asia*, 55 INT'L ORG. 81 (2001).

Menon, Jayant, *Assessing ASEAN's Economic Performance*, ASIAN DEV. BANK (2018), www.adb.org/news/op-ed/assessing-asean-s-economic-performance-jayant-menon.

Menon, Jayant & Rodolfo Severino, *The ASEAN Community: An Overview*, *in* THE ASEAN ECONOMIC COMMUNITY: A WORK IN PROGRESS (Sanchita Basu Das, Jayant Menon, Rodolfo Severino & Omkar Lal Shrestha eds., 2013).

Menski, Werner, COMPARATIVE LAW IN A GLOBAL CONTEXT: THE LEGAL SYSTEMS OF ASIA AND AFRICA (2nd ed. 2006).

Mercurio, Bryan, *Trade Liberalization in Asia: Why Intra-Asian Free Agreements Are Not Utilised by the Business Community*, 6 (1) ASIAN J. WTO & INT'L. HEALTH L. & POL. 109 (2011).

Merry, Sally Engel, *Measuring the World: Indicators, Human Rights, and Global Governance*, 52 CURRENT ANTHROPOLOGY S83 (2011).

Meyer, John W., et al., *World Society and the Nation-State*, 103 AM. J. SOC. 144 (1997).

Michaels, Ralf, *The Functional Method of Comparative Law*, *in* THE OXFORD HANDBOOK OF COMPARATIVE LAW 339 (Mathias Reimann & Reinhard Zimmermann eds., 2008).

Minor, Michael S., *The Demise of Expropriation as an Instrument of LDC Policy 1980–1992*, 25 J. INT'L BUS. STUD. 177 (1994).

Mintzberg, Henry, *Power and Organizational Life Cycles*, 9 ACAD. MGMT. REV. 207 (1984).

Miroudot, Sébastien & Håkan Nordström, *Made in the World?: Global Value Chains in the Midst of Rising Protectionism*, 57 REV. IND. ORG. 195 (2020).

Mitzen, Jennifer, *Ontological Security in World Politics: State Identity and the Security Dilemma*, 12 EUR. J. INT'L REL. 341 (2006).

Mohamad, Juita, *ASEAN Waits for RCEP Ratification – and Post-Pandemic Integration*, HINRICH FOUNDATION (Sept. 7, 2021) www.hinrichfoundation.com/research/article/ftas/asean-waits-for-rcep-ratification-and-post-pandemic-integration/.

Moravcsik, Andrew, *Taking Preferences Seriously: A Liberal Theory of International Politics*, 51 INT'L ORG. 513 (1997).

Ness, Gayl D. & Steven R. Brechin, *Bridging the Gap: International Organizations as Organizations*, 42 INT'L ORG. 245 (1988).

Newcombe, Andrew & Lluis Paradell, LAW AND PRACTICE OF INVESTMENT TREATIES – STANDARDS OF TREATMENT (2009).

Nguitragool, Paruedee & Jürgen Rüland, ASEAN AS AN ACTOR IN INTERNATIONAL FORA: REALITY, POTENTIAL AND CONSTRAINTS (2015).

Nicholls, Alicia, *RCEP Investment Rules: Help or Hindrances to A'ia's COVID-19 Recovery?*, AFRONOMICSLAW (Feb. 17, 2021), www.afronomicslaw.org/category/analysis/rcep-investment-rules-help-or-hindrances-asias-covid-19-recovery.

North, Douglas C., INSTITUTIONS, INSTITUTIONAL CHANGE AND ECONOMIC PERFORMANCE (1990).

Nottage, Luke & Sakda Thanitcul, *An Introduction, Special Issue: International Investment Arbitration in Southeast Asia*, 18 J. WORLD INVESTMENT & TRADE 767 (2017).

OECD, *Making Global Value Chains Work for ASEAN* (June 13, 2016), www.oecd.org/trade/events/making-global-value-chains-work-for-asean-13-june-2016.htm.

Ohnesorge, John K.M., *The Rule of Law, Economic Development, and Developmental States of Northeast Asia*, *in* LAW AND DEVELOPMENT IN EAST AND SOUTHEAST ASIA 70 (Christoph Antons ed., 2003).

Palmer, Norman D., THE NEW REGIONALISM IN ASIA AND THE PACIFIC (1991).

Pangestu, Mari & Sudarshan Gooptu, *New Regionalism: Options for East Asia*, *in* EAST ASIA INTEGRATES: A TRADE POLICY AGENDA FOR SHARED GROWTH 48 (Kathie Krumm & Homi Kharas eds., 2004).

Pangestu, Mari, et al., *A New Look at Intra-ASEAN Economic Cooperation*, 8 ASEAN ECON. BULL. (1992).

Paulsson, Jan, *Arbitration Without Privity*, 10 ICSID REV. 232 (1995).

Pelkmans, Jacques, THE ASEAN ECONOMIC COMMUNITY: A CONCEPTUAL APPROACH (2016).

Peng, Shin-yi, *The WTO Legalistic Approach and East Asia: From the Legal Culture Perspective*, 1 ASIAN-PAC. L. & POL'Y J. 13 (2000).

Petri, Peter A. & Michael G. Plummer, *RCEP: A New Trade Agreement That Will Shape Global Economics and Politics*, BROOKINGS (Nov. 16, 2020).

Trade War, RECP and CPTPP: Will East Asia Decouple from the United States? (Nov. 28, 2020), https://papers.ssrn.com/sol3/papers.cfm?abstract_id=3630294.

Piei, Mohd Haflah, *An East Asia FTA: A Malaysian Perspective*, *in* EAST ASIAN REGIONALISM: FEASIBILITIES AND CHALLENGES 109 (Choong Yong Ahn, Richard E. Baldwin & Inkyo Cheong eds., 2005).

Pilling, David, *The Fiction of a Unified, Harmonized ASEAN*, FIN. TIMES (Dec. 10, 2015).

Piris, Jean-Calude & Walter Woon, TOWARDS A RULE-BASED COMMUNITY: AN ASEAN LEGAL SERVICE (2015).

Pistor, Katharina & Philip A. Wellons, The Role of Law and Legal Institutions in Asian Economic Development *1960–1995 (Executive Summary) – Prepared for the Asian Development Bank* (1998), www.asianlii.org/asia/other/ADBLPRes/1998/3.pdf.

Poulsen, Lauge, BOUNDED RATIONALITY AND ECONOMIC DIPLOMACY: THE POLITICS OF INVESTMENT TREATIES IN DEVELOPING COUNTRIES (2017).

Powell, Walter W. & Paul J. DiMaggio, THE NEW INSTITUTIONALISM IN ORGANIZATIONAL ANALYSIS (1991).

Prado, Mariana Mota & Michael J. Trebilcock, *Path Dependence, Development, and the Dynamics of Institutional Reform*, UNIV. TORONTO L. J. (2009).

Pratt, Travis C., et al., *The Empirical Status of Social Learning Theory: A Meta-Analysis*, 27 JUSTICE Q. 765 (2010).

Quah, Jon S.T., *Why Singapore Works: Five Secrets of Singap're's Success*, 21(1) PUBL. ADMIN & POL. 5 (2018).

Quah, Jon S.T. & David Seth Jones, *Organising the Public Bureaucracy to Ensure Effective Implementation and Compliance with ASEAN Commitments* (July 23, 2019) (unpublished manuscript) (on file with author).

Radaelli, Claudio M., *Whither Europeanization? Concept Stretching and Substantive Change*, 4 EUR. INTEGRATION ONLINE PAPERS (2000).

Radin, Margaret Jane, *Reconsidering the Rule of Law*, 69 B.U.L. REV. 781 (1989).

Ramcharan, Robin, *ASEAN and Non-interference: A Principle Maintained*, 22 CONTEMP. SE. ASIA 60 (2000).

Randeria, Shalini, *The State of Globalization: Legal Plurality, Overlapping Sovereignties and Ambiguous Alliances between Civil Society and the Cunning State in India*, 24 Theory, Culture & Soc'y 1–34 (2007).

Raustiala, Kal, *The Architecture of International Cooperation: Transgovernmental Networks and the Future of International Law*, 43 VA. J. INT'L L. 1 (2002).

Reed, John, *Vietnam Prepares for Supply Chain Shift from China*, FIN. TIMES (Dec. 28, 2020).

Reed, Mark S., et al., *What Is Social Learning?*, ECO. & SOC'Y,. vol. 15, no. 4 (2010), www.ecologyandsociety.org/vol15/iss4/resp1/.

Ren, Xin, TRADITION OF THE LAW AND LAW OF THE TRADITION: LAW, STATE, AND SOCIAL CONTROL IN CHINA (1997).

Ress, Georg, *The Interpretation of the Charter*, *in* THE CHARTER OF THE UNITED NATIONS – A COMMENTARY 28 (Bruno Simma et al. eds., 1994).

Roberts, Anthea, *Power and Persuasion in Investment Treaty Interpretation: The Dual Role of States*, 104 AM. J. INT'L L. 179, 186 (2010).

Rudner, Martin, *Institutional Approaches to Regional Trade and Cooperation in the Asia Pacific Area*, 4 TRANSNAT'L L. & CONTEMP. PROBS. 159 (1994).

Ruggie, John Gerard, *Territoriality and Beyond: Problematizing Modernity in International Relations*, 47 INT'L ORG. 139 (1993).

Embedded Liberalism and Postwar Economic Regimes, *in* CONSTRUCTING THE WORLD POLITY: ESSAYS ON INTERNATIONAL INSTITUTIONALIZATION (John Ruggie ed., 1998).

Rüland, Jürgen, THE INDONESIAN WAY: ASEAN, EUROPEANIZATION AND FOREIGN POLICY DEBATES IN A NEW DEMOCRACY (2018).

Coping with Crisis: Southeast Asian Regionalism and the Ideational Constraints of Reform, 16 Asia Eur. J. 155 (2018).

Sachs, Lisa & Karl Sauvant, *BITs, DTTs and FDI Flows: An Overview*, *in* The Effect of Treaties on Foreign Direct Investment: Bilateral Investment Treaties, Double Taxation Treaties and Investment Flows (Karl P. Sauvant & Lisa E. Sachs eds., 2009).

Scalapino, Robert A., *Regionalism in the Pacific: Prospects and Problems for the Pacific Basin*, 26 Atl. Cmty. Q. 174 (1988).

Scheuerman, William, *Economic Globalization and the Rule of Law*, 6 Constellations 1 (1999).

Schimmelfennig, Frank, *The Community Trap: Liberal Norms, Rhetorical Action, and the Eastern Enlargement of the European Union*, 55 Int'l Org. 47 (2001).

Schneiderman, David, *International Investment Law as Formally Rational Law: A Weberian Analysis*, *in* Research Handbook on the Sociology of International Law (Moshe Hirsch & Andrew Lang eds., 2020).

Scoles, Samuel, *15 Asia-Pacific Countries Sign World's Largest FTA; A Closer Look at RCEP's Key Outcomes and Implications*, White & Case (Nov. 25, 2020).

Scott, Richard W., Organizations: Rational, Natural, and Open Systems (3rd ed. 1991).

Sellier, Elodie, *The ASEAN Economic Community: The Force Awakens?*, The Diplomat (Jan. 12, 2016).

Setboonsarng, Suthad, *ASEAN Economic Cooperation: Adjusting to the Crisis*, Southeast Asian Aff. 35 (1998).

Severino, Rodolfo C., Southeast Asia in Search of an ASEAN Community: Insights from the Former ASEAN Secretary-General (2006).

Sewell, William H., Jr., *Three Temporalities: Toward an Eventful Sociology*, *in* The Historic Turn in the Human Sciences 245 (Terrance J. McDonald ed., 1996).

Shaffer, Gregory C. & Mark A. Pollack, *Hard vs. Soft Law: Alternatives, Complements, and Antagonists in International Governance*, 94 Minn. L. Rev. 706 (2010).

Shelton, Dinah, *Introduction: Law, Non-Law and the Problem of Soft Law*, *in* Commitment and Compliance: The Role of Non-Binding Norms in the International Legal System 1 (Dinah Shelton ed., 2000).

Shepsle, Kenneth A., *Rational Choice Institutionalism*, *in* Oxford Handbook of Political Institutions (R.A.W. Rhodes, Sarah A. Binder & Bert A. Rockman eds., 2008).

Shihata, Ibrahim F.I., *The Dynamic Evolution of International Organizations: The Case of the World Bank*, 2 J. His. Int'l L. 217 (2000).

Shockey, John E., *Bank Regulatory Examination and Enforcement after Barings and Daiwa*, *in Financial Services Litigation*, 935 Corp. L. & Prac. Course Handbook 681, 708 (Practicing Law Institute 1996).

Simmons, Beth, *East Asia, investment and International Law: Distinctive or Convergent?*, 13(3) Kor. J. Int'l. Stud. 461 (2015).

Simmons, Beth A. & Richard H. Steinberg, International Law and International Relations (2007).

Slaughter, Anne-Marie, *A Liberal Theory of International Law*, 94 Am. Soc'y Int'l L. Proc. 240 (2000).

Snape, Richard, *Which Regional Trade Agreement?*, *in* Regional Integration and the Asia Pacific (Bijit Nora & Christopher Findlay eds. 1996).

Solingen, E., *The Genesis, Design and Effects of Regional Institutions: Lessons from East Asia and the Middle East*, 52 Int'l Stud. Q. 261 (2008).

Sornarajah, Muthucumaraswamy, *Mutations of Neo-Liberalism in International Investment Law*, 3 TRADE L. & DEV. 203 (2011).

de Sousa Santos, Boaventura, TOWARD A NEW LEGAL COMMON SENSE: LAW, GLOBALIZATION AND EMANCIPATION (2002).

Steinberg, Richard H. & Jonathan M. Zasloff, *Power and International Law*, 100 AM. J. INT'L L. 64 (2006).

Stubbs, Richard, *Signing on to Liberalization: AFTA and the Politics of Regional Economic Cooperation*, 13 PACIFIC REV. 297 (2000).

Tai, Benny Y.T., *Developing an Index of the Rule of Law: Sharing the Experience of Hong Kong*, 2 ASIAN J. COMP. L. 1 (2007).

Tan, Lay Hong, *Law and Policy in ASEAN Economic Integration*, 38 ASIA BUS. L. REV. 3 (2002).

Tangkitvanich, Somkiat & Saowaruj Rattanakhamfu, *The ASEAN Economic Community and the East Asian Agenda*, *in* ASIAN ECONOMIC INTEGRATION IN AN ERA OF GLOBAL UNCERTAINTY 190 (Shiro Armstrong & Tom Westland eds., 2018).

Teitel, Ruti & Robert Howse, *Cross-Judging: Tribunalization in a Fragmented but Interconnected Global Order*, 41 N. Y. J. INT'L L. & POL. 959 (2009).

Tetsuo, Abo, *Spontaneous Integration in Japan and East Asia: Development, Crisis, and Beyond*, *in* THE OXFORD HANDBOOK OF ECONOMIC GEOGRAPHY (Gordon L. Clark et al. eds., 2000).

Thompson, Edmund R., *ASEAN after the Financial Crisis*, 17 ASEAN ECON. BULL. (2000).

Tourk, Khairy, *Asia-Pacific Pact Is a Triumph for the Region's "Quiet Diplomacy,"* FIN. TIMES (Nov. 19, 2020).

Trachtman, Joel P., *The Constitutions of the WTO*, 17 EUR. J. INT'L L. 623 (2006).

Trebilcock, Michael J. & Robert Howse, THE REGULATION OF INTERNATIONAL TRADE (3rd ed. 2005).

Trubek, David M., *Max Weber on Law and the Rise of Capitalism*, 1972 WIS. L. REV. 720 (1972).

Toward a Social Theory of Law: An Essay on the Study of Law and Development, 82 YALE L.J. 1 (1972).

Tzouvala, Ntina, *A False Promise?: Regulating Land-Grabbing and the Post-Colonial State*, 32 LEIDEN J. INT'L L. 235 (2019).

U.N. Conference on Trade and Development, Incentives and Foreign Direct Investment (1996).

UNCTAD, *Incentives and Foreign Direct Investment*, U.N. Doc. UNCTAD/DTCI/28 (1996).

International Investment Instruments: A Compendium Vol. I, U.N. Doc. UNCTAD/DTCI/30(Vol. I) (May 31, 1996).

International Investment Instruments: A Compendium, Vol. III, U.N. Doc. UNCTAD/DTCI/30(Vol. III) (May 31, 1996).

Bilateral Investment Treaties 1959–1999, U.N. Doc. UNCTAD/ITE/IIA/2 (2000).

International Investment Law Rule-Making: Stocktaking, Challenges and The Way Forward, U.N. Doc. UNCTAD/ITE/IIT/2007/3 (2008).

FDI Statistics Division on Investment and Enterprise (April 2, 2016), http://unctad.org/en/Pages/DIAE/FDI%20Statistics/FDI-Statistics.aspx.

United States Department of State, *Model Bilateral Investment Treaty* (2004), https://ustr.gov/sites/default/files/U.S.%20model%20BIT.pdf.

United States International Trade Commission, PUB. NO. 4176, ASEAN: REGIONAL TRENDS IN ECONOMIC INTEGRATION, EXPORT COMPETITIVENESS, AND INBOUND INVESTMENT FOR SELECTED INDUSTRIES (2010).

Vander Kooi, Joel, *The ASEAN Enhanced Dispute Settlement Mechanism: Doing It the "ASEAN Way,"* 20 N.Y. INT'L L. REV. 1 (2007).

Vandevelde, Kenneth J., *The Political Economy of a Bilateral Investment Treaty*, 92 AM. J. INT'L. L. 621 (1998).

Sustainable Liberalism and the International Investment Regime, 19 MICH. J. INT'L. L. 373 (1998).

Van Rijckeghem, Caroline & Beatrice Weder, *Corruption and the Role of Temptation: Do Law Wages in the Civil Service Cause Corruption?*, IMF WORKING PAPER WP/97/73 (1997).

Verico, Kiki, THE FUTURE OF THE ASEAN ECONOMIC INTEGRATION (2017).

Viterbo, Annamaria, *Iceland's Capital Controls and the Constraints Imposed by the EEA Agreement*, 6 CAP. MAR. LAW J. 214 (2011).

How to Make the GATS a Code of Conduct for Capital Controls, *in* CAPITAL ACCOUNT REGULATIONS AND THE TRADING SYSTEM: A COMPATIBILITY REVIEW 20 (Kevin Gallagher et al. ed., 2013).

Tensions between International Investment Protection and Financial Stability, *in* THE FUTURE OF ICSID AND THE PLACE OF INVESTMENT TREATIES IN INTERNATIONAL LAW 192 (N. Jansen Calamita et al. eds., 2013).

Wade, Robert, GOVERNING THE MARKET: ECONOMIC THEORY AND THE ROLE OF GOVERNMENT IN EAST ASIAN INDUSTRIALIZATION (1990).

Wallerstein, Immanuel, THE MODERN WORLD SYSTEM (1974).

Waltz, Kenneth N., THEORY OF INTERNATIONAL POLITICS (1979).

Wardekker, Willem L., *Identity, Plurality, and Education*, *in* PHILOSOPHY OF EDUCATION 1995 (Alven Neiman ed., 1995).

Watson, Alan, Law in Books, Law in Action and Society (Apr. 12, 2006) (paper presented as part of the Faculty Colloquium Series, School of Law, Univ. of Georgia, Apr. 12, 2006, Paper No. 1), https://digitalcommons.law.uga.edu/conf_coll_symp_colloquia/1/.

Wells, Louis T. & Rafiq Ahmed, MAKING FOREIGN INVESTMENT SAFE: PROPERTY RIGHTS AND NATIONAL SOVEREIGNTY (2007).

Wendt, Alexander, *Anarchy Is What States Make of It: The Social Construction of Power Politics*, 46 INT'L ORG. 391 (1992).

Collective Identity Formation and the International State, 88 AM. POL. SCI. REV. 384 (1994).

THE SOCIAL THEORY OF INTERNATIONAL POLITICS (1999).

The State as Person in International Theory, 30 REV. INT'L STUD. 289 (2004).

Weber, Max, *Science as a Vocation*, *in* FROM MAX WEBER: ESSAYS IN SOCIOLOGY 139 (Hans Heinrich Gerth & Charles Wright Mills trans. & eds., 1946).

Weintraub, Andrew N., POWER PLAYS: WAYANG GOLEK PUPPET THEATRE OF WEST JAVA, SOUTHEAST ASIA SERIES, VOL. 110 (2004).

Westerman, Pauline, INTRODUCTION IN OUTSOURCING THE LAW: A PHILOSOPHICAL PERSPECTIVE ON REGULATION (2018).

Williamson, Oliver E., THE ECONOMIC INSTITUTIONS OF CAPITALISM (1985).

Wilson, Bryan R., *A Sociologist's Introduction*, *in* RATIONALITY x (Bryan R. Wilson ed., 1970).

Wolfe, Robert, *See you in Geneva! Legal (Mis)representations of the Trading system*, 11 EUR. J. INT'L REL. 339 (2005).

Wonnacott, Ronald, *Trade and Investment in a Hub-and Spoke System versus a Free Trade Area*, 19 WORLD ECON. 237 (1996).

Working Party on GATS Rules, *Negotiations on Emergency Safeguard Measures: Report by the Chairperson of the Working Party on GATS Rules,* WTO Doc. S/WPGR/9 (Mar. 14, 2003).

World Bank, *Worldwide Governance Indicators,* http://info.worldbank.org/governance/wgi/.

World Bank Group, *Global Value Chain Development Report 2017: Measuring and Analyzing the Impact of GVCs on Economic Development* (2017), https://openknowledge.worldbank.org/handle/10986/29593.

WTO, *The Relationship between Trade and Investment,* WTO Doc. WT/WGTI/W/7 (Sept. 8, 1997).

Xuetong, Yan, *Xun Zi's Thoughts on International Politics and Their Implications,* 2 CHINESE J. INT'L POL. 135 (2008).

Yackee, Jason Webb, *Do Bilateral Investment Treaties Promote Foreign Direct Investment? Some Hints from Alternative Evidence,* 51 VIRG. J. INT'L L. 405 (2010).

Yen, Trinh Hai, *Fragmented Approaches to Investor-State Dispute Settlement Mechanisms in Intra-ASEAN and Extra-ASEAN Investment Treaties, in* ASEAN LAW IN THE NEW REGIONAL ECONOMIC ORDER: GLOBAL TRENDS AND SHIFTING PARADIGMS 252 (Pasha Hsieh & Bryan Mercurio eds., 2019).

Yerkey, Gary G., *Sen. Baucus Calls WTO "Kangaroo Court" with Strong "Bias" against the United States,* 19 INT'L TRADE REP. (BNA) 1679 (2002).

Yuzawa, Takeshi, *The Fallacy of Socialization?: Rethinking the ASEAN Way of Institution-Building, in* ASEAN AND THE INSTITUTIONALIZATION OF EAST ASIA 75, 81 (Ralf Emmers ed., 2012).

INDEX

www.ingramcontent.com/pod-product-compliance
Lightning Source LLC
LaVergne TN
LVHW052250200926
848481LV00002B/327
* 9 7 8 1 0 0 9 2 2 3 3 6 2 *